To **Rose Arnett**

From _____

Date **5/16/22**

Dear friend, I pray that you may enjoy good health
and that all may go well with you,
even as your soul is getting along well.

~ 3 John 2

Apples OF GOLD

DR MICHAEL MOL
DALENE REYBURN

CHRISTIAN ART
PUBLISHERS

Published by Christian Art Publishers
PO Box 1599, Vereeniging, 1930, RSA

© 2020
First edition 2020

Designed by Christian Art Publishers
Cover designed by Christian Art Publishers

Images used under license from Shutterstock.com

Scripture quotations marked NLT are taken from the *Holy Bible,* New Living Translation, copyright © 1996, 2004, 2015 by Tyndale House Foundation. Used by permission of Tyndale House Publishers, Carol Stream, Illinois 60188. All rights reserved.

Scripture quotations marked ESV are taken from the Holy Bible, English Standard Version®. ESV® Text Edition: 2016. Copyright © 2001 by Crossway, a publishing ministry of Good News Publishers. Used by permission. All rights reserved.

Scripture quotations marked NIV are taken from the *Holy Bible,* New International Version®, NIV® Copyright © 1973, 1978, 1984, 2011 by Biblica, Inc.® Used by permission. All rights reserved worldwide.

Scripture quotations marked BSB are taken from The Holy Bible, Berean Study Bible, BSB copyright © 2016, 2018, 2019 by Bible Hub used by permission. All rights reserved worldwide.

Scripture quotations marked MSG are taken from The Message, copyright © 1993, 1994, 1995, 1996, 2000, 2001, 2002 by Eugene H. Peterson. Used by permission of NavPress. All rights reserved.

Scripture quotations marked CEV are from the Contemporary English Version. Copyright © 1991, 1992, 1995 by American Bible Society. Used by permission.

Scripture quotations marked HCSB are taken from the Holman Christian Standard Bible®, Used by Permission HCSB ©1999, 2000, 2002, 2003, 2009 Holman Bible Publishers. Holman Christian Standard Bible®, Holman CSB®, and HCSB® are federally registered trademarks of Holman Bible Publishers.

Scripture quotations marked *New Heart English Bible* are taken from the New Heart English Bible New Testament and are in the Public Domain.

Printed in China

ISBN 978-1-4321-3099-2

20 21 22 23 24 25 26 27 28 29 – 10 9 8 7 6 5 4 3 2 1

A word fitly spoken

is like

apples of gold

in settings of silver.

~ Proverbs 25:11

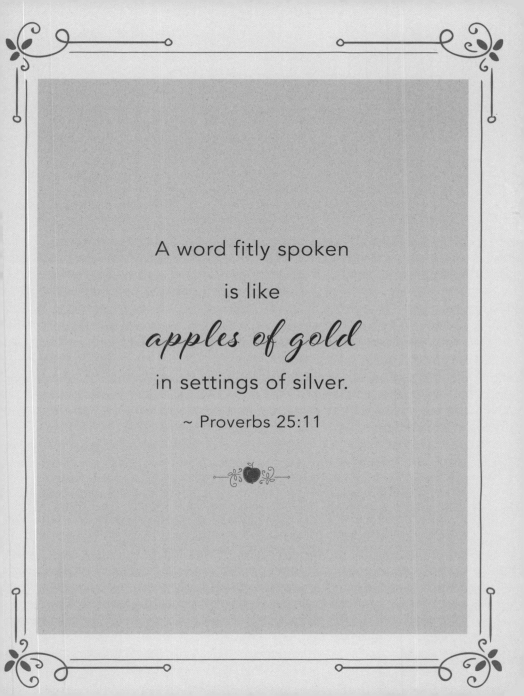

A NOTE FROM THE AUTHORS

We each have *just one body*, to live out our one life on the planet.

You're in the skin you're in, and your one beating heart is all you have to show the love of Jesus to the other humans you meet, marry, or pass once in a mall. That's why we're passionate about inspiring you to live out your days in splendid health, fulfilling the call of God on your life in the best and most bountiful ways.

We know that sickness and suffering are part of our reality in a broken world (Romans 8:20-21). We know God causes all things to work together for our good and His glory (Romans 8:28).

We know that in Him are all the treasures of wisdom and knowledge – *medical* wisdom and knowledge too (Colossians 2:3). And we know there's incredible joy to come because one day God will renew, restore and redeem all things, and it will be glorious (Revelation 21:4).

May this daily devotional encourage you to walk closely with Jesus, our Healer, to live a life worthy of the calling you have received, and so to echo Paul's inspiring words – with high fives and fist bumps – *'For we are God's handiwork, created in Christ Jesus to do good works, which God prepared in advance for us to do'* (Ephesians 2:10).

With love and every good wish for abundant health,

~ *Dalene and Michael*

5/16/22

NEVER TOO LATE

... I have not achieved it, but I focus on this one thing:
Forgetting the past and looking forward to what lies ahead,
I press on to reach the end of the race and receive the heavenly
prize for which God, through Christ Jesus, is calling us.
Philippians 3:13-14, NLT

Maybe things went down last year that you wish you could forget. Perhaps there was tragedy and grief. Gnawing concerns. Ordinary disappointment-turned-cynicism.

It's not too late. It's *never* too late for you to square your shoulders and start again – because God's mercies are fresh like morning coffee, with every sunrise (Lamentations 3:23). And if you're *facing* the sunrise, your shadow is behind you. That's exactly where the shadows of your past belong: behind you. Your *one thing* this year might simply be to make sure you're facing the Son?

Lying ahead is the gift of 365 days wrapped up in good decisions waiting to be made. Here's to ripping the wrapping like a kid at Christmas. Here's to a healthier you – body and soul.

🍎 THIS ONE THING

What's the *one thing* you need to concentrate on this year, more than anything else, in terms of your health? Fitness? Food? Fatigue? Having too many goals is unrealistic, overwhelming and unwise. Focusing on *just one thing* energizes and encourages. And remember, your body looks different from all the other bodies around you, and your *one thing* will look different too. It's yours alone, and so it should be.

OVERFLOWING

The thief comes only to steal and kill and destroy.
I came that they may have life and have it abundantly.
John 10:10, ESV

God is not on rations, and He doesn't ration us. He doesn't eke out a miserly existence, doling out love scraps to His starving children. He's the boundless God of everywhere, all-the-time power, wisdom and kindness. He wanted so much to show us His lavishness that He sent His only Son to pour that limitless love into our lives.

And you don't ever need to fear that God's life in you will run dry – that there won't be quite enough of His peace and joy to see you through another year, and then some. The Greek word *perissos*, translated *abundantly* in this verse, means *over and above, more than is necessary, superadded, superior, extra-ordinary, surpassing, uncommon*.

That's the kind of existence your Heavenly Father has designed for you. Your glass certainly isn't half empty. It's not even half full. It's overflowing.

FIRST PRIZE FOR POSITIVE

Positive people are more likely to exercise and eat well, which enhances their health and longevity. Sure, no one can be happy all the time, but everyone can make small trajectory changes for a happier life course. Optimism is part genetic, part learned. So even if you were born into a glass-half-empty family, you can persist in tweaking your negative thoughts until you're in the habit of seeing the opportunity instead of the ominous.

LOOK UP, LOOK OUT

The heavens declare the glory of God;
the skies proclaim the work of His hands. Day after day
they pour forth speech; night after night they reveal knowledge.

Psalm 19:1-2, NIV

Our self-help culture is insidiously insular. We hardly notice anymore how self-obsessed we're encouraged to be – how self-absorbed we really are. We're so bent on improving ourselves that we're trapped by the navel-gazing that breeds narcissism.

C.S. Lewis writes, 'I had not noticed how the humblest, and at the same time most balanced and capacious, minds praised most, while the cranks, misfits and malcontents praised least … I had not noticed either that just as men spontaneously praise whatever they value, so they spontaneously urge us to join them in praising it: "Isn't she lovely? Wasn't it glorious? Don't you think that magnificent?" The Psalmists in telling everyone to praise God are doing what all men do when they speak of what they care about.'

Let's look up to God and out towards others – declaring with our lives the wonders of our Creator.

OUTSIDE FOR OPTIMISM

The great outdoors is a substantiated stress-reliever and a natural way to alleviate depression. The more you're outdoors, the better your mental outlook. Those who walk, bike, or run in nature have a significantly lower risk of poor mental health than people who work out indoors on the 'dreadmill'. Evidence also suggests those who exercise outside are more likely to return for future workouts than those who hit the gym.

CLUTTER OR CALM?

For God is not a God of disorder but of peace ...
everything should be done in a fitting and orderly way.
1 Corinthians 14:33, 40, NIV

This verse has to do with how people were worshipping and using their gifts within the context of the Corinthian church — but it applies to all of life. God's never dazed or confused, disorganized or in disarray. That doesn't mean He's cold, calculating and clinical. And it doesn't mean there's no room for spontaneity in lives surrendered to Him.

But it may be wise to extricate yourself from life's untidiness so you've got margin to move. Ask God to show you where you need to declutter spiritually (because you don't have to commit to every church program), relationally (because you may be exhausting yourself unnecessarily, carrying another's emotional load), financially (because maybe this is the year you finally pay off that thing and determine not to take on any more debt), and of course, physically.

MINUTE TO WIN IT

Physical clutter often means mental clutter, so getting organized is unquestionably good for both body and mind. One of the greatest benefits of decluttering is simply the sense of getting something done. But if tackling your chaos feels too much so early in the year, try following the one-minute rule. Make a list of tasks that can be completed within one minute. You don't have to do them all, but accomplishing even one will boost your happiness.

STARVING SLAVES

So Christ has truly set us free. Now make sure that you stay free,
and don't get tied up again in slavery to the law.
Galatians 5:1, NLT

Instead of enjoying their newfound freedom in Jesus, the Galatians had gone back to their old ways, putting themselves on a strict diet of impossible law-keeping that made them *feel* holy (and hungry).

New Year's resolutions can make us legalistic like that. If we get things right, we think we're super-spiritual. If we get things wrong, we self-flagellate. We enslave ourselves to impossible ideals and when we (predictably) don't reach them we think, *I'm such a loser!*

We somehow believe we need to go on a grace detox, starving ourselves of the rich fruit God supplies, in an attempt to pay for something He already paid for, in full. Jesus died so we'd be free and filled – never deprived of His love.

DETOX DISASTER

Google *detox*. You'll go, 'Wow, detoxing must really be a thing, right?' Wrong! Despite its popularity, there's very little science to support detoxing – because there's no such thing as a build-up of toxins in your body. If something toxic does arrive in your system, your skin, liver and kidneys work together to get rid of it. The true benefit of detox diets is what you *don't* eat during the process. So instead of a dedicated 'detox', make healthy food choices your new normal. It's more sustainable, and far more likely to give you the results you're looking for.

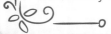

FOOD FOR THOUGHT

Detox dangers:

- There's a distinct difference between a 'detox diet', and something like intermittent fasting. Detox diets, often promoted by glossy mags and celebrities, are not backed by any solid science. Some require you to buy magic fat busting pills or shakes, while others require you to drink lemon water for 3 days. If you've done either and felt the 'benefits', it was more likely a result of what you *aren't* putting in (sugar, excess carbs, takeaways) than what you are. The reality is that your body doesn't really need a detox. Your internal 'detoxers' (your kidneys and liver) do an excellent job of detoxing already, meaning you won't have a 'build up of toxins'.

- Detox diets and weight loss remedies are to your body what diluted petrol is to your car. The main reason people choose to do a detox is because they haven't been eating well in the first place. With your body already running on empty, taking away nutrients from the mix means you slow down because you lack the necessary fuel. Once your body reaches starvation mode, the fatigue that the detox first caused might dwindle, but only because your body recognizes the starvation.

- Detox diets, besides making you feel grumpy, result in poor immune function, lethargy, skin problems, brittle nails, confusion and sickness. If you yo-yo on and off cleansing plans, shifts in your weight and metabolism can lead to weight gain and obesity-related problems, such as high blood pressure, sleep apnea and even heart disease.

Do this instead:

- Eat. This allows your digestive system to cleanse itself.

- Turn to whole foods, or 'clean eating'. Eat more fruits, vegetables, nuts and fish, and fewer processed foods, refined grains and added sugars.

- Get rid of the toxins you *can* control, like smoking or those extra swigs of alcohol.

TIME TO REFLECT ...

As you reflect, journal and pray over what you've read in the past week, thank God that He's the God of second chances. *It's never too late.* Thank Him for the abundant life He pours – and keeps on pouring! – into you. Thank Him that He's made Himself known to us through the splendor of the great outdoors.

And ask God for wisdom. Where is there chaos and confusion in your life? What one thing could you do today to begin to declutter? What toxic thought or habit could you toss, feasting instead on God's goodness?

DUTY OR DELIGHT?

You do not desire a sacrifice, or I would offer one. You do not
want a burnt offering. The sacrifice You desire is a broken spirit.
You will not reject a broken and repentant heart, O God.

Psalm 51:16-17, NLT

My deepest longing, as a parent, is for my kids to love God
with their lives. I'm convinced everything else falls into
place – somewhere, somehow – if He has their hearts. I want them
to obey Jesus because it delights them, not because it's their
duty. I want them to know in the marrow of their bones *why* they
make the good choices they make – as opposed to knowing why
they *should*.

I also know my kids need to see me living this way: free,
because of God's favor. I need to be sure I've found the *why* that
underpins my worldview and all my ways, never trapped by habit
or obligation but energized by God's splendid love.

I LIKE TO MOVE IT, MOVE IT!

Exercise is a simple solution to countless health issues. Yet for many,
exercise is a chore, not a choice. Even understanding the impressive
benefits of exercise doesn't always galvanize us into becoming more
active. Why? Because we haven't identified our own *why*. Knowing *why* we
exercise is different to knowing why we *should*. We have at our disposal
everything we need to exercise – our bodies. So let's figure out our *why*.
Then all that's left is to get moving.

BRIGHT EYES

Your eye is a lamp that provides light for your body.
When your eye is healthy, your whole body is filled with light.

Matthew 6:22, NLT

Jesus explains that our eyes are the gateway to our minds and hearts. So it's wise to watch out for what our eyes are watching – and what our eyes are watching a lot, are *a lot of screens.*

We live in a screen world, and that's fine. Moses had stone tablets. We have smart tablets. God calls each new generation from time's beginning and high tech doesn't surprise Him (Isaiah 41:4). But whether we're navigating the digital dimension or sitting around someone's dining room table, we should be consistently Christ-like in character.

You've got app icons all over your phone or laptop, right? Our word *icon* (meaning *picture* or *representation*) comes from the Greek word meaning *window.* Let's live so that, when people (metaphorically) click on the icon of your life and mine, a window to Jesus opens.

STAY SCREEN SMART

Screen-gazing can result in digital eye strain. Flicker, glare, fuzzy text, viewing distances and screen angles all make your eyes work harder than they do for old-school print-on-paper reading. To stay screen smart, follow the 20-20-20 rule: Every 20 minutes, take 20 seconds to check out what's going on 20 meters away from you. Also, blink! Your blinking rate halves when you're staring at a screen, and without regular lubrication, that tired-itchy-scratchy feeling only gets worse.

NOW I LAY ME DOWN

In peace I will lie down and sleep,
for You alone, O LORD, will keep me safe.
Psalm 4:8, NLT

If something's keeping you up at night, you may be somewhere on the control freak spectrum. Because sleep is a form of surrender.

When you finally give in to sleep … and drift off … *you can't do anything.* You may have disturbed dreams, but really, you can't plot, plan or solve. You can't worry or wonder or work out what to do. When you sleep, you surrender to sleepiness. You surrender consciousness. And you surrender to God – accepting that He's sovereign over your circumstances. He's far beyond the confines and limitations of your finite body – the body that desperately needs sleep.

Ultimately, only God can keep you safe. So perhaps you could see your shut-eye as a form of trust: a nightly recalibration of your resolve to fling yourself on the mercy of a good, strong God.

SNOOZE OR LOSE

Sleep isn't a luxury. It gives your body the chance to repair and maintain itself. Poor sleep is associated with everything from lowered immunity, to high blood pressure and diabetes. When it comes to heart disease, sleeping can be as beneficial to your health as not smoking. Aim for seven to nine hours of sleep each night. Try setting a *go-to-bed* alarm for eight hours before you need to wake up, and get the best night's sleep you can by keeping your room cool, dark and quiet – just like Batman!

QUIET CONTROL

The LORD replied, 'My Presence will go with you,
and I will give you rest.'

Exodus 33:14, NIV

We have no control over heaps of life's happenings – globally, locally, personally.

But we *do* have control over our actions, attitudes, thoughts and words. We *do* have control over our immediate environments, making sure our homes, work settings and social spaces are – as far as it depends on us – places of peace, where Christ is King.

As for the rest of our crazy busy noisy life, we *can* control how we choose to respond to the things we *can't* control. When it's hard to find time to rest, or impossible to turn down the din blaring round you, remember that God's presence goes with you, all the time, and you can rest in it, anytime.

Ask God to teach you how to live in two places at once: the chaos of life, and the quiet of His presence.

YOUR SLEEP STATION

Temperature, light and noise are as important as your bed and pillow in determining how well (or restlessly) you sleep. The ideal sleeping temperature is between 18 and 22 degrees Celsius. The darker the room, the better. Darkness triggers the release of your key sleep hormone, melatonin. When you use electronic devices close to bedtime, they trick your body into thinking it's still light and sunny outside, making it difficult for your mind to unwind. Finally, a quiet bedroom (no buzzing of notifications!) is a healthy bedroom.

UP STRAIGHT

But you must continue to believe this truth and stand firmly in it.
Don't drift away from the assurance you received
when you heard the Good News …
Colossians 1:23, NLT

I'm standing as I type this. My laptop's perched at eye level and my keyboard comfortably one level lower than that. When I got this 'standing desk', it came with a workout. *Day 1 – stand for one hour only!* Over two weeks I slowly built up to standing for five hours. That's because I wasn't initially 'standing fit'. I was used to sitting … slumping … slouching. Standing was rigorous. I discovered different muscles. And I was glad I did.

Spiritually, we're not always standing fit either. That's why Paul encourages and reminds the Colossians to *stand firm*. We're quick to forget. Quick to tire … and slump back into old habits or bogus beliefs. Would you practice today – even for a few minutes – allowing a promise of God to help you stand up straight?

GET FIT DON'T SIT

It's true: sitting is the new smoking. Sedentary times of six to nine hours per day are associated with a higher risk of cancer, diabetes and heart disease. That's because even small movements, like standing up, activate significant metabolic processes responsible for regulating hormones, and burning energy and fat. Take regular standing and walking breaks. Limit your sitting episodes to no more than sixty minutes at a time. Sit less, move more. Don't tweet it, do it.

FOOD FOR THOUGHT

What's your why to exercise? Which one of these reasons to exercise makes the most sense to you?

- *Depression or mood swings.* You're feeling a bit down. Enter exercise! Being active boosts your mood and can keep it elevated, in some cases just as well as anti-depressant medication.

- *Weight loss.* You're feeling a bit podgy. Exercise isn't the magic bullet for weight loss, but it makes a significant contribution to getting you back in shape. Plus, it puts you in the right frame of mind to eat better and be healthier overall.

- *Stress and fatigue.* You're tired and tense. You guessed it: exercise gives your energy-making machinery an extra boost, and it stops the stress hormone cortisol in its tracks. Exercise also improves sleep quality, which is just as important as sleep quantity.

- *Low immunity.* You can't go a month without feeling sick. That magical vitamin E (exercise!) arms your immune system with all it needs to keep germs at bay.

- *Anxiety.* You're worried about your heart or your brain or some other part of your body. There's no better medication than being more active. Of course, if your gut feeling (or you mom) tells you to see a doctor, best you listen!

TIME TO REFLECT ...

Heavenly Father, help me find my why —
so that I'll never lose my way.
Keep me resolved to manage what goes into my mind,
through my eyes.
Keep me resolved to stand up and stand firm,
for You and for others.
Keep me resolved to sleep deep and move more.
Amen.

_____

_____

_____

_____

_____

_____

_____

_____

_____

_____

EARN YOUR STRIPES

Gray hair is a crown of glory; it is gained by living a godly life.
Proverbs 16:31, NLT

God's Kingdom is fantastically counterculture. Where the world idolizes youth and beauty, God honors age and experience. He *created* youth and beauty, so of course they're wonderful things, in and of themselves. But it's helpful to be aware that we tend to fixate on these elusive traits – exhausting ourselves and wasting our lives chasing them.

It's also helpful to remember that we all get the *same amount of time* in our twenties, thirties, eighties … Don't despise that beautiful thirty-something woman (because you're fifty-something). She'll get a full beautiful decade in her thirties – like you did. Once she's had her turn, she'll move on. Like you did.

Time is fair that way. Instead of being jealous, celebrate the signs that you've lived – filled up your years and earned your silver streaks and laughter lines. You've got more to offer the world than you once did, because you've lived a bit.

🍎 SILVER LINING

Stress is more likely to be the cause of hair loss than any color change – so you might be able to blame your boss for your receding hairline, but not for the gray. Gray hair is mostly determined by genetics and a complex series of cell chemistries. If you have this genetic predisposition, a significant stressful event *may* speed up the graying process – but for most of us, we can justifiably blame our parents when we go gray!

CUP OF COURAGE

You prepare a feast for me in the presence of my enemies.
You honor me by anointing my head with oil.
My cup overflows with blessings.

Psalm 23:5, NLT

Psalm 23 is a rich, multisensory depiction of a confident, coura-geous David, not at all threatened or insecure in his enemies' presence. He's brave and assertive because his cup is brimming with satisfaction in God's providence, provision and protection. He's got nothing to fear, because he has found ultimate fulfillment and assurance in his Heavenly King.

What's filling your cup? What are you relying on to keep you spiritually or emotionally energized and engaged? The truth is, God fills your cup so you can fill others. You get to do His work, His way, in His strength and for His glory. Let the thrill of that privilege keep you drinking deeply at the Source of every blessing.

JAVA JUNKIE OR BRILLIANT BARISTA?

Coffee has a long history of being blamed for many ills, but the truth is it's a potent source of antioxidants, the vital compounds that prevent cell damage. Antioxidants help maintain the health of your liver, heart, immune system and blood vessels. Coffee's also good for your brain: improving attention, reaction time and reasoning. If you're healthy, you can drink up to six cups a day. Of course, if you feel stressed, can't sleep, or get tremors, cut back on the caffeine! And don't forget, it's the *coffee* that's good for you, not the *sugar* you add!

UNPLUG

But Jesus often withdrew to lonely places and prayed.
Luke 5:16, NIV

Jesus wasn't antisocial. He engaged with crowds of thousands. He hung out with close friends. He took time to chat to individual men, women and kids. He also never abdicated His responsibilities, opting for escapism. He was just boundary smart: wise about managing His time and His emotional, physical and spiritual resources.

He calls us to *follow Him*. Let's follow Him in this. Let's guard some time to think and pray – so we do more responding and less reacting. If we step away from social media for a bit, or take a break from city life, or decline an invitation in favor of family downtime – the world will keep spinning on its axis. God will continue to write history, working out His plans for us and the rest of the human race.

And we'll be able to join Him in His work far more effectively, once we've taken time to unplug.

DIGITAL DETOX

Many of us spend more time on digital devices than we do on sleep. We're sitting, slouching and scrolling far too much, and our health has taken a hit. Ironically, social media has us suffering from *disconnectedness*, anxiety, depression, poor self-esteem and stress. Consider including a regular digital detox into your media diet: a periodic shut down of all devices. Taking a brain break from digital multitasking elevates thinking, and improves your memory and mood. You may also get a whole new perspective on your life.

MIND RIGHT

Even though the fig trees have no blossoms,
and there are no grapes on the vines; even though the olive crop
fails, and the fields lie empty and barren; even though
the flocks die in the fields, and the cattle barns are empty, yet I will
rejoice in the Lord! I will be joyful in the God of my salvation!
Habakkuk 3:17-18, NLT

The prophet penning these words clearly made a choice. He said, 'Even though life sucks, I'm choosing to praise God!' He wasn't delusional. He was eyes-wide-open to the challenges, difficulties and tragedies of real life in a wrecked world. But he chose *anyway* to keep his eyes on his sovereign, wise and loving Heavenly Father.

God is so much more powerful than any amount of positive thinking we can muster. But He's given us minds made in His image. We have astute faculties and the power of choice. Taking our toxic thoughts captive (2 Corinthians 10:5) changes us, and that changes the atmosphere in which we find ourselves.

LIVING ON UPBEAT STREET

It's impossible to be perpetually cheerful. But it *is* possible to adjust your self-talk and approach unpleasantness in a positive, productive way. Studies show that patients who adopted a positive outlook while dealing with heart disease lived 58% longer – and stronger – than those who didn't look on the bright side. Other studies have linked silver-lining thinking to improved immunity and quicker recovery from illness. Smile – it's good for your health.

WELLSPRING

Jesus replied, 'Anyone who drinks this water will soon
become thirsty again. But those who drink the water
I give will never be thirsty again. It becomes a fresh,
bubbling spring within them, giving them eternal life.'

John 4:13-14, NLT

Jesus asserts that anything earthly eventually runs out. If we
hook our hope onto *anything* other than Jesus (like, a career,
a country, a church leader, a spouse or friend), we'll end up
disappointed – and thirstier than before.

For sure, we can hope for good things for a person we love. We
can hope for good things to arise from a particular situation. But
we can't expect anything or anyone other than Jesus to provide
our peace, wellbeing or security. He's the hope that does not
disappoint (Romans 5:5).

Isaiah wrote, 'Is anyone thirsty? Come and drink – even if you
have no money! Come, take your choice of wine or milk – it's all
free!' (Isaiah 55:1). It's not too good to be true: the water of life
is not only accessible and available – it's *free*.

WATER IS LIFE

Water covers 70% of the Earth's surface, and our bodies are made up
of around the same percentage. Water is involved in everything from
regulating body temperature to carrying nutrients and waste products
throughout your body. It allows metabolic reactions to occur, acts as a
lubricant and cushion around joints, and forms the amniotic sac surrounding
a fetus. Obey your thirst. It's life-giving.

FOOD FOR THOUGHT

De-bunking health and beauty myths: These things are so not true!

✤ *I must drink eight glasses of water a day.*

The eight-glasses-a-day rule dates back to 1945. The original guidelines came from a misinterpretation of a recommendation from the Food and Nutrition Board in the USA, which stated that a person should have around 1ml of water for each calorie he or she consumes. The average diet at the time was approximately 1900 calories, meaning you needed about 2 liters of water per day. What the guidelines also said was that most of this water could be found in foods. If that last, crucial part is ignored (as it was), the statement could be interpreted as clear instructions to drink eight glasses of water a day.

✤ *If I pluck out this gray hair, three more will grow back in its place.*

Plucking a rogue silvery strand will not result in three more popping up in its place. Each hair has a single follicle, and we can't add to our number of follicles. Also, plucking one out won't magically transform the color of any of its neighbors! Plucking can traumatize the follicle, and repeated trauma to any follicle isn't ideal. Over time a message is sent to the hair follicle that there's no need to produce hair and the follicle goes into rest, eventually shrinking and no longer producing a hair shaft. This is great for limiting your gray hair, but not so great when it leads to a bald spot.

TIME TO REFLECT ...

Substantial evidence shows that people who meditate daily display more positive emotions than those who don't. So, make yourself a cup of coffee, and take even just ten minutes to reflect, journal and pray over what you've read in the past week.

Have there been times that you've felt dehydrated – physically, relationally, emotionally or spiritually?

Are you thankful for a positive experience you've had this week? *Write it down.*

We're great at scheduling meetings, conference calls and other weekly events into our calendars. Could you schedule some time to play? Or time to unplug – even for a couple hours – from the urgency of online life?

Where do you need to give yourself permission to *smile a little more?* (The worst that could happen is that you'll feel a little better and live a little longer ...)

_____

_____

_____

_____

_____

SWEET POISON

Do you like honey? Don't eat too much,
or it will make you sick!
Proverbs 25:16, NLT

Sugar has crept into almost every food we eat. While it's made our lives much tastier, it's also made them much shorter. If you're typical, you're eating between 100-200g of sugar every day, consciously or not. There's sugar in unobvious places like cereals, ketchup, yoghurts and salad dressings. And sugar shows up in masks called sucrose, dextrose, fructose, maltose, lactose and glucose, even masquerading behind products labeled 'natural'.

God created sugar. It's a good thing. But all His good gifts – friendship, amusement, sex, sport – can be twisted into idols by our natural bent towards sin and self. Also, Satan's oldest trick is sugarcoating the hook, baiting us with things that look, taste and feel good – but are *not* necessarily good for us.

Are you doing too much of something that's essentially *good* – but *not good for you*? Pray for discernment – recognizing the danger – and discretion – knowing what to do about it.

BUT EVERYBODY'S DOING IT ...

Sugars you eat are broken down into glucose – providing instant energy – and fructose – which gets sidetracked by first being converted into glucose in the liver. If you consume more sugar than you burn through activity, your liver converts the excess glucose into fat. Not cool. You heard that right – sugar makes you fat, not fat. Besides the sugar hangover you'll get from sweet stuff, sugary diets are associated with diabetes and inflammation, which lead to heart disease. Grab a small apple instead!

ADDICTED

Dear children, keep away from anything that
might take God's place in your hearts.
1 John 5:21, NLT

To figure out if you're addicted to something, ask yourself these two questions: Am I willing to sin to get it? And, will I sin if I don't get it?

If we're readjusting our lifestyles – our coming and going, our spending, our socializing or working – around a particular activity or substance, that may be an indication that we've developed an unhealthy dependence on it. So, if the corner store is out of your favorite candy, do you get mad? Are you willing to cut into work hours to sneak a smoke even though that's breaking regulations and you'll need to lie on your time sheet? Is there a website you know you need to block?

We're made to need God desperately – to wholly depend on Him. Let's not choose to wholly depend on anything else.

I CAN QUIT ANY TIME ...

Sugar travels the same chemical pathways as alcohol and heroin, and studies show that high glycemic index foods, which cause a rapid spike in blood sugar and insulin, also result in hunger and cravings for up to four hours after they've been noshed. There's also evidence that one of the sugars, fructose (often used as a sweetener in processed foods), can suppress leptin, the hormone that carries the *stop-eating-you're-full* message to your brain. So if you're caught with your hand in the cookie jar, at least you now know why!

STRESS HAPPENS

'I have told you these things,
so that in Me you may have peace.
In this world you will have trouble.
But take heart! I have overcome the world.'
John 16:33, NIV

Losing your job. Losing a loved one. Losing your car keys or a lane in the traffic. Finding out you owe the taxman way more than you thought. Finding a zit on your forehead the morning of a job interview. Finding a text message you weren't meant to read, or a tumor, or a truckload of creased clothes that won't iron themselves. Life is full of the complications and unravelings of things going wrong and beyond our power to manage.

We can't always know what's coming and we certainly can't always control it – but we can determine to make the best choices around those events and eventualities. And we can determine to trust Jesus, who assured us that He has overcome all the things that threaten to overcome us.

STRESS INSIDE, SPOTS OUTSIDE

Students experience significantly more skin breakouts around exam time, as stress increases the hormone production involved in inflammation. But stress also results in poor sleep, less exercise and dicey dietary choices (when last did you see someone stress-eat a salad?) Eating a single slab of chocolate won't cause acne, but regularly eating foods high in refined carbohydrates (and the resulting inflammation) will. So, you can't wish away real-life stress or do much about hormonal changes, but you can control your exercising, snacking and sleeping.

YAWN ...

As a door swings back and forth on its hinges,
so the lazy person turns over in bed.
Proverbs 26:14, NLT

Stress is an undeniable, largely unavoidable part of our lives, so the sooner we learn to manage it – gathering all the tricks and tools we can to do so – the better. It helps, even, to view some stress *positively*. Demanding situations or encounters – deadlines and drawbacks – can galvanize us into action and force us to find creative solutions.

Except, sometimes we'd rather stay in bed, hoping all the lousiness goes away. If you've ever done that, you'll know that stress is happy to wait for you to surface. And when you do, you find that stress has invited a few of its friends – like fear, anxiety and depression. Why not ask God to show you if or where you're opting for sleep or some other escapism instead of facing what's in front of you, in His strength, head on?

TOO MUCH OF A GOOD THING

Sleep is crucial for almost all aspects of our health, from the physical to the emotional. But it's possible to get *too much* of a good thing. Being horizontal for extended periods (more than 9 hours) means much less time for other healthy behaviors, like exercise. Also, because your body slows down while you sleep, too much sleep can have a knock-on effect on your metabolism, increasing your risk of conditions like insulin resistance, diabetes and heart disease. Aim for seven to nine hours a night, no more, no less.

BREATHE IN, BREATHE OUT

Understand this, my dear brothers and sisters:
You must all be quick to listen, slow to speak,
and slow to get angry.

James 1:19, NLT

It's mostly just irritating when you're (legitimately or not) losing your cool and someone tells you to 'Just breathe!' Yet, in stressful situations, don't dismiss this advice as simplistic. Sometimes it's the most spiritual thing you can do.

How many parent-child relationships, co-worker partnerships or marriages might have been set on different – better – trajectories – if one or both parties had just taken a deep breath in … and out … to curb the harsh or hurtful or otherwise regrettable thing they were about to unleash?

Breathing deeply – diaphragmatically – gives you time to think. It helps you pause to consider the consequences of the conversation you're caught up in. It slows your heart rate and gets oxygen to your brain so you can think more clearly. Just one deep-in-and-out breath might be Jesus to someone today.

DREAM ROUTINE

Sleep apnea is a sleeping disorder in which you experience one or more pauses in breathing while you sleep. Breaks can last a few seconds or minutes, and can happen up to 30 times an hour. As your body realizes it's running out of oxygen, you start breathing normally again, but not before you've moved out of deep, restorative sleep, which disrupts your hormones, and can increase your risk of high blood pressure and heart disease. Losing weight, stopping smoking and reducing alcohol consumption all ease the condition.

FOOD FOR THOUGHT

Slash your sweet cravings:

- ✤ *Zero in on your sugar sources.* Get honest with yourself about the two teaspoons of sugar in your morning coffee. That sweetened cereal you like. Your daily pick-me-up soda at work and those biscuits in your child's lunchbox.

- ✤ *Consider slowly cutting back on each one.* Start by adding just *one* sugar to your morning fix. Sweeten your cereal with fresh fruit. Choose water at work and rather give your kids something more filling like a boiled egg or nuts. The key is to eliminate or reduce, systematically, all obvious added sources of sugar, and to slowly self-train to appreciate less of it. You *can* teach old taste buds new tricks!

- ✤ *Don't drink yourself fat.* Possibly the biggest change you could make is to kick the fizzy beverages and vitamin enhanced sugary juice traps to the curb and reach for good 'ole H_2O instead. You have to chuck your sugar addiction sometime, so it may as well be now. That's the bad news. The good news is that your teeth, heart and waist will all be thanking you. (Your dentist and cardiologist, maybe not so much!)

TIME TO REFLECT ...

Almighty God, thank You that You're strong enough
to break the chains of any addiction.
I know You lend me every breath I take,
and I want to use each one to magnify Your great Name
above my troubles, so I submit to You every source of stress
currently stealing my joy. I don't want to use sleep
or anything else as an escape. Make me brave!
Amen.

_____

_____

_____

_____

_____

_____

_____

_____

_____

_____

GRACE FOR DISGRACE

Suddenly, a man with leprosy approached Him and knelt before Him.
'Lord,' the man said, if You are willing, You can heal me
and make me clean.' Jesus reached out and touched him. 'I am
willing,' He said. 'Be healed!' And instantly the leprosy disappeared.

Matthew 8:2-3, NLT

The leper described in this passage would've been mortified about his condition. Leprosy was so embarrassing – so hideously obvious. Lepers were ostracized, shamed and disgraced. *Dis-included*, as my youngest son would say. And yet Jesus wondrously *included* the leper – encircling him with help and healing. Jesus was unaffected by his imperfections, and His love for him was unwavering. Jesus covered his shame, and restored his dignity.

Perhaps you're living with a condition you feel to be in some way physically shameful. Or maybe you carry *inside* shame no one knows about. The same Jesus who loved the leper is your Friend and Redeemer. He gave up His life to woo you with grace for disgrace. Call out to Him today. *He's willing.*

THE SKIN YOU'RE IN

Psoriasis is an autoimmune disease causing raised, red, scaly patches on your skin. It can range from mildly annoying to disfiguring and debilitating. The causes are a combination of genes, your immune system and environmental triggers. Triggers can be external (skin injuries, severe sunburn, a scratch, or infections), lifestyle factors (stress, smoking and excessive alcohol consumption) and certain medications. It's vitally important to figure out your triggers so you can manage the condition well.

BLEMISH TURNED BEAUTIFUL

… Christ loved the church. He gave up His life for her to make her holy and clean, washed by the cleansing of God's word. He did this to present her to Himself as a glorious church without a spot or wrinkle or any other blemish. Instead, she will be holy and without fault.

Ephesians 5:25-27, NLT

I've never seen a bride with acne. Maybe that's because makeup works magic. But mostly it's because a bride has left the worst of her teenage acne behind her. She's grown and gorgeous – her skin aglow with love.

Stunningly, this is how Jesus presents His bride, the church, to Himself too. We're far from flawless and we won't be anything close to perfect until heaven, but by covering for us – taking our place on the cross that should have been our torture, not His – Jesus ascribes to us *His* perfection. He makes His bride beautiful: pure, shame-free, forgiven, transformed, completely accepted, and welcomed into an eternal love relationship with Him, regardless of the pimples of the past, literal or figurative.

MANAGING MOUNT VESUVIUS

Pimples happen when the sebaceous glands at the base of hair follicles, become overactive. These overactive glands, which moisturize your skin, get blocked up with bacteria, setting off an immune response resulting in inflammation, redness and voila … your common pimple. People prone to acne are especially sensitive to blood levels of the hormone testosterone. See a doc if your acne is severe, as a simple antibiotic could do wonders.

BREATHE SWEET

She opens her mouth with wisdom,
and the teaching of kindness is on her tongue.

Proverbs 31:26, ESV

Solomon is describing the wonder woman of Proverbs 31, but this verse can encourage us all. Think about what you'd love for people to say about you at your office farewell party one day. *'Dude, whenever you opened your mouth, we knew it would be worth listening!'* Or at your funeral. *'She had a wise, witty word for every person she interacted with!'*

Jesus says that one day we'll each give an account for every empty word we've spoken (Matthew 12:36). That makes me want to *shut my mouth* – then slow down, and think. It makes me want to choose carefully and kindly, and to speak only what strengthens the soul of the listener. Pray that you'd be the sweet aroma of Christ (2 Corinthians 2:15) in every arbitrary or crucial conversation you're part of today.

SCRUB THE STINK

Bad breath affects one out of four people. It's caused by gases emitted by bacteria living in your mouth. These bacteria produce gas when they meet food particles on your gums, teeth or tongue. Brush your teeth twice a day, sure, but *don't forget to brush your tongue*, which is the biggest bacteria breeding ground in your mouth. Also, what you put in your mouth influences what comes out. Swap sugary foods for carrots and celery, which help scrub away gas-producing bacteria that your toothbrush may have missed.

DIFFERENT BY DIVINE DESIGN

He created them male and female,
and He blessed them and called them 'human.'
Genesis 5:2, NLT

*B*oth *kinds* of human being were made in God's image. And yet we've exhausted ourselves over millennia trying to find our place and our pecking order. For too long, women were degraded and disregarded. So they jumped on the pendulum and made sure it swung right to the other side – where men were belittled, beleaguered and emasculated.

The truth is, there are glorious overlaps between the ways of men and women. But sometimes what we do and how we do it differs. What we *feel* and how we feel it differs. Instead of comparing and criticizing (husband-bashing at ladies' nights or making derogatory jokes about wives in the locker room), let's honor and celebrate each other, grateful for how our differences makes us stronger, more secure versions of our distinct selves.

CHANGE OF HEART

There are definitive differences when it comes to heart disease in both sexes. Men are more at risk than pre-menopausal women because estrogen works on white blood cells to stop them sticking to the insides of blood vessels, which leads to dangerous blockages. However, once women are past menopause, there's no risk difference, and more women than men die of heart disease each year. Women are, in fact, nine times more at risk of developing a heart condition than breast cancer. Thankfully, 80% of premature heart disease can be prevented through healthier lifestyle choices.

BAD TO WORSE

' ... lies instead of truth prevail in the land,
for they proceed from evil to evil,
and they do not take Me into account,' declares the LORD.
Jeremiah 9:3, BSB

These are harsh-but-true words from the prophet to God's people (and us). We tend to lie to ourselves more than we lie to others. We can talk ourselves into and out of almost anything. We convince ourselves that our lifestyle choices, for example, 'aren't hurting anyone'. Except, you're an *anyone* too, and they're probably hurting you. If we're honest, we can admit that when we fall, we don't fall far. We 'proceed from evil to evil', little by little, decision by decision.

Let's decide to be better than that. Hebrews 3:13 (NIV) reminds us to 'encourage one another daily, as long as it is called 'Today,' so that none of you may be hardened by sin's deceitfulness.' Let's hold each other accountable. This day is still called 'Today', so it's not too late.

ONE THING LED TO ANOTHER ...

Our greatest health risks are seldom stand-alone conditions, and often when we fail to manage one condition, it leads to another. Diabetes, for example, increases the risk of heart disease in women more than it does in men, perhaps because women with diabetes more often have added risk factors, such as obesity and hypertension. Start by reassessing your bed time. Night owls are at increased risk of both diabetes and heart disease, mostly because they have more time to eat more, snack more and drink more.

FOOD FOR THOUGHT

Skin solutions: Tips for treating psoriasis and acne

- *Sleep deep. Move more. Eat well.* This applies to both acne and psoriasis. Focus particularly on eating fewer foods that cause inflammation, like sugar and processed carbs.

- *Know your psoriasis triggers.* Firstly, infections like strep throat are associated with psoriasis flare ups. Then there are lifestyle factors causing inflammation (lack of sleep or exercise, stress, smoking and alcohol consumption). And lastly, certain medications (used to manage bipolar disorder and prevent malaria) trigger psoriasis. Of course, the benefits of managing bipolar symptoms and preventing malaria *far* outweigh the risks of triggering psoriasis, so always talk to a doc before tinkering with meds.

- *Inside and outside treatments.* Psoriasis can be managed with topical creams, phototherapy and medication. The treatment course will depend on the severity of the psoriasis, and on *you.* Your skin doesn't fit anyone else, and there isn't a one-size-fits-all approach to how it's treated. Ideally, stay out of the sun and opt for cool showers.

- *Keep it clean.* When it comes to zits, keep your face, hands and hair clean. A splash of water isn't enough: add soap to the mix. Think about how many times a day your fingers touch your face. Then think about what else those fingers have touched. It's a bacteria party out there! The more bacteria on your face, the more likely the chance of infection.

- *Speak up.* The treatment and management of both acne and psoriasis is important, but don't lose sight of your emotional response. Self-esteem and mood can both take a blow during flare ups. Asking for help, speaking out and recognizing the emotional side of things can help you take back some control.

TIME TO REFLECT ...

No doubt you know someone who has survived cancer, is battling cancer today, or has passed away from cancer. Perhaps *you* are in the fight of your life right now.

Could you be a breath of fresh air to a struggling someone today? How might you try to understand what the world feels like rubbing up against their skin?

_____

_____

_____

_____

_____

_____

_____

_____

_____

_____

_____

_____

_____

POWERFUL IN THE PRESENT

Don't brag about tomorrow,
since you don't know what the day will bring.
Proverbs 27:1, NLT

It's not fatalistic to say none of us knows how much time we've got left. It's actually empowering. It reminds us not to wish away time, or fixate on the possibilities of approaching disaster. It reminds us to stay humble – grateful for the breath and the blood flooding our bodies this instant.

Moses wrote, 'Teach us to number our days, that we might gain a heart of wisdom' (Psalm 90:12). He's saying, 'This moment – *now* – is all you have, so choose wisely how you spend it – for the win!'

It's also not fatalistic to remind ourselves that there are no guarantees. In a broken world, crazy terrible stuff happens to all of us at some time, in some way. That's all the more reason to determine – *today* – to build excellent, beautiful lives in all the ways we know how.

REDUCE THE RISK

Four in ten cancer cases are preventable. Healthy living isn't a cast-iron guarantee against cancer, but it heavily stacks the odds of avoiding it in our favor. Some years ago a study calculated how people who ticked four healthy behavior boxes – not smoking, being active, drinking in moderation and eating five fruits and veggies a day – lived on average fourteen years longer. Fourteen years! That's watching your kids graduate, walking them down the aisle and getting a chance to hold your grandkids. Your choices today might ensure that kind of tomorrow.

THIS FAR, NO FURTHER

Temptation comes from our own desires,
which entice us and drag us away.
These desires give birth to sinful actions.
And when sin is allowed to grow, it gives birth to death.
James 1:14-15, NLT

When things go wrong, it's so much easier to blame, or play the victim. It's uncomfortable to ask ourselves, 'Could I have done something differently to prevent this?' Or even, more honestly, 'Am I actually entirely at fault?'

You've almost certainly unfairly reaped what someone else has sown. That sucks. But truthfully, at the end of more than a few bad days, I've soul-searched and had to admit that *my* words, attitudes or actions had a lot to do with things going pear-shaped. I've asked God to show me the source of my sin, deep beneath the external behaviors. Is it greed? Jealousy? Anger? Pride? If I know where and why the sin begins in me, I can trace its ugly flourishing – and cut it off at the roots.

CRUSH THE CULPRIT

Understanding how cancer starts and grows helps us understand how to make it stop and shrink. The vast majority of cancers are triggered by DNA damage that accumulates during your lifetime. DNA is a molecular instruction manual for our cells. Damaged DNA can make cells grow and divide uncontrollably – the hallmark of all cancers. Healthy living reduces our exposure to things that damage DNA (like cigarette smoke, ultraviolet radiation in sunlight, and hormonal changes associated with carrying extra weight).

YOU'RE IN THERE SOMEWHERE

The LORD will work out His plans for my life –
for Your faithful love, O LORD, endures forever.
Don't abandon me, for You made me.

Psalm 138:8, NLT

I feel useless. My life's going nowhere. I just don't have it in me to reach for the stupid stars!' If your thoughts have gone down these kinds of dirt roads, maybe you need to stop them in their tracks and hear the truth:

God's strands of wonder are woven into your DNA. In conceptualizing the universe, He dreamed you up too. He's a faithful Father and Creator, never abandoning His children or His creation. All the potential in you – *He placed it there* in the first place. Why would He *not* fulfill His purposes in you and through you, as you surrender your dreams (crazy or legit) to Him?

Beneath your imperfection is the Christ-like person God created you to be. You can freely enjoy spending the rest of your life becoming that masterpiece.

SIX OF THE BEST

Exercises targeting your abdomen can tone and strengthen those muscles, but if there was a quick fix for killer abs, surely we'd see more six packs and fewer beer bellies. Our bodies can't slim down in one area exclusively. Fat loss is a full body phenomenon. To minimize belly fat? Lose fat *all over*. How? By the myth-free approach of combining cardiovascular training, resistance training and selective calorie choice. You definitely have a six pack; it may just be hiding beneath some unnecessary padding!

SAY WHAT NOW?

And the people of Berea were more open-minded
than those in Thessalonica, and they listened eagerly
to Paul's message. They searched the Scriptures day after day
to see if Paul and Silas were teaching the truth.

Acts 17:11, NLT

The Bereans' example can shape how we do life. They were curious and open-minded. They were keen to learn, and assimilate knowledge into lifestyle. And they were grounded. They checked their facts. They weighed up everything they heard against the immutable truth of the Word. They made an effort to study, think, question and apply.

We absolutely need to do the same. Check the context of every verse in this devotional, if you can! We're all just grace-saved pilgrims finding our way through this life to eternity. None of us is above mistakes and misinterpretations.

In a deceptive age fraught with false teaching, we need each other's checks and challenges. More than that, we need to keep going back to God's infallible Word.

SO NOT TRUE

Myth-busting time! If you stop exercising, *muscles don't turn to fat*. Muscle and fat are two different tissue types. The one can't magically become the other. But when people stop exercising, muscles shrink, clearing the way for adipose tissue (fat). Couch potatoes are also inclined to continue eating as much as they did during their active days, despite less energy expenditure. All this creates the illusion that a lean six-pack and bulging biceps have turned to fat. The solution to avoid the illusion: stay active!

DO RIGHT ANYWAY

For it is better, if it is God's will,
to suffer for doing good than for doing evil.
1 Peter 3:17, NIV

Nobody *loves* suffering. You don't hear people cheering, 'Bring on the misery!' Suffering's roads lead through horrid landscapes – like disappointment, grief and fear – turning people all kinds of bitter and disillusioned. You may feel *especially* cheated if you're suffering for doing the *right* thing. Totally unfair.

Imagine how Jesus felt. He never did one wrong thing. He only ever did all the right things, all the time. Yet He suffered more than anyone in history, taking upon Himself the shame and blame of all humanity. (And just imagine where we'd be, in our suffering world, if He hadn't.)

When you suffer for doing right – like, you end up paying tons of tax because you're honest about your earnings – you're in good company. God will do right by you, judging your case with divine justice (1 Peter 2:23).

YOU'RE NOT A NUMBER

Your weight may go *up* even when you're eating all the right things. Your body's a complex machine, and the number on your scale is a combination of your true weight plus *weight variance* – determined by water retention, what you've eaten, muscle glycogen stores, certain days of the month (for women) and even the weather. So your weight can fluctuate wildly over a couple days. There's more to health than an ideal scale weight – and one of the best yardsticks is quite simply how great you feel!

FOOD FOR THOUGHT

Put this in your pipe and smoke it ...
These three lifestyle changes can reduce your risk of cancer:

* *Stop smoking.* Smoking is by far the most important preventable cause of cancer in the world. Quitting may be one of the hardest things to do, but it's a no-brainer if you want to grow old with someone. Five years after quitting, your risk of throat, esophageal and bladder cancer is halved; after ten years your risk of lung cancer is halved; and after fifteen years your risk of lung, throat, esophageal or bladder cancer is the same as for a non-smoker.

* *Cut back on the booze.* Along with smoking, drinking alcohol causes the majority of mouth and esophageal (food pipe) cancers. People who smoke *and* drink multiply the harm, because tobacco and alcohol work together to damage the cells of your body. Alcohol makes it easier for your mouth and throat to absorb the cancer-causing chemicals in tobacco.

* *Keep a healthy body weight.* Carrying extra weight around your abdomen has serious health risks, more so than fat anywhere else on your body. Belly fat is associated with increased risk for heart disease, diabetes and certain cancers. The good news is that, as weight loss and fat reduction kicks in, the first place it usually happens is around your belly, which is far more valuable than simply helping you get your six pack back!

TIME TO REFLECT ...

*Lord, thank You that You hold the future and You've placed
in me the potential to greet what's coming.
Give me grace to manage the external influences in my life,
well and wisely, and honesty to acknowledge when what's
making me worry or waver is really coming from within.
You are the source of all wisdom and information
(Colossians 2:3). Help me check my facts against
Your timeless truth. Strengthen me to keep on
choosing obedience, even when the benefits aren't
immediately apparent. Jesus, You said I could cast
all my anxiety on You, because You care for me (1 Peter 5:7).
Here are my health worries:*

_____

_____

_____

_____

_____

_____

_____

_____

BEEN THERE, FELT THAT

He comforts us in all our troubles so that we can
comfort others. When they are troubled, we will be able
to give them the same comfort God has given us.
2 Corinthians 1:4, NLT

I get migraines. So when someone pops an over-the-counter pain pill and flippantly laments, 'I've got such a migraine!' – I happen to know they really *don't* have a migraine. Migraines involve vomiting. Blinding, unspeakable pain. (Literally – since migraine sufferers often experience loss of vision and speech.) You can take days to recover.

I've been comforted before by *real* migraine sufferers. And I've been able to comfort others.

A hug plus I-know-how-you-feel goes a long way to assuring someone they're not alone. And somehow, that helps us know everything's going to be ok in the end.

If you're human, you've experienced pain of your own. Could you be brave enough to ask God to transform it into another's comfort?

NO BRAIN, NO PAIN?

Your brain doesn't feel pain. There are no pain receptors in brain tissue itself. This is why neurosurgeons can operate on brain tissue without causing the patient (who is sometimes awake!) discomfort. But millions of pain triggers hide in the protective shield *around* your brain. So headache pain results from a complex conversation between your brain and its surrounding blood vessels and nerves. There are about 150 diagnostic headache categories (like tension headaches, migraines and sinus headaches). Naming the pain and knowing its cause are the first steps towards relief.

SATURDAY NIGHT FEVER

Then a leader of the local synagogue, whose name was Jairus, arrived. When he saw Jesus, he fell at His feet, pleading fervently with Him. 'My little daughter is dying,' he said. 'Please come and lay Your hands on her; heal her so she can live.'

Mark 5:22-23, NLT

Once we had kids, 'Saturday night fever' no longer meant *party time*. It meant *another trip to the ER*. Because babies have a way of picking inconvenient moments to get sick. They say a mom is only ever as happy as her unhappiest kid. True story.

Yet Jesus loves our kids even more than we do. The story Mark records unfolds with Jesus heading to Jairus's home, even though He's been told the little girl is already dead. He raises her to life.

Jesus had so much compassion for kids it was considered scandalous (Matthew 19:13). He has that same scandalous compassion for your kids too.

FEVERS AND FEBRILE CONVULSIONS

It's your worst nightmare: your child's temperature spikes causing short bursts of abnormal electrical activity in her brain. She loses consciousness and starts twitching. Febrile convulsions affect around 3% of children aged six months to six years. Stay calm — and stay with your child. Most seizures stop within seconds or a couple of minutes without medical treatment. Take note of what happens so you can describe it later. Call a doctor if the seizure lasts more than five minutes, as something other than fever, might be in the mix.

SHAKE IT OFF

You have turned my mourning into joyful dancing.
You have taken away my clothes of mourning and clothed me
with joy, that I might sing praises to You and not be silent ...
Psalm 30:11-12, NLT

Years ago, my husband trudged through a season of grief. He was angry, sad and desperate to fix things. He started mountain biking. He trained hard for several multi-stage races, coming home sweaty, muddy, exhausted – and at peace. We often talk about how his cycling was central to getting him through those years. His bike was pure grace with pedals on.

Sometimes we have to make movement a sacrifice of praise – *sacrifice* being the operative word. If you're facing trauma, betrayal, depression or disillusionment, you won't *feel* like pulling yourself up by your bootstraps to keep going.

Ask God to help you move forward *just one step*. He'll give you strength for just that step. And then the next. Until you've found your rhythm, momentum and joy once again.

MOVE YOUR MOOD

If you're feeling down, boost your mood instantly without paying a single cent: *just move!* Exercise delivers a 'runner's high': that euphoric feeling caused by a release of happy hormones, or endorphins, which reduce the sensation of pain. Exercise also interferes with the release of certain immune system chemicals that can make depression worse, plus it increases body temperature, which has a calming effect. Possibly the greatest benefit of exercise is that it improves confidence and helps take your mind off your worries.

GEARED FOR GLAD

Jesus stood still, and said, 'Call him.' They called the blind man,
saying to him, 'Cheer up. Get up. He is calling you.'
Mark 10:49, New Heart English Bible

Our happiness fluctuates with circumstance and season. That's normal. But there's an unchanging reality supplying unrelenting joy that we can lean into constantly: the fact that Jesus is calling us, all the time.

Some days it's tough to answer His call, because it involves sacrifice, or very little tangible reward. Some days it's super exciting to answer His call, because He's leading us into adventure. But walking in the footsteps of the Redeemer who is also the source of all power and joy and who dreamed up human happiness will ensure a measure of serenity despite what our conditions dictate. It may even result in rampant delight.

Cheer up. Get up. He's calling you.

HAPPY HORMONES

There are four key happiness hormones: dopamine, serotonin, oxytocin and endorphins. They're neurotransmitters, meaning they work directly on and within your brain to generate good vibes. These hormones are driven in part by your genes, and in part by your lifestyle. Exercise, for example, creates a tsunami of endorphins. Cuddling with your favorite person or pet generates oxytocin, while going outside and soaking up sunshine boosts both dopamine and serotonin. Simply put, the things that make you happy are also the things that make you healthy: nature, exercise and social interaction.

DON'T FORGET TO REMEMBER

Repeat [these commands] again and again to your children.
Talk about them when you are at home and when you are on the road,
when you are going to bed and when you are getting up. Tie them to
your hands and wear them on your forehead as reminders.

Deuteronomy 6:6- 8, NLT

If humans were perfect at remembering things, we wouldn't need instructions like this. We're so easily distracted by oh look a shiny thing! (See?) God knows all the intricacies and simplicities of our finite brains. He created them. And He knows we need to put systems in place – feast days, festivals, Sunday communion and Google calendar – so we don't forget His goodness and greatness.

Consider creating a remembrance trigger – like, every time you flick a light switch, draw a curtain or start your car. Use the moment to remember God's most recent kindness to you, or allow the habit to prompt you to pause and pray.

LOSING YOUR KEYS, AND POSSIBLY YOUR MIND?

Memory declines after the age of 30, and genetics & lifestyle both play a role. Ongoing exposure to stress hormones changes the structure of the brain area responsible for your memory, by destroying nerve endings involved in information flow and memory recall. Stress also interferes with sleep – which is when your brain discards or stores information. Be proactive. What's stressing you out? How can you manage it? Tackle it. And (don't forget to) aim for 150 minutes of moderate intensity exercise a week.

FOOD FOR THOUGHT

Eat on the run, out of the sun ...

Four more lifestyle habits, to reduce your risk of cancer:

- *Eat a balanced diet.* A diet filled with a variety of plant foods (vegetables, fruits, whole grains and beans) lowers the risk for many cancers. Try drinking green tea. It contains high levels of catechins, which prevent DNA damage by mopping up free radicals, blocking the growth of tumor cells and stopping the activation of cancer-causing chemicals. On the flip side, a raft of research urges us to avoid processed meats, which increase bowel cancer risk.

- *Get your heart beating.* A study of 40,000 men found that daily physical activity significantly reduced the chances of dying from cancer. It showed that people who walked or cycled for just half an hour a day were 35% more likely to beat the disease. Today, based on current evidence, health organizations recommend we do at least 30 minutes of moderate physical activity, five times a week, to reduce cancer risk. Too much? Anything's better than nothing. Start by taking the stairs instead of the elevator.

- *Stay safe in the sun.* At least 80% of sun-induced skin damage happens before the age of 18! Slip on a shirt, slop on sunscreen and slap on a hat.

- *Get wise.* The most effective weapon against cancer is knowledge. One in four people may be affected by the disease during their lifetime, which means knowledge about risk reduction, prevention and early detection can be lifesaving.

TIME TO REFLECT ...

Reflect on what you've read over the past week.

Can you hand over your headaches? What nagging worries can you give to God?

In which area of your life is God convicting you to *move*? Commit it to paper. You may be surprised by how the very thing you've been avoiding will energize you, once you get up and get going.

Pray that God would *bring* to mind people who've *slipped* your mind. Who needs your attention? Even now – who are you suddenly remembering?

_____

_____

_____

_____

_____

_____

_____

_____

_____

_____

NOTE-WORTHY

Sing a new song to the LORD,
for He has done wonderful deeds.
His right hand has won a mighty victory;
His holy arm has shown His saving power!

Psalm 98:1, NLT

Hans Christian Andersen said, 'Where words fail, music speaks.' God could've created the universe without melodies and voice ranges and the human inclination towards rhythm and song, but He made music part of our humanity because it's a matchless vehicle for expressing desire, aspiration and celebration: *worship*.

And worship – living lives that express the truth that God is praiseworthy and noteworthy and worthy of our every note – is the very point of our existence.

Your musical talents may be entirely average. Still, are you making music part of how you do life? In the traffic this morning, or while you cook tonight, could you sing to God a new song – or an old song – making way for immediate worship?

MUSICAL MEDITATION AND MEDICATION

Music has been part of medicine since the days of Pythagoras and Hippocrates. Neuroscientists have discovered that listening to music heightens positive emotion through your brain's reward centers, stimulating 'dopamine hits' that make us feel fantastic. Listening to music also lights up other areas of your brain, with knock on effects for everything from stress relief to improving both cognitive and physical performance. Music can meaningfully reduce your perceived intensity of pain, and is especially effective in the care of the elderly, for chronic pain conditions like fibromyalgia and even recovery from surgery.

BAD FOR WORSE

Did you receive the Holy Spirit by obeying the law of Moses?
Of course not! You received the Spirit because you believed the
message you heard about Christ. How foolish can you be?
After starting your Christian lives in the Spirit, why are you now
trying to become perfect by your own human effort?

Galatians 3:2-3, NLT

The Galatians weren't going to die wondering what Paul thought. He comes on pretty strong, and for good reason. He's saying to them, 'Jesus set you free from sin and the law's impossible standards. Why would you want to go back to legalism for your holiness hit? Replacing your sinful lifestyle with ego-driven works righteousness – that doesn't please God either!'

Let's ask God to help us trace habits of legalism or perfectionism that may have crept into our lives: ways we try to get a divine pat on the back, all the while superciliously patting ourselves on the back too.

'HEY POT. THIS IS KETTLE. YOU'RE BLACK.'

Many food items marketed as 'healthy' are usually a bit better nutritionally, than say, a packet of chips. But the problem with these pseudo-healthy foods, especially the 'fat free' versions, is that it's the fat that generally makes something taste good. When you take fat out, you have to replace it with something equally tasty: *sugar!* To add insult to injury, we mistakenly think these fat-free (sugar-loaded) foods are healthier and lower in calories, and we tend to eat more of them. Don't swap bad for worse.

LAMBING, OR SELF-LAMBASTING?

He tends His flock like a shepherd: He gathers the lambs
in His arms and carries them close to His heart;
He gently leads those that have young.

Isaiah 40:11, NIV

Perhaps as a parent, you've cried out with the psalmist, 'I am slipping!' (Psalm 94:18). You've felt as if raising these kids to be even semi-human is hopeless – maybe because you feel like a hopeless human yourself.

The psalmist finishes his sentence: 'but Your unfailing love, O LORD, supported me.' The Shepherd is gently leading you, and your young. Try to let go of perfectionism. Get the best advice you can, and go with your gut.

Remember parental guilt is only appropriate when you've sinned. You're likely doing the best you can, and one day you'll look back on these years and think, 'I wouldn't change a thing.' Today, do a little less lambasting (of yourself and your lambs). Whatever pasture you're in, just enjoy the green grass beneath your feet.

BEATING BABY BLUES

80% of women experience mood disturbances after pregnancy, but 30% of new moms develop postnatal, or postpartum depression, which interferes with your ability to care for yourself and your baby. Rapid hormonal changes occurring after birth, sleep deprivation, and changes in blood pressure, immune system functioning and metabolism may trigger postpartum depression. The symptoms are outside your control. They don't make you a bad mom. They DON'T make you a bad mom. The choice to get treatment is something you *can* control. Don't wait to reach out.

WHERE IT'S AT

The one thing I ask of the LORD – the thing I seek most –
is to live in the house of the LORD all the days of my life,
delighting in the LORD's perfections and meditating in His Temple.

Psalm 27:4, NLT

Most of us are drawn to action and adventure, entertainment and the latest endeavors. We're keen to cash in on life where we see it being lived. But there's no better place to be than in the center of God's will. Wherever God has you, you'll be missing out on something, somewhere. But you can't possibly be missing out on anything *better* because you're in the best place, according to His best plans for you.

When you're heading to any big or small event, ask God to choose the conversations you'll be part of, or who you'll sit next to. You probably won't get to talk to everyone. You'll miss some jokes and feel out. That's ok. Be where God has you, and be there well.

FOMO OR JOMO?

The fear of missing out can negatively impact your health. A survey on the dramatic increase in sales of over-the-counter cold and flu medication showed that FOMO weakens our immune system. We push ourselves, even when we're sick, to be everywhere, doing everything, and so take even longer to recover. FOMO causes anxiety and depression, and may contribute to violence and feelings of shame. Forget the status updates and profile pictures. Embrace JOMO: the *joy* of missing out.

HOT FRESH BUTTERED

'Yes, I am the bread of life! Your ancestors ate manna in the wilderness, but they all died. Anyone who eats the bread from heaven, however, will never die. I am the living bread that came down from heaven. Anyone who eats this bread will live forever … '

John 6:48-51, NLT

We tend to cram our lives with all sorts of stuff, to cheer us up or induce euphoria. But Jesus explains that He's the only limitless source of perfect peace, comfort, satisfaction, strength and joy. Anything else wears off, and eventually disappoints. He's our hot fresh buttered bread of life. Irresistible.

So *resist* the inclination to be satisfied with Jesus Lite: a nibble or a sip here or there, with no commitment or investment. That will leave you hungry. Rather, feast on the Word. If you're really not Word-hungry, give it a try anyway. You might find that after a few bites you won't want to stop.

MOOD FOOD

Your brain needs a constant energy supply and the better the quality of the food you eat, the better the quality of your brain fuel. Your food can also change your brain's structure and function, directly impacting your mood and behavior. Processed, sugary foods will give you a buzz – but when the sugar high wears off you'll feel flat and down. The more fresh food you eat, the calmer and happier you'll feel. Energizing, nutrient-dense foods (eggs, nuts and fish) are your brain's – and your mood's – best friends.

FOOD FOR THOUGHT

Headache triggers and treatments

* *The ice-cream headache.* Ice-cream is often served with brain freeze. Your favorite ice cold treat can cause a very quick dilation of one of the major arteries supplying your brain, which then gets flushed with blood – causing pain. Eat cold things slowly … to give your mouth chance to warm up whatever you're about to swallow. If the pain hits, hold your tongue on the roof of your mouth or drink a warm-ish beverage.

* *Migraines.* Migraine triggers are different for different people, and range from things like irregular sleep or bright lights to anything that puts your body under stress, like illness or an intense workout. Specific foods may also set off a migraine (like chocolate, certain cheeses and alcohol). If you're sensitive to any of these foods, best to avoid them like the plague.

* *Stress and tension headaches.* These could be caused by most careers, lifestyle or environmental stress, like intense screen work, noise, extreme heat or cold, or poor posture when sitting or driving. Small tweaks to your desk setup or work environment, not to mention a bit of time management to ease anxiety, can make a world of difference. Relaxation techniques; a balanced, healthy diet; and rest can all help too.

* *Sinus headaches.* Once your breathing pipes are clear, this headache should disappear. In the meantime, a steamy shower helps get that air flowing freely again.

TIME TO REFLECT ...

Father God, I don't want to stay stuck in my old ways.
And I don't want to invent a religion that I think will please You.
Teach me how to enjoy Your grace,
so my whole life is a song about You.
Please take the reins of my mood today.
I know You won't leave me in the mud pit of depression
(Psalm 40:2). Rescue me! Put my feet on a rock.
Fill me again with the joy of Your salvation (Psalm 51:12).
And God, thank You that I can live without FOMO. I trust You
to place me exactly where I'm meant to be, every moment.
Amen.

_____

_____

_____

_____

_____

_____

_____

POWERFUL POSTURE

And so, dear brothers and sisters, I plead with you to give your
bodies to God because of all He has done for you.
Let them be a living and holy sacrifice – the kind He will find
acceptable. This is truly the way to worship Him.
Romans 12:1, NLT

Whether we're all alone or center stage or just doing our daily doings, our demeanor should be unassuming confidence. Because we're sons and daughters of the High King. That's some serious street cred right there. And we're dust-to-dust sinners wholly dependent on grace. That should keep us humble every moment.

I wonder if the world wouldn't sit up – wide-eyed – if all Jesus-followers everywhere – in their homes and work spaces and grocery stores – began to walk out their days with a posture of easygoing, natural graciousness born of being deeply comfortable in the acceptance of a Savior who's working in us and through us, to bless the world.

STOMACH IN, CHEST OUT

To look good, feel good, and de-stress: sit up, or stand up, straight. Chest out, stomach in, like your mom always said. Try this: take a breath. Now, sit up straight and take another. Notice the difference? Slouching reduces your lung capacity by around 30%. With less fresh oxygen flowing through your body, you have less energy, less focus and a lot less function. Slouching doesn't only make you look sad, it can spark negative emotions too. So square those shoulders and stand tall – it'll boost both your self-esteem and your mood.

FULLY COMPLETELY

Don't you remember ... how hard we worked among you?
Night and day we toiled to earn a living so that we would not be a
burden to any of you as we preached God's Good News to you.
1 Thessalonians 2:9, NLT

You've heard older folks lamenting the evils of a younger generation. 'In *my* day,' they say – followed by a diatribe against youths with no staying power, no sense of loyalty, responsibility or resolve. *Those older folks are usually right.*

We don't like to admit that we spend too much time scrolling inanely through other people's feeds on our phones – but we do. We don't like to admit that we're hesitant to agree to an invitation in case something more *happening* comes up – but that's often how we behave.

I think we can be better than that. Let's shock the world by working as if we're looking to God for a glowing reference letter. Let's commit to being committed. When we're there, let's be *all there*.

THE LIGHTS ARE ON BUT NOBODY'S HOME

When you're down with flu or a tummy bug, your productivity plummets. But day-to-day niggles (allergies, fatigue or headaches) can also seriously affect your output. Minor health complaints don't necessarily keep you away from the office but can keep you away from productive work. Being physically present at work but not fully functional is called *presenteeism*. If this is you, see a doc. Work out your work-life balance, and commit to healthier living.

PAST, PRESENT, PARENTS?

Parents are not to be put to death for their children,
nor children put to death for their parents;
each will die for their own sin.

Deuteronomy 24:16, NIV

This is one of those feel-good Scriptures often shared at weddings. *Not!*

It's part of a miscellany of laws God gave His people for managing their society. The point is, although we are doubtlessly affected by the DNA and decisions of our forebears, you and I are standalone people and we'll each be held accountable for the lives we lead.

You may need to do a bunch of forgiving, when it comes to how your parents raised you, or rejected you. It may be absolutely true that you were oppressed or abandoned or misunderstood. But traipsing through life blaming your folks or others for every misfortune or misdemeanor will get you nowhere. You'll stay stuck in your sin or self-pity – when you were destined for progress and profusion (John 10:10).

There's more to your story than the thickening plot of your past and your parents. Turn the page. God is writing a brand new life.

BIG FAT BLAME GAME

Genetics do play a role in obesity, but generally to a much smaller degree than most people believe, or hope! So far, research reveals that your genes are most definitely not your destiny. Many people who carry these so-called 'obesity genes' (I'm one of them) don't become overweight, simply because healthy lifestyle choices can effectively counteract, or turn off, many of these genetic effects. It's lame to blame.

FUTURE FAMILY FEATURES

'You parents – if your children ask for a loaf of bread,
do you give them a stone instead? Or if they ask for a fish,
do you give them a snake? Of course not!'
Matthew 7:9-10, NLT

We read yesterday that we'll be held responsible for what we did with all our days, and our kids will be held responsible for what they did with theirs. But that doesn't let us off the hook. God has entrusted to us the stewardship of the small humans in our homes.

What dreams do you dream for your kids? Are you *living* those dreams? Like, if you dream of raising men who'll make dinner for their wives one day, are you living the dream by teaching your boys to cook? Our decisions, directions and lifestyle choices *will* rub off on our kids, for better or worse. Let's give them bread and fish – not stones and snakes.

(FAT) APPLES DON'T FALL FAR FROM THE TREE

Three key factors shape a baby's nutritional profile and future health. Firstly, smoking during pregnancy is associated with a 50% higher risk of childhood obesity. Secondly, children of women who gained excessive weight during pregnancy are four times more at risk of being overweight as toddlers. Thirdly, rapid weight gain in infancy is associated with a higher risk of obesity later in life. As your kids grow up, they'll absorb your attitudes towards food and physical activity. Be the leader you'd love them to follow.

EPIC FAIL

Examine yourselves to see if your faith is genuine.
Test yourselves. Surely you know that Jesus Christ is among you;
if not, you have failed the test of genuine faith.

2 Corinthians 13:5, NLT

Epic spiritual fails are entirely avoidable, if we'd just stop for long enough to be honest. But it's easy to coast, as a Christian, riding on the momentum created by church, and churchy friends and churchy activities. It's easy to keep busy and avoid pausing, to take stock.

Could you make time to ask yourself what you believe, and why you believe it? Could you self-examine your life and spot where you've covered dirt or doubt with external cleanliness or trendiness? If necessary, preface your soul test with a frank conversation that may sound like, 'Lord, some days I wonder if this whole Jesus thing is for real. What if I've built my life on something fictional?'

God's big enough to handle your misgivings. Rather be real (He knows anyway). Determine not to cheat, and you'll pass with flying colors.

KNOW YOUR NUMBERS

Chronic kidney disease affects 10% of the world's population. It's a silent killer because its most common causes are also silent: uncontrolled diabetes and high blood pressure. Both of these damage the delicate blood vessels supplying your kidneys with important nutrients. Without enough nutrients, your kidneys become damaged, preventing them from performing their crucial duties. Get tested! Knowing your blood pressure and blood glucose numbers is vital for long term health.

FOOD FOR THOUGHT

Don't kid your kidneys

You only need one kidney. If you happen to lose one of yours, or give it away, the other picks up the slack. Still, these little organs are vital to your overall health, so here's how you can look after them:

❧ *Consume plenty of fluids.* This helps your kidneys to clear sodium, urea and toxins from your body. However, while it's a good idea to stay hydrated, there is no need to *over*-hydrate. Over-hydration carries its own risks, so the general recommendation is to drink moderately, to thirst – and stick to water.

❧ *Reduce the tax of toxins on your kidneys.* Cigarette smoke is the most common toxin, so if you're a smoker, or are regularly exposed to second hand smoke, you know what to do! Smoking also doubles your risk of kidney cancer – just saying. Another source of toxins is medication, specifically over-the-counter medications commonly used for pain relief. If you have healthy kidneys and take an anti-inflammatory every now and then, don't stress. But if you're taking pain killers regularly, your kidneys will be taking strain, so best to have yourself checked out by a professional to find out what's really going on.

❧ *Eat a balanced diet, exercise regularly and control your weight.* These lifestyle choices support your kidneys both directly, by supplying them with nutrients, and indirectly, by lowering your risk of those chronic diseases that damage them. A healthy kidney works best in a healthy body!

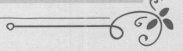

TIME TO REFLECT ...

In which areas of your life could you sit up a little straighter and be fully *in the moment*? With your kids? Your spouse? A friend or fellow volunteer worker?

Do you need to practice a posture of humility, where your ego has gotten the better of you? Do you need to practice a posture of confidence in God, where your assurance has been shaken?

Are there toxic relationships or situations, best filtered out of your life?

How could you fatten up on truth that leads to life, love and long-term wellbeing?

_____

_____

_____

_____

_____

_____

_____

_____

_____

_____

DON'T STOP NOW

So let's not get tired of doing what is good.
At just the right time we will reap a harvest
of blessing if we don't give up.

Galatians 6:9, NLT

If you've ever stuck at something against all odds and despite zero rewards for the longest time – you'll know the ecstasy and surprise of one day realizing, *I'm finally winning at this thing!* It's as if the seeds have been hidden in dark soil. You've watered … and waited … You've been tempted to walk away – but you kept watering, and waiting. Then one day: green shoot! And the rest is history.

If God's given you ground to plow, the green shoots will come. He grows things in the dark all the time. It might *feel* like nothing's happening – like, your kids aren't responding, or your boss isn't noticing – but God doesn't say things He doesn't mean, and He assures us that at just the right time, we'll reap the good harvest we've sown.

TAKE YOUR MEDS AS PRESCRIBED, NOT AS YOU LIKE

Modern medicine is amazing. It can cure illness, prevent infections and even help our heart beat in time. As a result, we are living longer and healthier lives. There is one catch though … for medicine to work, you need to be taking it! Compliance isn't only about taking your medication; it's also about how much you need, when to take it, what to take it with and how long it will last. The type and amount of medication that your doctor gives to you is unique to only you, so definitely a case of sharing is not caring. If you start feeling better, that is a sign that the medication is working, and not that you can stop taking it!

IMMUNE

I have hidden Your word in my heart,
that I might not sin against You.
Psalm 119:11, NLT

Flu is a great leveler, rendering even the strongest person pretty useless. And flu can come with dire medical complications. By far the most effective flu prevention is the annual flu vaccine. It does need to be annual, because the vaccine itself changes each year. A group of germ geeks study virus samples from around the world, tweaking the vaccine recipe every year based on the viruses most likely to wreak havoc that season.

God's Word is like a spiritual flu jab. If we take it preventatively – preemptively – it immunizes us against every virus of temptation that tries to take us out. It has comfort, answers, warnings, and instructions, and it's relevant to every cultural strain of sin, in every season. If we recognize its power to keep us safe from evil and its complications, we won't want to skip a daily truth shot.

VIRUS SHMIRUS …

The flu vaccine is recommended for everyone, especially the elderly and those with underlying medical conditions (like heart disease, HIV and diabetes). It's safe for children over the age of 6 months, and for pregnant women in any trimester. Protection offered by the vaccine in healthy adults is 70%-90% when the recipe is well matched to the actual strains that come along, reducing hospital admissions by 90% and days off work by 43%. Hard to sneeze at those numbers, isn't it?

DELIGHT IN THE DIFFERENCE

… you husbands must give honor to your wives.
Treat your wife with understanding as you live together.
She may be weaker than you are, but she is your
equal partner in God's gift of new life. Treat her as you
should so your prayers will not be hindered.

1 Peter 3:7, NLT

What theologians call the Trinity is a perfect relational equilibrium of complementary character traits and strengths. Made in God's image, our relationships – particularly with the opposite sex – are designed to reflect the same beautiful balance.

No amount of feminist bra-burning or male chauvinism will change our male-female differences. We'll lead happier lives if we gratefully – graciously – embrace our dissimilarities. Regardless of the buff or beautiful body you're in, you're required to do your best with it, offering it to God as a living sacrifice (Romans 12:1). That means, ladies: don't use your feminine charms to manipulate. Gentlemen: don't use your brute force to abuse.

Let's flabbergast the rest of the human race by affirming each other with exceptional kindness.

BUFF OR BEAUTIFUL – BE YOU

Adult men, on average, are 20% larger than women. Women have smaller muscles – around 50% of men's upper body strength. No matter how much iron she pumps, a woman won't beef up (or grow facial hair) to the same extent as a man because she has only a tenth of his testosterone (which promotes muscle development and inhibits protein break down, resulting in muscle growth and strength).

FIT US FOR HEAVEN,
TO LIVE WITH THEE THERE

Physical training is good, but training for godliness is much better,
promising benefits in this life and in the life to come.

1 Timothy 4:8, NLT

Getting fit can only do you good. Strengthening your body will make you look better, feel better, think better and sleep better. But why not let whatever efforts you're making *physically* be a reminder that your *spiritual* fitness is even more important, and longer lasting? Spoiler alert: no matter how healthy you are (and please make every effort to be healthy) eventually you're going to die. Me too. And then perhaps we'll wish we'd taken excellent care of our *spiritual* health too.

Don't get all fatalistic, or defeatist in your thinking! Rather, every time you head outside with your running shoes, your skipping rope, your dumbbells or your swimming stuff, let them prompt you to *live* outside of yourself too – to pray, to praise, to serve and strengthen others, and to find ways to live selflessly and compassionately.

A LOAD FOR THE LADIES?

The very real threat of osteoporosis means women *must* look after their bone health. Despite numerous studies on the benefits of strength training, most women still opt for cardio over weights. Any exercise is good for you, strengthening bones as well as muscles, but weight-bearing exercise has particular bone benefits. As your bones are exposed to these forces, they adapt by building more cells and becoming denser. So don't take a load off for osteoporosis, put some load on!

LESS IS LOVELY

LORD, You alone are my portion and my cup;
You make my lot secure.
Psalm 16:5, NIV

We live in a supersize world of buy-one-get-one-free-with-an-extra-side-of-chips. Size counts. If we're not aware and intentional, we can quickly get trapped in the consumerist cycle of believing more is better.

God owns the cattle on a thousand hills (Psalm 50:10). That doesn't mean we need to own them all too. He's a well-resourced God in every way – which just means you can trust Him to give you your allotted portion.

Before every meal, treat or temptation, I try to pray: *Choose my weight; choose my plate.* I try to trust God to provide for my needs, lending me wisdom to take only what I need and share generously. Maybe we could pray like that when we shop for clothes, cars or décor too? Our God is Jehovah *Jireh*. He *provides*. He knows just what you need, and He knows just how to spoon out a satisfying abundance.

PORTION DISTORTION

Sometimes the problem isn't *what* we eat – it's how *much*. Even healthy foods have calories – which contribute to weight gain! A frisbee-sized piece of fish isn't going to make your skinny jeans more comfortable. Massive restaurant and supermarket portions also distort our ideas about healthy platefuls. You might leave a *nouvelle cuisine* restaurant still feeling peckish. But chew on this: the French are amongst the skinniest in Europe. They're definitely on the right track when it comes to smaller portion sizes.

FOOD FOR THOUGHT

Move more. Grow young. Here's how.

The bad news:

On a cellular level, as you get older, telomeres (the protein endcaps of your chromosomes) get shorter. Each time a cell replicates, you lose a tiny bit of the endcaps. Also, mitochondrial activity slows with age. Mitochondria are your cells' batteries. It's their job to generate energy and ensure your cells use it efficiently. As these mitochondria slow down, you slow down too.

The good news:

The more physically active you are the less biological aging happens within your body. High intensity exercise rejuvenates aging cells, which means you may have celebrated *forty* birthdays, but your body is only blowing out *thirty* candles! Studies have shown that people who have high physical activity levels have telomeres that are biologically nine years younger than those who are couch potatoes, and seven years younger than those who are only moderately active. High intensity exercise also boosted the ability of mitochondria to generate energy by up to 70%.

The *get going* news:

High intensity interval training (HIIT) workouts involve short intervals of maximum intensity followed by recovery periods of low intensity. Provided you stick with the pattern of alternating high intensity exercise with recovery, you can do whatever gets you moving (cycling, sprinting, climbing stairs, or even using your own body weight to do jump squats). Before you start, make sure you're in good health. Check your technique. Start slowly, gradually increasing your number of intervals and intensity so your body adapts without injury.

TIME TO REFLECT ...

*Jesus,
Be my strength on days I want to give up, or give in.
I don't want to postpone my obedience.
Help me do all I can do to bolster my spiritual
immunity so I can stand, robust and resilient,
against temptations and enemy attacks.
I trust You to know just what I need,
and how much. Be my portion.
Amen.*

TRUTH IN FOCUS

Open my eyes to see the wonderful truths in Your instructions.
Psalm 119:18, NLT

No one knows for sure, but many scholars believe the apostle Paul had an eye disease or some measure of failing vision (Galatians 4:13-15, 6:11, Acts 14:19-20). Whether or not Paul could see clearly in the natural, *we know he could see clearly in the spiritual*.

My own son has glaucoma, and I'd do anything for his help and healing. But even more than I long for the full restoration of his *physical* sight, I want him to have 20/20 *spiritual* sight – to see the glory and the goodness of God in the land of the living (Psalm 27:13).

Let's take full responsibility for the two windows to our souls, doing all we can to keep our eyes healthy.

Let's also sharpen our spiritual vision by focusing and re-focusing on the clear and defining truths of God's Word.

🍎 BRAVING THE BLUR

After cataracts, glaucoma is the second leading cause of blindness. It's the name given to a group of eye diseases in which the optic nerve is slowly destroyed by a build-up of fluid pressure, which blocks blood supply to the nerve fibers or damages them directly. Glaucoma sufferers can lose up to 40% of their sight (peripheral vision is affected first) before they notice something's amiss – because our eyes are pretty good at covering for each other – so regular screening is essential.

CHECKUP

If you think you are standing strong, be careful not to fall.
The temptations in your life are no different from what others
experience. And God is faithful. He will not allow the temptation
to be more than you can stand. When you are tempted,
He will show you a way out so that you can endure.
1 Corinthians 10:12-13, NLT

Too often we're unaware of 'silent killers' like glaucoma and high blood pressure, until it's too late. We needn't become paranoid. We should just go for regular checkups because knowledge is power. Once we know what we're dealing with, we can treat it effectively. There's a *way out* of the physical danger.

Our spiritual lives aren't without silent killers: like pride, denial and complacency. We'd be fools to assume we're always doing just fine. Check in with your heart's Physician who promises to comfort you, and lead you into all truth (John 16:13). Allow Him to prod you and prompt you with His inescapable love.

UNDER PRESSURE

Blood pressure is the force of blood against artery walls. High blood pressure develops if larger arteries' walls lose elasticity, and smaller blood vessels narrow. This puts strain on your blood vessels, causing tiny scratches. As the body heals these microscopic tears, scar tissue forms – on which fatty material and blood cells gather and stick, increasing your risk of stroke or heart attack. You can't tell if your blood pressure is up without a blood pressure test – so get tested!

PASS THE SALT

'You are the salt of the earth. But what good is salt
if it has lost its flavor? Can you make it salty again?
It will be thrown out and trampled underfoot as worthless.'
Matthew 5:13, NLT

Too much salt is one of the factors plaguing our health, and research shows that almost everyone needs to cut back.

But in the Ancient Near East culture that Jesus was part of – in a time before processed food, consumerism and excess – salt was a critical flavor enhancer and natural preservative. And that's what we're called to do and be. We're called to preserve the good ways of a good God in a rotting, rancid world – building lives and homes that are beautiful receptacles of His grace, love and peace.

We're called to bring the flavor of joy and expectation to people living in bland hopelessness. And when we're shaken? We should just sprinkle all that goodness, all the more.

 ## THIRSTY BLOOD

When you consume excess salt, it stays in your bloodstream. Your blood gets 'thirsty', sucking up more water to dilute the saltiness. This creates a greater volume of blood, which has to flow through the same sized blood vessels, pushing up your blood pressure as your heart and arteries work harder. This increases the likelihood of a blood vessel clogging or rupturing. Limit your salt consumption to about one teaspoon per day – and don't forget that salt hides in many of the cans and condiments in your pantry.

MINDFUL OF A MINDFUL GOD

Can a mother forget the baby at her breast
and have no compassion on the child she has borne?
Though she may forget, I will not forget you!
Isaiah 49:15, NIV

The busier we get, the less we remember. We forget to switch off the oven. (We forget to pick up our kids!) We forget meetings and car keys and anniversaries and the promises of God – which is why His words to us through Isaiah are pure joy, deep comfort, and sublime refreshment.

We might forget all sorts of things, but *He never does*. Our omniscient, omnipresent, omnipotent Creator-King never loses track of any of the crazy tracks running through our lives at any given moment on any given day. Though we may feel abandoned or alone – or like we're losing our minds and the plot – God's gracious attention never wavers. He's remembering you, and rejoicing over you, even now.

MAINTAIN YOUR (PAINLESS) BRAIN

Unhealthy behaviors (smoking, alcohol in excess, unbalanced eating and lack of exercise) lead to the narrowing of your blood vessels, which reduces blood flow to your brain and leads to hardening of your brain's arteries. This results in memory malfunction and overall cognitive deterioration. The good news is your brain's a dynamic organ. Healthy habits encourage your brain's neurogenesis, or neuroplasticity. No matter your age, you can train your brain to become faster and more efficient. Don't forget, your brain literally can't feel pain. So don't worry about working it too hard!

FELLOWSHIP TRUMPS FOOD

Those who feel free to eat anything must not look down
on those who don't. And those who don't eat certain foods
must not condemn those who do, for God has accepted them.

Romans 14:3, NLT

Paul isn't saying we can do *anything*. (Or eat *anything*. Like, your kid's hamster. Because that would be weird.) This verse has to do with criticizing fellow believers for their personal preferences or convictions.

Paul reckons, 'Each to his own. Let God be the judge.'

A friend told me once, very seriously, 'I'm allergic to sugar. I break out in fat.' It's pretty normal these days for everyone to be avoiding one food group or another. Most functions and Friday night suppers cater for keto, paleo or gluten-free vibes. But firstly, let's not call what's just an aversion, an 'allergy'. Secondly, let's be gracious and accepting, trusting our fussy friends have good – and possibly private – reasons for their food choices.

ALLERGY ALERT

Sometimes our immune system glitches, seeing a harmless food protein as a potential threat. It goes into overdrive to protect you, producing an allergic reaction (itching, swelling, wheezing or dizziness). Most food allergies are mild; some are fatal. Over 90% of anaphylactic reactions are caused by milk, eggs, peanuts, tree nuts, fish, shellfish, soy and wheat. Food allergies are easy to control, by excluding the offending food from your diet. But if you're allergic, *learn all there is to know*, including what to do if you eat something you shouldn't.

FOOD FOR THOUGHT

Pressure management tips and treatments:

Glaucoma:

Once glaucoma damage is done, it can't be undone. However, with early detection, correct treatment and proper compliance, vision loss can be stopped in its tracks. Glaucoma doesn't discriminate, but you may be more at risk if … you have a family history of it, you've had an eye injury, you have high blood pressure or diabetes, you use cortisone or steroids, or you're over forty. Go for a glaucoma test every two years, and once you hit 60, it's a good idea to do an annual check.

Blood pressure:

The best thing you can do for your blood pressure is cut out processed foods. That way, you'll be avoiding a type of sweetener regularly used in these products, known as high fructose corn syrup. Some studies have found that these types of sugars can contribute to an increase in heart rate, salt retention and vascular resistance — which interact to increase your blood pressure.

Added to that, the more processed food you eat, the higher your risk for both heart disease and stroke. There's a flipside bonus: we use up to 50% *more* energy breaking down *real* food, so besides reducing your salt and sugar intake, you'll be upping your metabolism.

Food without loads of salt and sugar needn't be bland. Get creative in the kitchen. Lemon juice activates the same sensors as salt, giving the same flavor without the nasty side effects. And of course, it goes without saying: Quitters live longer — so quit smoking, quit drinking alcohol excessively, and quit making excuses not to exercise!

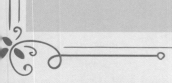

TIME TO REFLECT ...

Consider what you've read over this past week.

When it comes to your health or any other aspect of your life: *is the pressure mounting?*

Where is God nudging you to flavor conversations with His kindness and easygoing grace? Where are you called to preserve truth, where deception's decay has set in?

What truth do you need to remember never to forget?

_____

_____

_____

_____

_____

_____

_____

_____

_____

_____

_____

_____

WASTING OR SPENDING?

Look carefully then how you walk, not as unwise but as wise, making the best use of the time, because the days are evil.
Ephesians 5:15-16, ESV

We only get so much time on the planet. So when somebody *wastes* some of that time, it's infuriating. When we could be getting something constructive done, and circumstances dictate that we wait … and wait … debilitating frustration sets in.

Maybe we could reframe time wasted as time *spent*. We might actually maximize it, as moments or minutes to think or plan. And it's never a waste of time to pray for someone who keeps cropping up in your thoughts, or to ask for wisdom for the next conversation you'll have or decision you'll take.

Time we could've spent doing something supposedly more valuable may have been paused deliberately by a loving Father who wants us, as the song goes, to *stop – collaborate –* and *listen*.

TICKED OFF

A global survey calculated that on average, humans spend an extra 13 minutes per hour in traffic jams. That means ten whole working days ticked by each year … while we're getting ticked off by traffic. Studies also show that mental health can take a serious hit from too much traffic time – so your daily commute could actually be driving you crazy. Reframe your thinking. When else, in your frenetic day, do you have to do absolutely nothing, besides get yourself from A to B? Take a deep breath. Embrace your alone time.

THE ROOT (AND ROUTE) OF RAGE

Stop being angry! Turn from your rage!
Do not lose your temper – it only leads to harm.

Psalm 37:8, NLT

This isn't a confusing verse. God's instruction is uncomfortably clear. Anger doesn't result in the righteousness God desires (James 1:20).

It feels almost dangerous to screech to a halt when our tempers go from zero to a speeding fine in a few seconds – but it can be done. Count. Breathe. Remind yourself that you *can* make a decision to control your anger (the way I can pause yelling at my kid to answer the phone politely).

Make sure you're eating well, drinking water, sleeping enough, and *talking* to someone – ideally God – about your frustrations. Find the root of – and the route to – your anger. How did you end up so mad? Do you feel life, or another person, *owes* you something? How can you cancel the account, or hand it over to a righteous debt-collecting judge (1 Peter 2:23)?

CALM COMMUTE

Navigating traffic, day after day, can lead to increased blood pressure, blood glucose and triglycerides – all important markers for heart disease. Studies show the longer your commute, the lower your level of life satisfaction and the higher your risk for anxiety and depression. Not everyone lives close to work. For many, commuting is a necessity, not a choice. But you *can* spend your commute time proactively. Cranking up your favorite tunes improves patience levels and makes you more tolerant of others in your personal space.

NO HELP NO HOPE

Hear me, LORD, and have mercy on me. Help me, O LORD.
Psalm 30:10, NLT

Sometimes our anger or frustration comes from a feeling of helplessness. We're trapped in the traffic, or the turmoil of unresolved family relations, or financial downturns, or company restructuring – and we feel utterly, desperately powerless.

When Jesus died and rose again to reign on high with His Father – He didn't leave us alone. He sent us an Advocate, Helper and Comforter, the Holy Spirit (John 14:16-17). He's our ever present help in times of trouble (Psalm 46:1). *Ever present*. He's a racing heartbeat away from your stressed-out self. Call out to Him even now for the help, hope and comfort you need, knowing that no need is too massive or miniscule for His power and attention.

THIS IS WAR

Studies show that commuters suffer extreme stress, comparable to fighter pilots flying into battle, or riot police officers. The difference is that fighter pilots and riot police officers have some means of combating the stressful situation. As a driver or a passenger stuck in bumper to bumper traffic, there really isn't much you can do. It's this sense of helplessness that can be harmful to your health. Reset your expectations. If you sit in traffic every day, today's probably not going to be much different. Try leaving a little earlier to alleviate worry and time urgency.

FIRST FRIENDSHIP

Two people are better off than one, for they can help each other succeed. If one person falls, the other can reach out and help. But someone who falls alone is in real trouble.

Ecclesiastes 4:9-10, NLT

If we went to where time stretches endlessly backwards, we'd find that God the Father, Son and Holy Spirit have been in relationship since eternity past. There was *first* relationship – *then* the reality of substance. And *then* rules to live by, and cars, phones, takeout food, emails and the rest of ordinary life. Relationships (with God first, then others) are the foundation of – and reason for – our existence, and the only thing that will have any lasting worth, come close of day.

Social media positions us uniquely in history, because we've never before had access to so many people. But having a thousand Facebook friends doesn't mean you're a good friend, or that you're successful, and never lonely. It just means you have a thousand Facebook friends. Let's make building strong, IRL friendships and relationships a top priority.

FRIENDS FOR THE WIN

Strong social support networks can benefit your health to the same extent as exercising and giving up smoking. That's right! Studies on the impact of social networks have found the risk of heart disease, high blood pressure and diabetes was significantly higher amongst those who felt socially isolated. Loneliness generates an ongoing stress response, which increases your risk for disease. So phone a friend and thank them for being a friend!

DIFFERENT FOLKS, DIFFERENT STROKES

You have died with Christ, and He has set you free ... So why do you keep on following the rules of the world, such as, 'Don't handle! Don't taste! Don't touch!'? Such rules are mere human teachings about things that deteriorate as we use them.

Colossians 2:20-22, NLT

We use clichés that make us sound tolerant – like, 'Whatever floats your boat ...' But sometimes our hearts tell a different story. Sometime *we* tell a different story, behind someone's back. Because they don't parent or do church the way we do. They don't vacation or pursue education or play PlayStation the way we do. We invent for ourselves and others a set of life rules that, ridiculously, make us feel superior.

Except, our rules aren't God's. We don't have to be bound by them and neither does anyone else. Christ set us *free* (Galatians 5:1). We're free to worship God in Spirit and truth (John 4:24), in all the beautiful ways that fit our unique context, and so is everyone else.

FRESH OR FROZEN?

Frozen veggies are often underrated when they shouldn't be. Fresh vegetables are most nutritious just as they ripen. But they lose nutrients the moment they're picked, and exposed to heat and light en route to stores. Frozen vegetables are picked and flash-frozen closer to the peak of ripeness. This stops the ripening process, and nutrients are locked in. Whether fresh or frozen, steam your veggies quickly in just a little water. The crunchier, the better!

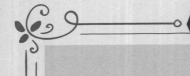

FOOD FOR THOUGHT

Top traffic tips for boosting health and reducing road rage:

Check your posture. To stop slouching while you drive, raise your rear-view mirror. This tiny adjustment forces you to sit up straighter to see clearly behind you, which in turn improves posture and can help reduce back and neck pain.

Multitask. Multitasking while you're driving is a really bad idea, except when you do car crunches! Tighten your abdominal muscles to scoop up your belly and pull in your waistline so that your navel moves toward your spine. This takes the stress off your lower, lumbar spine and contributes to strengthening that six pack, all while keeping both hands on the wheel.

Try the wheel grip. Clench your steering wheel as tightly as possible, then release. At the same time, relax your shoulders and sit up straight. Clench and repeat about 30 times a minute. Most people don't realize how hard they're gripping the wheel, and this exercise helps you relax, de-stress and creates body tension awareness.

Fidget. Drum your fingers on your steering wheel and move your body in time to your favorite tune. Why? It'll decrease your cortisol levels. Hopefully the person in the car behind you has read this too, and is doing the same thing. Muscle activity needed for these kinds of movements triggers important metabolic processes related to the breakdown of fats and sugars, which in turn minimizes the impact that a lengthy sit in the traffic has on your health.

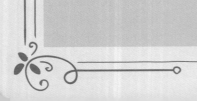

TIME TO REFLECT …

*Mighty God,
whether I'm microwaving veggies
or meeting friends for dinner,
stuck in traffic or transit,
remind me that the chief purpose of all my comings,
goings and doings is to know You,
and make You known. Help me do that
by loving others the way You have loved me.
Amen.*

_____

_____

_____

_____

_____

_____

_____

_____

_____

WEARY WORRIER

Have you never heard? Have you never understood?
The LORD is the everlasting God, the Creator of all the earth.
He never grows weak or weary. No one can measure
the depths of His understanding.

Isaiah 40:28, NLT

It's possible your life is brimming and so busy that you haven't realized how exhausted you are.

Perhaps chronic fatigue is not even your *new* normal – because it's been normal for quite some time.

Whether your tiredness is self-induced because of poor choices, or whether it's because of work or money worries or a mutinous teenager, let this truth flood you with fresh energy: there is always, *always* hope. Jesus died so you could be free. That means you're free today to begin doing things differently.

Your first move might be to cry out to the God who never gets tired. His energy never flags mid-afternoon. He never falls asleep at the wheel (or watching Netflix). Ask Him to teach you how to rest, and how to trust.

EXTREME ENERGY SLEEP-OVER

TATT (tired all the time) is one of the most cited complaints in doctors' consulting rooms. One in five people feel unusually tired. Mostly, there's nothing physically 'wrong'. Fatigue is linked to mood and accumulated stress. Boost your energy by improving the quality of your sleep: go to bed and wake up at the same regular times, seven days a week. This will reset your body rhythms. You'll be recharged when you need to be, and appropriately ready to sleep at lights out.

WEEPING WARRIOR

You keep track of all my sorrows.
You have collected all my tears in Your bottle.
You have recorded each one in Your book.

Psalm 56:8, NLT

The same God who defeated death wept at the graveside of His friend (John 11:35). He was victorious God: Master and Creator of the universe, unafraid and unlimited. And He was just a person like you and me: moved by sadness, and His own and others' distress.

It's profoundly consoling to know that because Jesus felt physical and emotional pain, He understands ours. He notices the tears you hide behind your sunglasses; He witnesses the ugliest of your ugly cries; and He loves you unfathomably. Even more wonderful is the guarantee that when we get home to heaven, He'll be waiting, with nail-pierced warrior hands, to count, and wipe away, the last of our tears (Revelation 21:4).

CRY ME A RIVER

You produce around 300ml of tears per day. That's over 100 liters per year. There are three types of tears: reflexive tears (think onion fumes, or a rogue eyelash), emotional tears, and continuous tears, which keep your eyes well lubed. Having a good cry has psychological and physiological benefits. Tears get rid of toxins, keep your nasal passages clean and clear, and successfully fight off bacteria. One study found that tears have such strong antimicrobial powers that they could even protect against anthrax. (But don't try that at home.)

AVAILABLE

Jesus wept.
John 11:35, NIV

On average, women cry thirty to sixty times – and men only five to fifteen times – per year. Men can turn off the waterworks after two or three minutes, compared to six minutes for women.

There's some evidence to show that testosterone inhibits crying; whereas the hormone prolactin, which women have a lot more of, promotes it. But whether you're a guy or a girl, you're an emotional being, because you're created in the image of an emotional God (Psalm 103:13, Jeremiah 32:41, Matthew 9:36).

If we're to love people the way Jesus loved people – and the way He loves us – we have to be willing to be emotionally available to them.

It will cost us courage and vulnerability. It will likely cost us tears. But maybe the honest tears of compassion are all that's needed to soften the hard heart-ground of someone desperate to be cherished or understood.

CRY, CALM DOWN, COMMUNICATE

The mood-boosting benefits of crying aren't instantaneous, according to recent research. Shedding a few tears actually leads to an immediate mood dip, but after about ninety minutes, people report feeling even better than they did before they had reason to cry. Crying calms your body down after a stressful ordeal by regulating body temperature and blood pressure. It's also a great communication tool. Feeling sadness and expressing it with tears can change the dynamic of a conversation or relationship, and is often a powerful call for help.

ALL THE LIVELONG DAY

From the rising of the sun to its setting,
the name of the LORD is to be praised!
Psalm 113:3, ESV

The psalmist is calling for a whole lot of praising – *all* the day-light hours? You don't have to be in church 24/7, and you needn't only listen to worship music in the car or the kitchen. The praise actually goes bigger, deeper and wider than that. Your *life* can be a praise offering (Romans 12:1) – your eating, exercising, waking up and working (Deuteronomy 6:7).

God takes His glory from your ordinary undertakings as you live with an awareness of being constantly in His presence – in your conversations and your quiet moments, on the loo, or while refreshing your inbox. *It all matters.*

Will any of us, this side of eternity, get it perfectly right to live and move and have out being in Him (Acts 17:28)? No way. Praise God we're forgiven and free. Praise God for fresh, begin-again grace that rises with the sun every morning.

SUN SMART

Vitamin D – the 'sunshine vitamin' – is made in your skin on exposure to sunlight. Its primary function is the uptake of calcium in your bones and various other systems. Most of us get adequate vitamin D from just a few minutes' daily exposure to sunlight. Even when you're wearing sunscreen, small amounts of UV rays still penetrate your skin, and that's usually more than enough to help your body produce as much vitamin D as it needs.

ASK FOR AN EGG

You fathers – if your children ask for ... an egg, do you give them
a scorpion? Of course not! So if you sinful people know how
to give good gifts to your children, how much more will your
heavenly Father give the Holy Spirit to those who ask Him.

Luke 11:11-13, NLT

Many of us grow up in the faith with an absolute aversion for the prosperity gospel – and rightly so. But we end up believing it's presumptuous, sacrilegious or selfish to *ask God for anything*.

In this passage, Jesus reveals the Father's gentle, generous heart. He loves us. He knows we can't do life alone and that most days we're frantic for help and mercy. That's why He gave us the priceless, ever-present gift of His Spirit. More than that, you can freely, humbly, approach His throne (Hebrews 4:16) any day of the week and tell Him *anything*, and ask for *anything*. He might say yes. He might say no. He will definitely, always, answer according to His wise and perfect plans for your life.

EGGZACTLY RIGHT

Eggs get a lot of bad press because of their high cholesterol content. Truth is, you can't function without cholesterol. It's produced by your liver, and plays a critical role in digestion, hormone production, and maintaining cell structure. Still, some believe that limiting egg consumption (and therefore cholesterol) keeps your arteries unclogged and your heart healthy. We've cracked that myth right open: daily egg-eaters have a *lower* risk of heart disease. Eggs have been egg-zonerated!

FOOD FOR THOUGHT

Energy makeover tips:

❦ *Allergy and asthma alert.* Anything that affects your breathing will impact your energy levels. Hay fever and allergy sufferers often feel sluggish. They spend so much energy trying to breathe, they don't have much oomph left for anything else. If you can relate, start by identifying your triggers and steer clear of them. There are several over-the-counter antihistamine medications that can effectively relieve congestion, and significantly improve quality of life.

❦ *Have a sweat session.* When you exercise you release adrenaline, which tells your body to ignore feelings of pain and fatigue, and boosts blood flow to large muscles. One study found that healthy, sedentary people who began exercising three days a week for 20 minutes a day, increased their energy levels by 20% after only six weeks.

❦ *Take a gum break.* Taking mini-breaks throughout your day will help improve energy levels, but if all else fails, chew some gum. This little hack raises alertness and improves concentration, possibly because chewing increases blood flow to your head.

❦ *See the doc.* There are a few conditions, like anemia and diabetes, that forty winks can't fix. Symptoms like chest, jaw or back pain, along with fatigue, call for immediate medical attention. And if your symptoms last longer than a few weeks despite healthy eating and sleeping, see your doctor. Ruling out anything serious will relieve you of a big stressor, and that could boost your get-up-and-go.

TIME TO REFLECT ...

Are you tired all the time? Are your tears particularly close to the surface lately? Take just five minutes to pour out your heart to God. He's waiting. He's listening. He's your 'refuge and strength, a very present help in trouble' (Psalm 46:1).

_____

_____

_____

_____

_____

_____

_____

_____

_____

_____

_____

_____

_____

_____

_____

_____

_____

HEART PATROL

Above all else, guard your heart,
for everything you do flows from it.
Proverbs 4:23, NIV

You're at least in part a product of your parents. Whether you're a tall brunette, or a petite blonde, is to some extent a gift from your folks. How your mom cared for you, both in the womb and during childhood, has also influenced how you've turned out. So, your genetic makeup *is* part of God's design for your destiny – *but you don't get to use your genes as an excuse.* None of us gets to say things like, 'I can't help it! I got my violent temper from my dad!'

If you're brave enough to get honest with the mirror and your Maker, you'll accept that you're pretty much solely responsible for your wise or foolish choices. *Guard your heart.* Decide from now on (start today!) to be intentional and proactive about determining which natural tendencies you'll surrender to and which external influences you'll allow to direct the course of your life.

HAND-ME-DOWN GENES?

Family history plays an important role in heart disease – *to a point.* Certain gene combinations *do* place you at risk. But mostly, environmental factors you expose yourself to will decide your cardiovascular health. Our everyday wellness decisions are crucial in determining which genes are switched on or off. Studies have shown that healthy habits are associated with an 80% reduction in heart disease risk for men, and 75% for women. Our lifestyle choices make all the difference!

DON'T QUIT QUITTING

Think carefully about what is right, and stop sinning.
1 Corinthians 15:34, NLT

Sometimes the most powerful thing we can do to make progress in our lives is to not give up on giving something up. *Don't stop stopping what you know you need to stop.*

Like, maybe you know you need to stop gossiping. *Don't stop stopping!* When you feel yourself getting sucked into a conversational vortex, don't give up your efforts to kick to the surface and swim away. (And have alternative topics in mind to divert the mud-slinging of any conspiratorial tête-à-tête.)

Or perhaps you need to *keep on quitting* when it comes to overeating or overspending or overindulging on episode after episode of a gripping series. Cut your meals in half. Cut your credit card in half! Cut your Netflix account, if you know that's the thing that trips you up. Do the drastic thing that needs doing, so you'll quickly see the benefits of being determined to quit.

🍎 GONE UP IN SMOKE

When it comes to smoking, there really are no butts about it ... you simply have to stop. Smoking isn't only bad for your lungs; it's bad for every single other part of you too. Roughly one in five deaths from heart disease is directly related to smoking. Thankfully within a year of quitting smoking, your risk of heart disease, heart attack, and stroke drops by 50%. Go on – be a *quitter!*

HOW CAN YOU MEND A BROKEN HEART?

He heals the brokenhearted and bandages their wounds.
Psalm 147:3, NLT

Let's never forget: we worship the great Physician. Our God can heal and repair – physically, socially, intellectually and spiritually. And He can restore and reconnect our hearts where there's been emotional damage – whether mild or severe.

No matter the heartbreak, there's always hope. No matter the relational devastation, there's always the possibility of recovery. Healing is possible. Forgiveness is possible. God causes all things – even the painful, unthinkable things – to work for our good, so that heartbreak doesn't just *age* us. It *grows* us.

And where spiritual arteries are clogged (because which of us hasn't fallen into bad habits?), trust Jesus to show you what to cut out. As much as you need a doc to check your cholesterol, you need Jesus and trusted others to hold you accountable to lifestyle decisions and directions that may be harming, or hardening, your heart.

REVERSE AND REPAIR

Your heart is a lot more forgiving than you might think. When adults in their 30s and 40s drop unhealthy habits that are harmful to their hearts and embrace healthy lifestyle changes, they can control and potentially even reverse the natural progression of coronary artery disease. On the flipside, adults who *don't* maintain healthy habits as they get older, increase their risk of disease. Make these health habits part of your everyday routine, rather than adopting them as a quick fix for an unhealthy ticker!

BETTER TOGETHER

And let us not neglect our meeting together,
as some people do, but encourage one another,
especially now that the day of His return is drawing near.
Hebrews 10:25, NLT

The narrative of our culture is all about self-sufficiency and individualism. And sure, that worldview has its strengths. Leeches are hard to love and we don't want to suck people dry with our neediness. But taken to its extreme, the autonomy lauded by society is just pride. And *foolishness*. It ends in relational, social, emotional and spiritual infertility, and failure.

God made us for community: friendship with Him and fellow planet-sharers. We're designed to need other humans to fill our gaps. Don't ever kid yourself into going it alone by self-medicating spiritually. You need the wisdom, guidance, encouragement and practical help of other believers who love you even with your blemishes and blind spots. They need you too.

SELF-DIAGNOSIS OR SERIOUS DANGER?

Instead of visiting the doctor for a sudden ache or fever, you go straight to your medicine cabinet, right? Taking medicine at home is convenient, and often helpful. It's also risky. The wrong medications taken in the wrong amounts for the wrong amount of time are bound to cause side effects. The recommended dose of medication isn't a suggestion; it's a careful calculation. Insufficient dosages may prolong recovery, while too much medication may cause permanent damage. There's a place for self-medication, but don't rely on it entirely. Speak to your doc!

TRUTH-NUMB

You stubborn people! You are heathen at heart
and deaf to the truth. Must you forever resist the Holy Spirit?
That's what your ancestors did, and so do you!

Acts 7:51, NLT

It's possible you've heard the truth so many times, *you no longer hear it*. Not one of us is above a can't-see-the-wood-for-the-trees kind of obtuseness. Familiarity can desensitize us to the holy, healing power of God's Word.

Let's pause, and pay attention. Let's ask the Holy Spirit to awaken us from apathy, and convict us if we're being stubborn. Then, let's have the humility to admit He's onto something. Are there people in your life who've been saying the same thing to you, over and over? *Might they be right?*

Pray God would show you if you're missing something – and resisting His leading – because, like the Jewish Council Stephen is addressing in Acts 7, you've grown deaf to the truth.

RESISTANCE IS FUTILE ...

Antibiotics are one of the most frequently prescribed medications. They've saved millions of lives and changed the course of global disease outbreaks. But their effectiveness is challenged by the rise in antibiotic resistance infections, which are complicated and very difficult to treat. We can all help curb antibiotic resistance! Firstly, don't take antibiotics when you don't need them. This speeds up your own antibiotic resistance. Secondly, take your medication exactly as prescribed. When it comes to antibiotics, sharing is *not* caring! Finally, look after your health any way you can, to avoid antibiotics all together.

FOOD FOR THOUGHT

Tipsy Health Tips

Smoking is definitely *bad* for your health. But can drinking alcohol be *good*? Here are the facts on alcohol and your health:

* Moderate alcohol consumption (no more than a single drink a day) has been shown to have some health benefits, including reducing the risk of heart disease. But the small benefit alcohol offers is matched and usually *bettered* simply by exercising. So if you don't drink, *there's no need to start*, and if you do, moderate drinking should be considered a small part – not a keystone – of a healthy lifestyle.

* Try to limit your alcohol consumption by following the 1,2,3 rule: one drink a day, no more than 2 at one time, no more than 3 days a week. One drink is more or less equivalent to 250ml of 5% beer, 100ml of 13% wine or 30ml of 40% spirits

* When it comes to alcohol, the dose denotes the poison! Alcohol is a 'fine line' substance: if things get out of balance, trouble awaits. Having more than four drinks in one sitting, for example, temporarily increases your blood pressure, but repeated binge drinking can lead to long-term increases, as well as increased inflammation and a lowered ability to heal. If you needed more encouragement, an increase in blood pressure means an increased risk of heart disease.

* Ethanol – the active, buzz-creating ingredient in alcohol – increases the number of triglycerides in your blood. Too many of these bad boys contribute to hardening of your arteries or thickening of your artery walls, which increases your risk of stroke, heart attack and heart disease. Paul offers excellent advice: 'Don't be drunk with wine, because that will ruin your life. Instead, be filled with the Holy Spirit' (Ephesians 5:18, NLT).

TIME TO REFLECT ...

*Heavenly Father, let's get honest.
I don't want to be in denial about what's
really going on inside of me. And I don't want to
keep on blocking up soul arteries with bad habits.
Please do the necessary surgery to repair my heart.
Forgive me for thinking I can go solo, spiritually.
Help me trust other imperfect humans. Help me lean on them,
humbly and cheerfully, and let them lean on me.
Where I've become immune to Your truth – desensitized and
unaffected by the promptings of Your Spirit – revive me!
Shake me out of the truth-resistance of my own making.
Amen.*

NO STOMACH FOR SIN

'Don't you understand either?' He asked.
'Can't you see that the food you put into your body cannot defile
you? Food doesn't go into your heart, but only passes through
the stomach and then goes into the sewer.' (By saying this,
He declared that every kind of food is acceptable in God's eyes.)

Mark 7:18-19, NLT

Jesus explains that it's not what goes into us (food) but what comes out of us (sin) that corrupts us. It's what spews from our hearts, minds and mouths – evil thoughts, sexual immorality, theft, murder, adultery, greed, deceit, lustful desires, envy, slander and pride (Mark 7:21-22) – that's the filth we can't simply swallow down with a drugstore health shake, because the muck of sin is cooked up in our hearts.

What if you worried less about your eating plan – and judged a little less the eating plans of others – and put that energy instead into ensuring nothing but honey flows from your heart?

GUT FEELING

Like Jesus said, food can't defile you. But it influences health enormously. Living inside your gut are around 500 different bacteria containing nearly two million genes. These and other micro-organisms make up your body's unique microbiome – a mini eco-system. Bacteria facilitate digestion and impact everything from fat loss to inflammation levels and mood. Exercise encourages a diversity of bacteria to grow, whereas diet can help or hinder the microbiome. So, skip the junk! Eat your greens. Your belly and body will thank you.

A SLICE OF SIMPLE

At about that time Jesus was walking through some grain fields
on the Sabbath. His disciples were hungry, so they began
breaking off some heads of grain and eating them.

Matthew 12:1, NLT

Jesus displays such freedom in this Scripture. The very next
verse tells us that the Pharisees freaked out, saying, 'Look,
Your disciples are breaking the law by harvesting grain on the
Sabbath' (Matthew 12:2). Jesus points out that when David and
his men were hungry? *They ate.*

Simple as that.

And it's really ok if we do the same. The Good News translation
of Ecclesiastes 7:29 reads: 'This is all that I have learned: God
made us plain and simple, but we have made ourselves very
complicated.' Life with Jesus is simple. We needn't overcom-
plicate it. Are you fabricating rules for your diet, your spiritual
disciplines or your discipleship, even though it's entirely unnecessary to enforce them?

CURB YOUR CARBS

Some folks give up gluten hoping to lose weight and improve their health,
but the perception that gluten-free foods are healthier isn't backed by
science. Gluten, found in wheat and grains, is a combination of two
proteins bound by starch. Gluten is a recipe for disaster for someone
with celiac disease (an auto-immune condition which causes your immune
system to attack the lining of your small intestine, causing inflammation
and poor nutrient absorption). For everyone else, simply reducing your
carbohydrates – which trigger insulin release (the fat storing hormone) –
can improve your health.

REAL DEAL

'Produce fruit in keeping with repentance.'
Matthew 3:8, NIV

The fruit of the Spirit that Paul describes in Galatians 5:22-23 is a crop cultivated in our characters by the Holy Spirit.

It's the evidence that God's grace is transforming us so that our lives produce a harvest of goodness to feed a hungry, hope-deficient world.

And when it comes to this fruit, we'd be fools to try to fool others with fake fruit. No one is impressed by a bowl of kitsch, plastic pineapples, am I right? And no one is helped or healed when we fake our life-fruit by pretending to be like Jesus – practicing behavior that isn't rooted in the rich soil of a right relationship with God.

If we've come to know Jesus – grasping something of the truth that He's holy and we're not – then there'll be fruit. There may be just a little – but it'll be the real, delicious deal.

TO JUICE OR NOT TO JUICE?

Drinking fruit juice seems like an efficient (quenching!) way to consume nutrients from fresh fruit. But it takes three oranges to give you a single glass of OJ, which means fruit juice is a concentrated source of sugar. What's more, it doesn't have the fiber of fresh fruit. So juice is more likely to fill you *out* than fill you *up*. Fiber in whole fruit slows sugar absorption. This prevents major sugar spikes and slows the release of insulin (which regulates blood sugar, and stores extra energy as fat).

GOOD GOD, GOOD GUARDS

The LORD will protect you from all harm;
He will protect your life.
Psalm 121:7, HCSB

Vaccinations aren't just good for the person being vaccinated, *but also for their community*. In the same way, when we live out our faith in God's promises and protection, it bolsters the faith of those around us.

Before a watching world, let's be living breathing examples of the faith that knows: God is our Father and Healer. No harm falls on our lives unless it has first fallen through His hands.

He's able to protect us from *all harm*. So if and when we *do* come to harm – as we inevitably will – we can be confident that it's been vetted by that same Father and Healer. There's a reason He's allowed hardship, and He'll use the unraveling it causes to knit together His good plans for our lives (Romans 8:28).

VACATION FROM VACCINATION?

Vaccines trigger your immune system to respond to a disease germ, in that way building immunity and saving millions of lives. A report published in the 1980s suggested a link between the MMR vaccine and autism. The report was heavily criticized, the doctor struck off the medical roll and the evidence tossed out as meaningless – but not before the public caught onto the idea and stopped vaccinating their kids. As a result, measles has become increasingly common, even in countries where it had been completely eliminated through vaccination. Further studies have shown the MMR vaccination to be completely safe. So don't vacillate – vaccinate!

LAUGH IT OFF

A cheerful heart is good medicine,
but a broken spirit saps a person's strength.
Proverbs 17:22, NLT

Once, we approached a family holiday carrying a mountain of stress. This holiday had to *fix* us! It might seem unspiritual, but we prayed, 'God, let us *laugh a lot!*' Because we needed reminders that He created craziness and silly jokes and good times. God answered that prayer: blessing us with hilarious, tension-melting moments of wonder.

Hawk Nelson sings the following lyrics, and they strike me as excellent advice: 'So go ahead and live like you're loved; it's ok to act like you've been set free ...' Because sometimes we take ourselves far too seriously. While we should do right by God – taking Him and His Word unbelievably seriously – we shouldn't forget that we've been set free, and that it's really ok for our lives to reflect the relief and exhilaration of that marvelous state of being.

🍎 RAUCOUS REMEDY

Laughter really is one of the best medicines on the market! Laughter lowers stress hormones, and boosts immunity by increasing your infection-fighting antibodies. It relieves physical tension, relaxes your body and improves blood flow. Laughter triggers endorphin release, giving you an overall sense of well-being and even temporarily relieves pain. Laughing can also give you a workout: it involves your entire body, not to mention fifteen muscles in your face alone. Let's find our funny!

FOOD FOR THOUGHT

Common myths about the common cold ... and crossing your legs!

Myth: If you go outside on a cold day with wet hair or without a jersey, you'll catch a cold.

Colds are caused by viruses, and viruses aren't attracted to wet hair! There's also a marked difference between *feeling* cold vs. *catching* a cold, and frankly, the first doesn't lead to the second. Ironically, it's spending more time inside that ups your risk of seizing the sneezes. Being in close quarters with someone carrying bugs makes it all the more likely that you'll catch the virus too. Turns out sharing *isn't* caring!

The best way to avoid catching a cold is to wash your hands regularly, and get everyone in your home to do the same. You can also beef up your immune system by exercising regularly and eating a balanced diet.

Myth: Crossing your legs is bad for you.

Blood pressure rises slightly when you cross your legs at the knee – that's why you're advised to uncross your legs. But there's no evidence that leg crossing contributes to an ongoing blood pressure condition. Once you unwind your legs, your blood pressure returns to normal.

You may have also heard that crossing your legs causes varicose veins. It doesn't! Varicose veins happen as a result of damage to the small 'one way' valves that normally keep the blood moving in one direction, straight back to your heart. In those with varicose veins, some blood squeezes out into the small veins on the surface which eventually balloon under the pressure.

TIME TO REFLECT ...

Have you been comforted or encouraged by the fruit of the Spirit in another person's life this week? Thank God; thank that person too.

For which areas of your life (relationships, finances, career, parenting) do you need to trust God for particular protection, at this time?

What lightens your mood without fail? What makes you laugh 'til your face aches? Could you plan to incorporate those happy triggers into this next week?

_____

_____

_____

_____

_____

_____

_____

_____

_____

_____

_____

SMALL SPARK, BIG BURN

… the tongue is a small thing that makes grand speeches.
But a tiny spark can set a great forest on fire.

James 3:5, NLT

Small things are usually taken un-seriously – yet they can do horrifying damage. A mosquito is *tiny* – about half a centimeter in length. Yet it's officially the most lethal creature on earth. Malaria – the parasite carried by some mozzies, in certain parts of the world – kills a child every 45 seconds in Africa, and a single malarial mosquito can infect more than 100 people.

Similarly, don't assume that it's the grand gestures of our lives that leave the greatest marks. Our tiny tongues can destroy, like mosquitoes. Not because we buzz annoyingly in other people's ears … But because our words can kill: slapping, slicing, bruising and blindsiding those within earshot. Our words can ruin lives. *They can also build and bless, inspire and encourage.* Let's light up the world with words that nourish and nurture and draw nations to Jesus.

DON'T BE MOZZTAKEN …

Once you're chomped by a malarial mosquito, parasites incubate in your liver before being released into your blood stream where they invade red blood cells and continue to multiply. There's no vaccine for malaria, and no way of telling which of those blood suckers is carrying malaria, so your best bet is prevention. There are many anti-malarial drugs available. Just remember: as good as these meds are, they don't work overnight. Visit your pharmacist long before you embark on your safari adventure!

FAKE OR FOR REAL?

And no wonder, for Satan himself
masquerades as an angel of light.
2 Corinthians 11:14, NIV

Y ou can probably think of a time when you were duped by
something that (or someone who) *looked* or *seemed* legit.
You were so sure that this was a good buy, a good person, a
good opportunity, a good deal. And then what you thought were
impressive qualities turned out to be the veneer of an alluring
user interface designed to draw you in, and deceive you.

This is the enemy's oldest trick, and you and I should never
think we're so mature, or so experienced, that we'll recognize
every ruse. Never stop praying for discernment and discretion,
because so long as we're in this world, there'll be visible and
invisible con artists bent on blinding us with the artificial light
that hides their darkness.

SWEETS FOR MY SWEET, SUGAR FOR MY HONEY ...

If you're cutting out sugar: fantastic! But if you're replacing sugar with
an artificial sweetener, you may be buying into just another problem
masquerading as a solution. Sweeteners are *super* sweet, delivering a much
sweeter hit than regular sugar. Overstimulation of sugar receptors from
frequent use of these hyper-intense sweeteners' limits tolerance for more
complex tastes – so you may start to find less intensely sweet foods (like
fruit) less appealing, and unsweetened foods (like vegetables) downright
unpalatable. Over time, artificially flavored foods with less nutritional value
become the norm, negatively impacting both your weight and health.

EARLY EXPECTATIONS?

Each morning I will sing with joy about Your unfailing love.
For You have been my refuge, a place of safety when I am in distress.
Psalm 59:16, NLT

We sometimes put unfair expectations on each other, when it comes to how we work out our faith.

Some say mornings are the best time to read Scripture and pray. The Bible does have a bunch of examples of morning praise, morning offerings, morning worship. But it also talks about evening praise, evening offerings and evening worship (Psalm 141:2).

The indisputable fact is that we all have different rhythms and temperaments and body clocks. We find ourselves moving intentionally or unbidden into different seasons – and each season comes with different lifestyle demands. Look and learn. Consider how others do things. Then ask God to show you what, when, where and how works best for you to carve out uninterrupted time with Him.

ANY TIME

Morning people leap from bed first thing and get their exercise over with. Others wouldn't dream of breaking a sweat before lunch. *One isn't better than the other.* You're naturally stronger and more flexible in the afternoon – but you're also more likely to let life get in the way if you leave exercise for later in the day. Early-exercisers tend to work out more consistently. You need to find a time that helps you make your training a fixture and priority in your life, regardless of when that fits into your schedule.

DON'T LOSE SLEEP

'Can any one of you by worrying
add a single hour to your life?'
Matthew 6:27, NIV

It's easier said than done, but we do know better than to fret, worry and stress – losing sleep over things we can't change. Regret has a nasty way of reaching up from the past and tugging your sleeves to keep you stuck and twisting your heartstrings to keep you tied up in thoughts of what could've been and should've been.

Perhaps it's time to ask God to show you what you need to face, and what you can leave in His hands so you can fall asleep. If His kindness is leading you to repentance (Romans 2:4), then repent. If it's in your power to bring necessary change, hope and healing to a hectic situation, then do all you can. But don't allow anxiety to detract from the mercies and opportunities of today. Also, get some sleep.

CATCH ME IF YOU CAN

Losing a few hours of sleep over time catches up with you. We tell ourselves, after a few late nights, that we can just sleep in over the weekend and reclaim those lost hours. But it's impossible to catch up on lost sleep. Once it's gone, it's not coming back! If you're skimping on sleep, you have to do more than just *sleep more*. To get the biggest bang for your sleeping buck, and cancel your snooze debt, concentrate on improving both your sleep quantity *and* sleep quality.

BRACE YOURSELF

Brace yourself like a man,
because I have some questions for you,
and you must answer them.
Job 38:3, NLT

God is about to interrogate Job – who won't have much to say in return (Job 40:4). He'll be gob-smacked by God's majesty, sovereignty and power. But God doesn't hold back! He forthrightly challenges Job's limited perceptions, stretching him – and possibly stressing him out.

Yours is the same God who cross-examined Job. He knows exactly where you need to be confronted, and what you can handle. And because He's a loving Father who wants to draw from you the very best, He won't soft-soap life if He needs to contest your comfort. As one pastor put it, God comforts the disturbed, and He also disturbs the comfortable. It's ok to let challenge and stress do their work, so you can grow.

GOOD FOR GROWTH

Stress comes from a perceived imbalance between a challenge and the resources you have to deal with it. Researchers identify two types of stress: bad stress (distress) and good stress (eustress). Chronic stress, or prolonged exposure to distress, is what we need to avoid. It's been linked to chronic disease and permanent changes to the size, structure and function of our brain. But moderate levels of daily, manageable stress can positively impact our motivation, problem-solving, confidence and health, even protecting us against oxidative damage linked to aging and disease. Keep perspective. Wiping out *all* stress may just wipe out a bit of meaning too.

FOOD FOR THOUGHT

Stressed out of your mind:

The stress hormone, cortisol, is involved in a range of processes, including metabolism, immunity and memory formation. A good dose of cortisol gets you going – *but too much can cause damage*. Ongoing chronic stress negatively impacts your brain and nervous system, and can even lead to a wasting away of brain mass, which affects your memory and learning ability.

Whenever you wake up, exercise or stare down a stressful event, your body enters the fight-or-flight state. Confirmation of what you've always suspected was true – waking up is stressful! Your pituitary gland signals the adrenal glands to release cortisol, helping your body adapt. This process continues until the stressful event subsides. But when there's ongoing stress? Cortisol is continually released, unabated. One study found that people who had higher levels of cortisol also had lower brain volume and cognitive function compared to those with lower levels of cortisol.

There's hope! Lower your stress – and regulate cortisol levels – with these lifestyle habits:

Get the right amount of sleep. The timing, quantity and quality of sleep all make a difference to cortisol levels.

- ❧ Exercise. Run, ride, dance, or dribble a soccer ball with your kids! Get outside as often as possible.

- ❧ Learn to relax and laugh more. A glass-half-full disposition is associated with lower cortisol, not to mention the added bonus of lower blood pressure, a healthy heart rate and a strong immune system.

- ❧ Eat less sugar and more greens.

- ❧ Don't compare yourself to anyone else today, only to yesterday's you.

TIME TO REFLECT ...

*Jesus, show me when and where the small things I say
and do are a danger to others, or myself.
Make me sincerely sweet – wholesome like honey. I don't want
to spoon artificial grace or kindness into conversations.
Balance my waking up, and my working out.
Help me manage my stress – so that instead of paralyzing me,
it spurs me on to greater love and good deeds.
Amen.*

_____

_____

_____

_____

_____

_____

_____

_____

_____

_____

OUCH, BUT OK

No discipline is enjoyable while it is happening – it's painful!
But afterward there will be a peaceful harvest of right living
for those who are trained in this way. So take a new grip
with your tired hands and strengthen your weak knees.

Hebrews 12:11-12, NLT

I once walked a two-day ultra-marathon, for charity. The event organizers and volunteers marshalling and manning water points obviously got their wires crossed. Nearing the end, a sign read, '5km to go!' I was jubilant. Not long now. I walked and walked … and walked … and got to another sign that read, '5km to go!' I burst into furious tears. But eventually I hobbled across the finish line. And I'd learned something. Crestfallen and exhausted – when I thought I couldn't possibly go any further – *I actually could.*

When life's all uphill, let's remember: we've got it in us to go just a little further. And maybe even a little further than that. We might not see the immediate benefits of perseverance, but our gracious, generous God promises to reward.

SOFAS ARE THE NEW CIGARETTES

A study of 120, 000 people revealed that those who smoked or had heart disease were more likely to die younger than those who didn't. *But,* the numerical risks of smoking or having a chronic disease were similar to those associated with being unfit. In a nutshell: being out of shape increases someone's risk of dying young as much as smoking or having heart disease does. Sitting is the new smoking. Let's get moving!

HEAD HELD HIGH

But You, O LORD, are a shield around me; You are my glory,
the One who holds my head high.

Psalm 3:3, NLT

Instead of looking down at your phone today – comparing your beautiful, ordinary, authentic, warm-bodied life to the highlight reels of social media – *look up*. Lift up your head and look up to your Father and King and remember who you are.

Remember you're loved and redeemed, and remember He's able to do immeasurably more, in the midst of your unique, run-of-the-mill life, than all you can ask or think (Ephesians 3:20).

You needn't be a poser – always trying to position yourself in the center or the spotlight – because your purpose and posture are found in Him, and He holds your head high.

TEXT NECK

When you text or scroll through feeds on your phone, in all likelihood your neck is bent, chin stuck forward, shoulders hunched and posture slouched. This cramped pose puts pressure on your neck, spine and lower back, which can lead to pain and injury. It also pinches nerves in your neck that run down to your arms and hands, increasing your risk for overuse injuries like carpal tunnel syndrome. Plus, your head's really heavy. Holding it up engages lots of muscles in your neck, shoulders and upper back. As your head dips forward, the pressure on these muscles is close to doubled. Instead of just staring at your phone, set reminders to get up and stretch!

EAT PRAY LOVE

*So whether you eat or drink, or whatever you do,
do it all for the glory of God.*
1 Corinthians 10:31, NLT

The biography-made-movie, *Eat Pray Love*, isn't Jesus-centered. But the title alone might inspire us to embrace life from a biblical perspective. Paul explains: 'Whether you eat or drink, or whatever you do, do it all for the glory of God.' Rushing through days, we forget we're *living sacrifices* (Romans 12:1). Even small, simple things – a bite of breakfast, or a slow dinner with friends – are our worship.

What works well for your body, in terms of best times to eat, the size of meals and snacks, and what fills your fridge? Trust God for wisdom and insight in your eating and drinking and whatever else you do, so that you'll have maximum energy to pray, love and enjoy His purposes for you in the world – knowing Him and making Him known – even in your eating and drinking.

STITCH GLITCH

A stitch is an irritation of the membrane lining your abdominal wall. The pain usually starts in your side, ranging from a dull ache to a sharp, stabbing sensation. To reduce the chance of irritating that membrane, don't eat or drink for two hours before you exercise. When you do drink, stick to water. While you exercise, take slow, regular breaths, channeling breathing from your belly, rather than your chest. Finally, stretch upwards and over, away from the stitch, until you feel some relief – then carry on!

BASIC INSTINCT

Even the stork that flies across the sky knows the time of her
migration, as do the turtledove, the swallow, and the crane.
They all return at the proper time each year.
But not My people! They do not know the LORD's laws.

Jeremiah 8:7, NLT

G od created instinct. Animals – even plants – have instincts.
Humans too. We have intuition and gut feelings that (subconsciously sometimes) steer our course. And when our lives are
supernaturally overhauled by the indwelling Holy Spirit, we can
have even greater confidence that He's guiding us through soul
promptings.

Unless we're too busy.

Because sometimes we eat anything, on the run – without
considering what it might be doing to our gut. And we *live* any
old how, on the run – without *listening* to our gut. What are you
rushing past? Could you linger ... and listen? Is God speaking to
you about specific people who need you to slow down, so they
can catch up? Don't ignore those basic instincts.

GUTTED

Convenience foods are (kind of) great, but they're loaded with hidden
salt, sugar and additives that wreak havoc with our gut health. Diets
high in processed foods not only cause intestinal problems, they also
aggravate underlying conditions. Crohn's disease causes inflammation
in your digestive system. Common symptoms include chronic diarrhea,
weight loss, fever, abdominal pain and bloating. There's currently no cure,
only management: the goal of treatment is to reduce the inflammation by
managing diet, stress levels and lifestyle habits (like smoking).

NURTURE YOUR NATURE

*I remember your genuine faith, for you share the faith
that first filled your grandmother Lois and your mother, Eunice.
And I know that same faith continues strong in you.*

2 Timothy 1:5, NLT

The nature versus nurture debate has raged for centuries. But if we look at Scripture, it's not an either-or debate. It's both.

God created genetics, family resemblances and inherited temperaments. Yet, also, so many of the outworkings of your life and mine are based on personal decisions and intrinsic motivation. Try not to blame your ancestors for who you are, or who you wish you were. Be grateful to God for the family He placed you in, and for all they've taught you, and passed on to you. Then ask Him for the strength to make the right choices – choices for which *you* will be held accountable, when all's said and done. Nurture your nature into its most excellent form.

OUTRUNNING YOUR ANCESTORS?

Genetics play a role in why some people are more active than others. So do other life-influencers, like environmental issues and social context. Internal motivation is definitely a determinant, but so many different things could've influenced that motivation. While growing up, were your parents active? Did you play school sport? What facilities were available? As you got older, what social pressure or support did you experience? Thank God no matter what external forces have been at play in your life, you have a choice today to get up and get moving!

FOOD FOR THOUGHT

Text neck and laptop look – it's a real thing.

✤ If you sit in front of a computer all day, a workstation make-over is a must. Ensure that you can sit comfortably with your hips and knees at ninety degree angles and your screen at an arm's length away. Your display should also be eye level so that you aren't forced to look downwards.

   While you're adjusting your screen, give it a quick clean. A layer of dust on a display affects its sharpness and contrast, which tricks you into thinking your screen is darker than it really is. Some people adjust the brightness, but most just squint more and lean in closer, exaggerating their poor posture pose.

✤ Aim to spend less time on your phone altogether! But when you *are* using your phone, give yourself a good posture check beforehand, and again after a few minutes.

   Social media can be so distracting that you often forget where you are, let alone how you're sitting. The other option is to use the good old tried and tested book-on-your-head technique, to perfect your posture.

TIME TO REFLECT ...

Is there just *one thing* you could do this week to galvanize you into being more active – as opposed to binge-watching a series on Netflix, or scrolling Instagram?

Where are you when you tend to spend too much time on your phone (your car, your cubicle, your kitchen, your kids' school car park)? How could you reorganize that space, so you spend your time better? Could it be a chance to pray with a friend, exercise or read a book?

Is there a nagging sensation in your gut that you need to take to God? Don't delay. Do it now.

_____

_____

_____

_____

_____

_____

_____

_____

_____

_____

KNOW YOUR STATUS

Test me, LORD, and try me, examine my heart and my mind;
for I have always been mindful of Your unfailing love
and have lived in reliance on Your faithfulness.

Psalm 26:2-3, NIV

Knowledge is power. If every person on the planet knew their HIV status, it would be a powerful way of massively reducing transmission of the virus, if not eradicating it altogether. (What would eradicate it for sure is if the human race held to God's worldview: enjoying sex within the beautiful boundaries of life-time marriage.)

Think, too, how it would change the world if we really grasped our status before the King of kings. We go to Him – hat in hand – and He gives us a crown. That's who we are. Children of the Most High and heirs with His Son, our Savior. Let's keep examining our hearts, minds and lives, eradicating anything that doesn't reflect our royal status.

EXAMINATION FOR ELIMINATION

In the absence of a viable HIV cure or vaccine, we need to focus on transmission prevention strategies. The good news is that we're making progress in the fight against HIV. Even though we have a long way to go, we can at least say the glass is half full! The latest statistics show that globally the numbers of HIV infections are *down*. Of course, the ARV program has made a significant impact on the lives of those living with HIV. But the most powerful and empowering step people can take is to get tested!

RHYME AND REASON

Oh, the depth of the riches of the wisdom and knowledge of God!
How unsearchable His judgments, and His paths beyond tracing out!
Romans 11:33, NIV

There are bits of the Old Testament that seem odd, unnecessary and confusing to me. I'm not sure why God's people had to follow such stringent commands – like circumcision, and a pork-free diet. Yet I've discovered that many Old Testament regulations were put in place to keep God's people safe from danger or disease. God's New Testament instructions, whether or not we like them or understand them, are also always to bless us, keep us safe and set us free.

God's wisdom and ways are *way* above ours (Isaiah 55:8) – and so often He reveals that wisdom when we trust and obey, *anyway*. Whether or not you understand what God's doing, or why, could you obey anyway, today, and trust that He'll show you the rhyme or reason, in this life or the next?

(FORE)SKIN DEEP SOLUTIONS

Studies done in South Africa, Kenya and Uganda found that the risk of HIV infection was reduced by up to 70% in circumcised men. Medical male circumcision (MMC) reduces the infection risk because the inner foreskin has a heavy concentration of HIV target cells. Also, viruses prefer a dark, warm, moist environment – something circumcised men are missing along with their foreskin. MMC isn't a 100% HIV prevention strategy. God's wisdom is perfect in this instance too: one man, one woman, for life.

STAYING POWER

And endurance develops strength of character,
and character strengthens our confident hope of salvation.
Romans 5:4, NLT

The most spiritual step you can take is probably just the next one. Don't give up. Keep praying what you're praying, and keep trusting for what you're trusting for. God's timeframe is supernatural and eternal. He seldom sticks to our two-dimensional (usually selfish) schedule – and for perfect, holy reasons.

But just because you're not seeing immediate prayer 'results' doesn't mean God hasn't heard your prayer. He hears loud and clear, and He *is busy answering* – in perfect, holy ways. Even if it feels like you're getting nowhere, keep going for a little longer. Get a little fitter. When you're tired and sore and close to giving up – you're probably getting stronger.

AN ACUTE COUGH IS NOT SO CUTE

Getting over a cough can take longer than you think – as long as three weeks! Don't despair, and don't be too quick to jump to antibiotics. If you start taking medication seven days into a cough, you may begin to feel better naturally three to four days later, with your cough disappearing after ten days. That coincides with the average duration of an acute cough, misleading you into believing that antibiotics cured your cough. You healed you – so don't give credit where it isn't due.

WHINE FEST

A quarrelsome wife is as annoying
as constant dripping on a rainy day.
Proverbs 27:15, NLT

This verse is true of cantankerous, confrontational wives – *and* husbands, bosses, employees, needy friends, kids and colleagues. Every one of us – with our own unique displays of irritability and petulance – can be the constant drip … drip … of a leaking roof.

To check if you're wallowing in gripe water: count your complaints and criticisms. Are you finding fault more than favor? Sometimes it's necessary and right to stand firm and speak truth to power. Jesus did (Matthew 23:27). But moaning is different to bravely having your say.

There's a certain *tone* to whining. A relentless dissatisfaction. Even a sense that you're actually *enjoying* being miserable. If you need to voice a wrong, use the recourse available to you. Then leave it with God. Let Him fight for you (Exodus 14:14). Then get busy finding something to celebrate.

DRIP ... DRIP ... DRIP

Postnasal drip is a common cause of chronic coughing. Sinus drainage – thick, salty stuff – flows down the back of your throat (instead of through your nose). The drip hits your voice box and irritates it, triggering a cough. Coughs from postnasal drip are wet-sounding, and you may produce some mucus (similar to the kind that comes out your nose). Coughing tends to be worse at night, and, if caused by allergy, probably accompanied by itchy eyes and sneezing. Try using an antihistamine, or natural remedies like saline washes and steam, to relieve congestion.

(IN)APPROPRIATE?

Whoever sings songs to a heavy heart is like ... vinegar on soda.
Proverbs 25:20, ESV

One theologian comments:
'The un-timeliness of singing songs to a heavy heart is illustrated by ... [the comparison which] teaches vividly that the action which is thus untimely is also irritating when it ought to be soothing, and hurtful when it ought to be helpful. It is like "vinegar on nitre," like acid on soda, which produces effervescence, calling into active exercise the natural antipathies of the substances, and destroying the virtue of the soda.'

We definitely won't always read people perfectly. We won't always get it right to comfort appropriately. But God promises to give wisdom to those who ask (James 1:5). We could start by asking for wisdom to know how to heal, not hurt, so that the words or actions we offer to others will be *right on*.

CAUSTIC COMFORT

We've all turned to food for comfort. Yet too often food causes us *dis*comfort. What we hope will ease our pain bites us with acid reflux – and a nasty cough. Gastroesophageal reflux disease (GERD) is the second most common cause of a chronic cough. Acids from your stomach travel up to your esophagus, burning the bottom of your voice box and triggering a dry-sounding cough. You'll be stoked to know that a few lifestyle tweaks make the world of difference to this kind of cough. Limit alcohol and caffeine, avoid spicy foods, and manage your body weight.

FOOD FOR THOUGHT

Debunking beauty myths:

❧ *Drinking from a straw causes lip lines and 'smoker's mouth' wrinkles.*

Straws can be effective in reducing stains on our teeth from certain drinks, but there's some evidence that repeated straw drinking causes wrinkles because of repetitive muscle motion. A bit like frown lines on your forehead. Smokers, however, have far more wrinkles thanks to free radical skin damage from chemicals in their smokes, and because of their repeated lip movement when inhaling. So straw or no straw? No straw is definitely better for the planet! You can easily sidestep staining your teeth by avoiding certain drinks in the first place. That said, if there was an easy way of avoiding wrinkles – even if the chance was slim – wouldn't you want to take it?

❧ *Toothpaste is good for clearing up spots.*

This is a common DIY pimple trick, but the science behind it is questionable. It's true that toothpaste will dry out a spot, attributable to ingredients like baking soda, alcohol and hydrogen peroxide. However, there are no ingredients in toothpaste that make this method any more effective than conventional treatments, which is why this zit-zapping scheme really isn't recommended. Toothpaste actually irritates the skin causing redness and peeling. Don't know about you, but I'd rather have the zit!

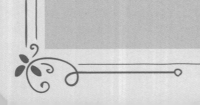

TIME TO REFLECT ...

*Father God, give me clean hands – and a clean heart –
to do all my doings today with integrity and kindness.
Give me patience to endure when my problems seem
chronic – dragging on with no end in sight. And help me be
quick to pounce on acute issues that suddenly crop up.
Amen.*

NO GRIEF NO GROWTH

In His kindness God called you to share in His eternal glory
by means of Christ Jesus. So after you have suffered a little while,
He will restore, support, and strengthen you,
and He will place you on a firm foundation.

1 Peter 5:10, NLT

Peter is writing to a suffering, persecuted church. He emphasizes God's *kindness* – because in His kindness He allows us to suffer, knowing what it will produce in us.

A good father will let his kid carry a heavy grocery bag now and then – to strengthen her muscles. God is a *perfect* Father. And sometimes He lets us suffer, to strengthen us. You can probably look back on something that was incredibly tough at the time, and though you'd never wish it on anyone or ask for a repeat experience, you actually wouldn't choose a different story, because the time of stiff, sore spiritual muscles wrought in you something nothing else would have.

 ## AFTER ACTION ACHE

Tried a new exercise, or trained harder than usual and woke up tired and sore? Stiffness starts around 24 hours after exercise, peaking at 48 hours. While your muscles are in pain, they're also weaker and less flexible. The pain is caused by miniature tears in individual muscle fibers, caused when your muscles do things they haven't done before, or done often. Your amazing body repairs these tears, and pain eventually dissipates. There's not much you can do to relieve stiffness, but there's also nothing to worry about!

BREATHE ON ME, BREATH OF GOD

The Spirit of God has made me;
the breath of the Almighty gives me life.
Job 33:4, NIV

Explaining the name God calls Himself – Yahweh – *I Am* – one commentator writes, 'Every time we hear the word Yahweh, or see LORD in the English Bible, we should think: this is a proper name ... built out of the word for "I am" and reminding us each time that God absolutely is. No beginning, no end, absolute reality and utterly independent. God is constant. He is the same yesterday, today, and forever. He cannot be improved. He is not becoming anything. He is who He is.'

Where there's breath, there's life. And where there's life, there's hope. Yahweh breathed the first breath into Adam (Genesis 2:7) and He lends us every breath we breathe too. While we have life and breath, we're living reminders that He is still the great I Am, and we have hope.

BREATHLESS

Asthma can be genetic, or brought on by environmental triggers and / or respiratory infections. An asthma attack sends muscles surrounding your airways into spasm, squishing them from the outside. Your body mounts a counter attack *inside*: swelling the lining of airways, producing mucous and a battle for breath. Breaths per minute can shoot up from 15 to 30, so your breathing bits work doubly hard. It's vital to know the warning signs of an impending attack – fatigue, persistent coughing, anxiety, and tightened neck & chest muscles – so you can keep breathing!

MANAGE AND MITIGATE

I know, O Lord, that Your regulations are fair;
You disciplined me because I needed it.
Now let Your unfailing love comfort me,
just as You promised me, Your servant.
Psalm 119:75-76, NLT

There are two types of asthma medications: controllers and relievers. The controllers keep the swelling and inflammation at bay and are used on a long-term basis. The relievers are used for temporary and immediate relief of any asthmatic symptoms. Controllers and relievers work together well to manage and mitigate the condition, keeping inflammation and irritation at bay and air moving smoothly.

God's Word has controllers and relievers too. It offers guidelines and guardrails – life handles that help us get a grip and keep it, and benchmarks against which we can measure our faith (2 Corinthians 13:5). And it offers great relief. What a privilege and joy to know we can dive into Scripture any time for hope and comfort when life has us all out of breath.

EASE YOUR WHEEZE

If you're asthmatic, you may need controllers, or relievers, or both. Firstly, keep taking your meds, even if you feel better! Secondly, identify what sends your chest into overdrive and avoid it. If it's dust, keep a clean house. If it's smoke, steer clear of smokers. And if it's your furry friend, wash Fido more often and limit bed and couch time. Thirdly, with colds and flu being one of the biggest triggers, do what you can to stay ahead of the germs.

WALKING THE LINE

'You won't die!' the serpent replied to the woman.
Genesis 3:4, NLT

This was the first lie Satan spat out to the human race. He still tells it. And we're adept at telling it to ourselves. *It's not hurting anyone. No one will even know. I won't die.*

It's our nature to see how close to the line we can walk to get by, or to *not* get into trouble. What we miss is that the line we're walking is a knife edge, and we'd be better served running safe and free into the wide open spaces of grace.

It's like – if we do just the *bare minimum* of exercise, we're not free to shop for smaller sizes, feel stronger, or not get out of breath climbing stairs. If we do the *bare minimum* spiritually (attending church on Easter and Christmas, and maybe rattling off pre-meal grace), we're not free to enjoy security, comfort, joy, help and wisdom.

The lie traps. The truth liberates. The choice is yours.

THE LEAST YOU CAN DO

The *need* for exercise isn't debatable, but *how much* you need, is. The answer depends on what you hope to achieve. We generally exercise for three reasons: to be healthy, lose weight, or win a gold medal. If you're a health-focused fitness minimalist, the global recommendations for health enhancing physical activity are 150 minutes of moderate intensity exercise every week, and muscle strengthening exercises on two or more days of the week.

BITE-SIZED

Study this Book of Instruction continually.
Meditate on it day and night so you will be sure to obey everything written in it. Only then will you prosper and succeed in all you do.
Joshua 1:8, NLT

No one eats a massive meal on Monday morning and expects it to fill them for the week. Same-same, spiritually. One massive Christian conference won't keep you fed, filled and sin-free for a year.

Daily chunks of Scripture keep us healthy. You probably don't remember exactly what you ate for lunch three Thursdays ago. But it's likely you ate *something* – whatever snack or smorgasbord was on offer – and it nourished you enough to keep you going, and here you are today.

Don't stress if you can't remember exactly what was preached three Sundays ago (one Sunday ago?), or even exactly what you read in the Bible yesterday. The regular, consistent – even bite-sized – truth you consume nourishes you nonetheless. Keep eating.

BREAK IT DOWN

It doesn't matter how you move, just get moving. But try not to do all your moving at once – for two reasons. Firstly, your risk of injury goes down if you don't shock your body into exercising suddenly after five days of lurking on the couch or at your desk. Secondly, it's probably going to be a lot more enjoyable to exercise throughout the week, which is a key factor in how likely you are to stick to it. Keep moving consistently!

FOOD FOR THOUGHT

Boost your breaks!

- *Schedule breaks.* Timing is critical. Studies have found that the more hours that elapsed before a break, the less energized people felt when returning to their desks. Earlier breaks were also associated with fewer unwanted symptoms such as headaches, eyestrain and lower back pain. Toiling through much of the workday before taking a breather is not as restorative as taking time out for breaks earlier in the day.

- *It's ok to take a break mid-task.* If you're on a roll, then by all means, get it done! But mental concentration is like a muscle. It becomes tired after sustained use, and needs a rest to recover, much like your bicep needs some R&R between reps. Taking a smart break improves productivity and creativity, which means a mid-task break could actually get the task done breezily and better.

- *Don't feel guilty.* Taking a break can induce guilty feelings because a break is 'me time'. But that's the whole point! To be the best you can be, you need to detach from work and your workspace every now and then. Cognitive recharging is a real thing, and your work can only benefit from it. Working long hours doesn't necessarily mean you're working efficiently or productively. Work smart, not long.

TIME TO REFLECT ...

Take a breather. Catch your breath. Maybe even light a candle – if that's a way for you to carve out a moment with God. And think about what you've read this week.

Are you breathless with busyness because life has picked up its pace – or breathless with excitement because of something God seems to be birthing?

Is there an area of your life where you've become sluggish? Is it time to get moving?

_____

_____

_____

_____

_____

_____

_____

_____

_____

_____

_____

_____

_____

BURNT BEAUTIFUL

I have refined you, but not as silver is refined.
Rather, I have refined you in the furnace of suffering.
Isaiah 48:10, NLT

Burn injuries are painful, traumatic, and sometimes fatal. And yet, spiritually, there's something satisfying about the idea of everything that's superfluous being burned away. It might not *feel* like a beautiful experience while we're being burned.

But we have to know that if God didn't love us, He'd just leave us in our mess. He'd watch and laugh (or not even watch, since He wouldn't care) as sin's consequences played out and we went from bad to worse, devolving into malice or misery.

It's only *because* He loves us that He wants to refine us into more useful and delightful instruments in His hands – by allowing what's ugly and unnecessary to be burned off in affliction's fire.

Stay mindful that we may not have a choice about how life burns us – but we do get to choose whether the fire makes us bitter or beautiful.

DEEP AND WIDE

Scalds, contact burns and flame burns are classified and treated according to two criteria: the depth of the burn, and the extent of the scorching (what percentage of the body has been burned – google the "rule of nines"). Special attention is always given to burns on the face, hands and genitals. Any burns on a baby or someone with compromised immunity should immediately be seen by a doc. Smoke inhalation and electrical burns are also cause to get immediate medical treatment.

PLAYING WITH FIRE

Let [wisdom and insight] protect you from an affair with an immoral woman, from listening to the flattery of a promiscuous woman.

Proverbs 7:4-5, NLT

Whether it's about fraud, adultery or addiction, you'll hear people say, 'I couldn't help how I felt!' or 'One thing led to another!' Feelings rise within us, sure. Doors open to desire. Sometimes, one thing really does lead to another.

But we make a mistake to think we can't do anything about that. You have a choice to walk away, no matter how overwhelmingly difficult or embarrassing that may be. You've a choice to immediately yell for help. A choice to be honest, or to rekindle romance in the fireplace it was designed to burn in. A choice to resign from your job, or to get new friends if your old ones keep enticing you to burn your fingers. It's within your power to stop playing with fire.

SCALDING SOLUTIONS

For any burn, immediately hold your painful parts under cool running water for 20 minutes to reduce swelling. Next, put on a protective gauze bandage. Don't use fluffy materials like cotton wool that may get stuck – or 'home remedies' like oil or butter! Anything you put onto a burn creates a barrier that retains the heat. Stick to first-aid burn ointments, and keep the infection risk down. Turn pot handles away from the stove edge, cover open plug holes, and put all kid-magnet temptations – like matches! – far out of reach of little hands.

UNDER THE INFLUENCE

Don't be drunk with wine, because that will ruin your life.
Instead, be filled with the Holy Spirit ...
Ephesians 5:18, NLT

Every human worships something – whether or not it's God. And every human is *mastered* by something – whether or not they're mastered by the Master of the universe.

Let's keep fighting the good fight to ensure we're mastered by nothing and no one but Jesus – who is not just the Savior, but Savior *and Lord.*

That means we can't be saying 'Yes Sir!' to anything or anyone other than Him. Like alcohol – which promises freedom, but has the power to master us, and change us. Too much of the stuff and we obey different impulses. Too much of the stuff and we can't think rationally. We lose dignity and inhibition and end up hurting others and making fools of ourselves. Let's not be led by the spirits – but only by the Spirit.

SOBER OR SMASHED?

Long ago, alcohol was used for almost anything: as a substitute for safe drinking water, as a preservative and even medicine. These days, however, there's a clear dose-response relationship between health and alcohol. This means that as you consume more alcohol, the health risks greatly outweigh any benefit. All of us intuitively know how much alcohol is meant by the term *moderate*: One drink per day for women and up to two per day for men. But keep in mind that even moderate alcohol consumption isn't without its risks. Drinking – any amount – whilst driving (or pregnant!) is *never* a good idea!

COLLATERAL DAMAGE

Do not be deceived: 'Bad company ruins good morals.'
1 Corinthians 15:33, ESV

As Kingdom pilgrims in Earth's countries, we *must* walk along-side those who don't know Jesus – so that perhaps something of the rhythm of our footfalls will have them following us, as we follow Him.

But even as we're reaching out to cynics, skeptics and unbelievers, we should take Solomon's advice and *guard our hearts above all else* (Proverbs 4:23). Because we'd be stupid to breathe in the secondhand smoke of other people's lives. We might convince ourselves it's ok to hang out with people caught up in sin of some sort. *As long as I don't participate*, we think, *or officially endorse their choices, then it's all good!* But inevitably we'll be affected – probably hurt.

Ask God to help you strike a balance, so you can stay spiritually healthy, with strength and capacity to love the lost.

HAND-ME-DOWN HEALTH RISKS

Kids exposed to secondhand smoke at home are twice as likely to start smoking themselves. Exposure to secondhand smoke affects brain function, decreases lung efficiency and increases both the number and duration of ear infections a child will experience. Little humans are particularly at risk because they have a faster breathing rate, taking in more air relative to their body weight, and so absorbing more smoke. If you smoke, stop now. If you're a parent, *stop yesterday and don't look back*. Your children's lives depend on it.

RIGHT ON TIME

For everything there is a season,
a time for every activity under heaven.
Ecclesiastes 3:1, NLT

We live two-dimensional lives – bound by the pressures of time and territory. We can do all sorts of things, but we can't do them all, everywhere, at the same time. We're limited or liberated by the season or the space we're in.

In many ways, this is a mercy. It reminds us to be slow to speak. It reminds us to take time to make a decision. Because circumstances vary and that makes a difference to our priorities, and our capacity. Whether you're in a high pressure season – managing a demanding job, parenting a colicky baby – or a low pressure season – enjoying some breathing room in your finances or your schedule – aim to be steadfast and consistent in character and values, but flexible to the demands and freedoms of life's time zones, and trust that God is always right on time.

WELL-TIMED

It's important to get an accurate blood pressure reading, as blood pressure is extremely variable and subject to a range of influences like time of day (almost always higher the earlier in the day you have it measured), temperature, how stressed out you're feeling, what you've just eaten, how many cappuccinos you've had and if you were running into your appointment because you were late. All these things have a short-lived but significant impact on blood pressure – usually making it shoot up.

FOOD FOR THOUGHT

How believable is your blood pressure reading?

❧ *Anger.* Your reading might not be accurate if you got mad at someone for nabbing the parking spot you wanted outside the doctor's office!

❧ *White Coat Hypertension.* This is a real condition, usually caused by bad experiences at hospitals, dentist chairs or a guilty conscience over unhealthy living. If thinking about a doctor makes you panic, it may result in a sky-high blood pressure reading.

❧ *A stress-free appointment.* Stressful situations or unhealthy behaviors at home may raise your blood pressure – only for it to return to normal levels when you're with your cool, calm and collected doctor. This is called *masked* hypertension – the antithesis of White Coat Hypertension.

❧ *Caffeine.* If you've had one too many espressos or cappuccinos, your reading may be raised for up to three hours after the last sip.

Perfect pressure ...

❧ Measure your blood pressure on at least three different occasions, at different times of the day.

❧ Ask your doctor to measure your blood pressure on both arms. New research suggests that a big difference (more than ten points) in blood pressure readings between your two arms might indicate heart disease.

❧ Relax. Rushing into the doctor's room without having had some time to rest first, will elevate your readings. Breathe. Slowly. Repeat.

❧ When having your blood pressure checked, rest your arm so your elbow is at the level of your heart, and sit with your back supported and both legs firmly on the floor. Crossing your legs can temporarily increase blood pressure, resulting in a false reading.

TIME TO REFLECT ...

*Jesus, I've been burned by the words
and actions of strangers and friends.
Help me to forgive. Help me to smell the smoke
when it's me who has set something
or someone on fire. Burn away muck and grime,
or meaningless fluff, from my life, so I can gleam.
Amen.*

FAMISHED

God blesses those who hunger and thirst for justice,
for they will be satisfied.
Matthew 5:6, NLT

Anyone who's sought solace in a pizza knows that food can be comforting. Food does more than fill our stomachs; it satisfies feelings. Sometimes the strongest cravings for food happen when you're at your weakest point emotionally. Research reveals that chocolate can actually taste 15% better when you're sad. Other studies have shown that certain foods can fend off negative emotions.

But what are you really hungry for, and why? Sometimes we're hungry to be around certain people and to have the connections, influence or stuff that they have. Or we're hungry for comfort and ease and pleasure so we gobble anything that promises those things. We eat up whatever scraps life throws for us – and we're left hungrier than before.

Let's rather ask for a holy hunger for God's justice and righteousness. He promises to satisfy that craving.

HUNGRY OR HURT?

Emotional eating is closely associated with obesity, so it's crucial to know the difference between emotional and physical hunger before you dive headlong into the ice-cream. Emotional hunger comes on suddenly, whereas physical hunger occurs gradually. When you're eating to fill an emotional void not an empty stomach, you crave a specific food. When you eat because you're actually hungry, you're open to options. When you're eating because you're (actually) hungry, you'll be more likely to stop when you're full – and you won't be plagued by feelings of guilt.

RIGHT TIME RIGHT PLATE

Blessed is the land whose king is of noble birth
and whose princes eat at a proper time –
for strength and not for drunkenness.
Ecclesiastes 10:17, NIV

Food is a necessity *and* a blessing. Food *is* comforting, and God has given it to us as a fantastic part of celebrations. That means it's totally ok to relish the delicious things God provides. (I'm particularly glad He didn't leave the human race without hot fresh bread and camembert cheese.)

The key to health and holiness is recognizing when your favorite food has become an idol, when we're turning to food to find meaning, hope or love, or when our comfort eating is affecting our health.

Ask yourself candidly, 'Why am I eating this thing, now?' Whether it's to be polite to hosts, or for strength or celebration, or just because *it's delicious* – use the occasion for worship. It's always the right time to chew on God's grace, with gratitude.

FEED YOUR FEELINGS

To deal with emotional eating, feed your feelings without food. Spoil yourself with something like a hot bath. If you're feeling down, reach out to a friend instead of for a packet of chips and if you're bored find something you enjoy doing and do it. Hit pause when cravings hit, and give them time to pass. Try the minute-to-win-it technique. Decide how long you believe it'll take your craving to pass and *just don't give in*, for one minute at a time.

TINY TROUBLE

This false teaching is like a little yeast
that spreads through the whole batch of dough!
Galatians 5:9, NLT

Yeast is just one ingredient in a loaf of bread – but the bread rises – or is ruined – with or without it. A virus is microscopic – but it can affect – even destroy – your whole body. It spreads and affects everything.

Spiritually, it's possible we're adhering to a teaching or believing a (small?) lie that's spreading rot throughout our lives. Or we may be succumbing to confirmation bias – seeing every experience or conversational nuance as evidence to support our grudge or grumblings.

What thoughts are permeating the different arenas of your life? Are they helpful and healthy, or noxious? It's never too late to dump what's damaging – no matter how deceptively small and seemingly insignificant it seems.

BED BUG

The health benefits of exercise are ostensibly endless and include keeping you healthy, happy and youthful. But exercising while you're not feeling 100% is never smart. When you have a fever, your heart works extra hard to get rid of extra heat. Furthermore, there are viruses that infect your nose and throat which can also infect your heart muscle when you exercise, resulting in permanent damage. This damage can cause disturbances of your heartbeat (cardiac arrhythmia), weakness of your heart muscle (cardiomyopathy) or sudden cardiac arrest. If you're ill, take you and your bugs straight back to bed!

MOBILIZED BY MANY

I commend to you our sister Phoebe,
who is a deacon in the church in Cenchrea.
Welcome her in the Lord as one who is worthy of honor
among God's people. Help her in whatever she needs,
for she has been helpful to many, and especially to me.

Romans 16:1-2, NLT

Paul was a project manager of a massive commission: taking the gospel across a continent and planting the early church.

He leaned heavily on people like Phoebe – friends, co-workers and faith-family who kept him motivated and mobilized. He could keep on keeping on because of their practical help, wisdom and encouragement. His community was a tapestry of people paying it forward to keep the gospel message on the move.

Don't underestimate the Kingdom-building role you can play by offering your gifts, ideas, hugs and help to God's people in your life. And don't be freaked out or afraid when hope and help are offered to you. We all need others to keep us moving.

MOTIVATED TO MOVE

To enjoy the benefits of exercise, you've got to stay motivated – and moving! Boost your enthusiasm by exercising with others. Besides being able to connect with someone while you huff and puff your way through a workout, you'll be less likely to let them down for those early morning sessions. There's also music that can reduce feelings of effort – especially when *that* song is on, you know the one! Always keep things interesting: try a new class or running route, and never let one missed workout turn into a month of them!

BOSOM BETRAYAL

Suppose someone secretly entices you – even your brother, your son or daughter, your beloved wife, or your closest friend – and says, 'Let us go worship other gods' … do not give in or listen.
Deuteronomy 13:6, 8, NLT

Deception can be very close to home. The King James version of the Bible translates 'beloved wife' in this verse as 'the wife of thy bosom' – a very intimate image.

It's not that we need to be paranoid, or live in constant suspicion of those around us. But we can check our interactions and perceptions against Scripture. We can test our thoughts, and we can pray for clarity.

Pray for those in positions of influence in your life – your leader or your lover. Because even our bosom-buddies are flawed – *as we are!* – and if they're not in a good place, it's not impossible that they'll want to take us there too.

BELIEVING THE BREAST

It's true that breast cancer is the most common cancer in women of all ethnicities. What's *not* true – no matter what you've seen on Facebook – is that antiperspirant deodorants and bras (underwire or not) cause cancer. Breast size also has no impact on breast cancer risk – *unless* your breasts have grown in size along with the rest of you as you put on excess body weight. Seriously. One out of every three cancer deaths is linked to excess body weight, poor nutrition, and physical inactivity.

FOOD FOR THOUGHT

Is it ok to exercise when I'm sick?

It's not a good idea to exercise if you're ill. But mild to moderate physical activity is safe if you have a garden-variety cold without a fever. Exercise might even help you feel better by temporarily relieving nasal congestion.

Not sure? Take the neck test:

- If your symptoms are from the neck up, you can exercise, but be aware that certain medications can increase your heart rate and when combined with exercise could cause your heart to work harder than normal. Consider reducing the intensity and length of your workout. Instead of going for a run, go for a walk.

- If your symptoms are from the neck down – with a deep chest cough or a fever – do not exercise! You most likely have inflamed tissue in your lungs and exercise will make it worse.

If you do decide to exercise, but have difficulty breathing before or after the session or generally feel worse, then *stop*. Taking a few days off until you feel better will not interfere with a strict training program. A heart infection on the other hand, which is the risk you run, will!

TIME TO REFLECT ...

Where do you turn first for comfort? If God has convicted you that your guilty pleasures are doing you no good, is there a life hack you could implement to steer you in a healthier direction?

Are you in a season of necessary rest from exercise? Talk to God about your fears and frustrations.

Are you in a season of consistently showing up to exercise? Ask God for wisdom and ways to stay motivated.

Is there someone close to your heart – or heavy on your heart – whom God is asking you to pray for today?

_____

_____

_____

_____

_____

_____

_____

_____

_____

_____

_____

PILLOW TIME

Jesus was sleeping at the back of the boat with His head
on a cushion. The disciples woke Him up, shouting,
'Teacher, don't You care that we're going to drown?'
Mark 4:38, NLT

This is a fantastic picture of Jesus' humanity. When Luke recounts this same event, he writes, 'As they sailed across, Jesus settled down for a nap' (Luke 8:23). I love that Jesus took naps. I love that He appreciated a good pillow. I love that He is unbelievably calm before the storm – and during the storm – and after the storm – despite the panicked, faithless accusations of His closest friends.

Where would we be, if we didn't have a God who isn't thrown by the winds and waves of life? Perhaps Jesus was able to sleep because He knew His Father never does (Psalm 121:4), and we can rest in the relief of that truth too, no matter how the storm blows.

DEEP SLEEP POSITION

Before turning out the lights, give some thought to your sleeping position of choice. If you're consistently waking up tired, there may be more at play than simply not getting enough sleep. How you "hit the pillow" is a major factor in the quality of your slumber. The best sleep position is on your back. It ensures proper circulation to your brain, maintains your back and neck in a neutral position, and combats acid reflux. If you're a snorer, try the second-best position: on your side.

AL FRESCO

On the glorious splendor of Your majesty,
and on Your wondrous works, I will meditate.

Psalm 145:5, ESV

Sometimes we arrive home from a vacation more exhausted than when we left – even though we've read books, slept late, walked on the beach and done all the other things the doctor ordered. Matt Chandler explains that unless we intentionally vacation to gaze upon the splendor of God, *we won't find rest*.

Amazingly, we don't have to save up time or money to go away in order to enjoy God's majesty. Just step out of your office. Breathe … in view of trees. Look down at weeds between paving stones – God made those too.

Poet Gerard Manley Hopkins reminds us that, despite how people have messed up our planet, 'nature is never spent; There lives the dearest freshness deep down things …' No matter where you live or work, you can always get outside and find something of God's glory.

OUT-OF-OFFICE NOTIFICATION

Bad day? Don't go to bed. *Go outside!* People who spend more time out-doors have lower levels of depression, stronger immune systems and a more positive outlook on life. Spending time exposed to natural daylight triggers vitamin D production, and helps you sleep better at night by syncing up your sleep-and-awake hormones. As little as five minutes of sitting in a sunny plant-filled setting will benefit your mental health. So instead of setting out-of-office notifications – get up and physically get out of your office!

SIMPLY SCRUB

Come close to God, and God will come close to you.
Wash your hands, you sinners; purify your hearts,
for your loyalty is divided between God and the world.

James 4:8, NLT

It's crazy that we've put people in space – but haven't cured the common cold. This is because a cold isn't a single illness but a number of symptoms caused by a number of viruses. Even the most common of these viruses has more than a hundred strains. So curing a cold would mean eliminating a very long list of respiratory viruses that all cause similar symptoms.

Life can be like this. Overwhelming. Where do we even *start* curing the world of evil? A lot can go simultaneously wrong in our lives. *So* many virus-like vices vie for our attention. It simplifies things enormously to *just get close to God*. Keep your hands scrubbed clean – consistently choosing a wholesome lifestyle – and keep the complications of evil away.

SOAP IT OFF

Until a cure for the common cold is discovered (never say never!), prevention is where it's at. The most effective way to keep a cold away is to wash your hands often. Germs can live up to three hours outside your body and take every opportunity they can to shift from surfaces to your hands – which then touch your mouth, nose or eyes – giving germs easy access *into* your body. Wash with soap, rubbing your hands for around 20 seconds to be sure they're germ-free!

GERMINATE

All the believers devoted themselves to the apostles' teaching,
and to fellowship, and to sharing in meals
(including the Lord's Supper), and to prayer.

Acts 2:42, NLT

As believers, we want to grow in love and fellowship, right? We want to share community, communion and the wisdom of God's ways. But we don't want to share germs. Be considerate when you're sick. Stay away, so you don't unwittingly pass on your flu virus, or start a community-wide vomathon.

And if you're healthy, be considerate to the sick. Don't keep them up all night. Let them rest. Cook them something delicious. Caring might not be your natural bent or gifting. You may not be a hospitality pro. But we're all commanded to be the hands and feet of Jesus to others in this world. You'll probably get better with practice, and prayer.

FRESH AIR, FRESH FOOD

To avoid catching a cold or the flu, prioritize quality nutrition. Winter or summer, whether you feel like it or not, crank up your fresh veggie intake! And hang out with your friends *outside*. The germs that cause the common cold are around most of the year, the reason we get sick more often in winter is because we spend more time indoors, with buddies and their bugs – mates and their microbes. Germs also enjoy warm environments – where they can plummet from person to person – so embrace those frosty mornings and chilly afternoons. There are far fewer germs in the wide open great outdoors.

LION OR LAMB?

[There is a] time to kill and a time to heal.
A time to tear down and a time to build up.
Ecclesiastes 3:3, NLT

Both fight-or-flight and rest-and-digest responses are crucial to how we function as humans. There's a time to be a lion, and a time to be a lamb. Sometimes we need to make a stand: be brave and speak truth to power (without ranting on Twitter and embarrassing ourselves, and our faith). And sometimes we need to keep quiet: trust God to fight for us (Exodus 14:14). Both are necessary and healthy. Both display God's glory and wisdom, grace and kindness. As each situation arises, pray for discernment and discretion to know whether a sympathetic or a parasympathetic response is required.

Furthermore, don't be suspicious of someone else's choice in this regard. Pray for them, and seek to understand and learn from their perspective.

YAY FOR YOGA

Yoga seems to be more breathing than sweating – but it's as good for you as something like running. Physical activity doesn't always have to be crazy vigorous to be effective. Yoga is an excellent weight-bearing, low-impact form of exercise, putting you in a relaxed state (called rest and digest – the complete opposite of fight or flight), which makes it ideally suited for people suffering from arthritis, fibromyalgia and high blood pressure. Yoga also lowers levels of stress hormones like cortisol, while increasing serotonin – a befitting formula for alleviating anxiety and depression.

FOOD FOR THOUGHT

You can't turn back time – but you can put the brakes on the ageing process:

- *Eat real food.* Skip processed foods in favor of fresh fruits and vegetables, which are all-in-one anti-ageing capsules, without the capsule! Try the one-ingredient rule. If a food contains one ingredient (apple, egg) it's probably a good choice. If you eat this way, besides *feeling* better, you'll likely shed a few kilos and start *looking* better too. Being overweight stresses your body, so losing a few pounds reduces your risk for conditions like heart disease and diabetes.

- *Get active.* Resistance (strength) training is extremely beneficial when it comes to ageing. It slows down the rate of age-related muscle wasting, boosts metabolism and reduces fat accumulation. That's the not-so-secret secret to preserving your physical youth.

- *Keep your brain engaged.* If you're active and eating well, you're already looking after your gray matter. You can show it even more love by taking up dancing. Why? Essentially, any activity involving creativity, movement and socializing has the potential to perk up the neuroplasticity of an ageing brain.

- *Stay connected.* Having meaningful, face-to-face (not just Facebook) relationships enhances longevity. One study found that people who were disconnected from others were about three times more likely to die earlier than people with strong social ties. Friends and family give us stress-busting emotional support and stimulate empathy, cooperation and trust. They also give us a reason to get up in the morning to do all these anti-ageing activities!

TIME TO REFLECT …

Lord, in my sleeping and waking –
my chilling and my to-dos –
let my position always be one
of total surrender to You.
Give me insight, and great ideas to manage
my health wisely and well.
Thank You for weaving so much beauty into the world.
Even today – open my eyes to notice lovely things.
Amen.

_____

_____

_____

_____

_____

_____

_____

_____

_____

COWBOYS TOTALLY CRY

Then Esau ran to meet him and embraced him,
threw his arms around his neck, and kissed him.
And they both wept.

Genesis 33:4, NLT

The book of Genesis alone has at least twelve references to men crying. Hardcore men. Powerful men. Heads of state, and men who fathered tribes and nations. Esau, Jacob, Joseph, Benjamin and his brothers.

I'm not sure when it became un-cool for men to cry, *but our Savior Himself wept* (John 11:35). We mistakenly equate courage with stoicism, when really, the root of courage is always humility and vulnerability, which come at a cost. Moral courage is the risk we take in exposing our hearts, knowing we might be scorned or rejected.

Let's be man enough – even woman enough – to wear our hearts on our sleeves from time to time, allowing God to use our uninhibited emotions to move the hearts of others.

MAN ENOUGH FOR A MEDICAL CHECKUP?

Some men are uncomfortable talking about their feelings. Research also confirms that, compared to women, men are less likely to see a doctor. Listen tough guy: *just because you don't feel sick doesn't mean you're healthy!* Many conditions display no symptoms until it's too late (the first symptom of high blood pressure is often a heart attack). Visit your doc at least annually to be sure you're in working order. Prostate cancer, as another example, is sneaky and slow growing, with few-and-far-between symptoms. Catch it early, and it can be treated successfully. Miss it, and you'll be missed.

IT'S NOT WHAT YOU THINK

Trust in the LORD with all your heart;
do not depend on your own understanding.
Proverbs 3:5, NLT

We live two-dimensional lives. Bound by time, space and our own limited perceptions of what's happened, what's going on around us, and what's likely (or not) to occur in the future, we never have a full picture of reality.

Only God sees every side of every story. He knows every heart – and its fallibility. Don't make the mistake of trusting your own judgment. Rather lean as heavily as you can on God's wisdom and understanding. Ask Him to adjust your interpretations. If something about a situation is more serious than you've judged it to be, rely on Him to show you. And if you're taking something far more seriously than you need to, relax into His more accurate assessment of the situation.

HOLLYWOOD HEART THROBS – OR NOT!

Hollywood has painted a classic heart attack picture: red faced man grabs chest in agony and collapses! Except, heart attacks aren't *always* accompanied by chest pain. Many people write off heart attack symptoms as anxiety, stress, heartburn or fatigue. Women in particular may not experience *any* pain – just nausea and difficulty breathing. Other heart attack indicators include hot flushes, cold sweats, body aches and dizziness. If you get pain in your chest, arm or jaw – plus any other weird symptoms – see a doctor! A real one. Not Dr. Google. Don't be that person that didn't, but should've …

COMFORTABLE QUIET

But I have calmed and quieted myself,
I am like a weaned child with its mother;
like a weaned child I am content.
Psalm 131:2, NIV

We can't accurately hear what's going on inside of us – *deep* inside our hearts and minds – unless we stop. And become absolutely still ... Before God.

Introspection can be super uncomfortable. But it's in the secret places – when you're not on duty or display – that God can really speak to you. When you're just you, before the throne of grace, and you've quieted the crazy noise of life, you're likely to *hear* His whisper. Don't be scared of the silence and the stillness – or of what God might say to you there. He's a mighty God – fearsome in splendor! He's also gentle, tender and consoling. *Come to Him.*

RESTING RHYTHMS

Take time to *listen* to your heart. Measuring your resting heart rate gives you a good idea of how efficient your heart is. The average resting heart rate for a healthy adult is 60-80 beats per minute. The lower the better! (A strong heart can contract with more force: it doesn't need to beat as often.) Before you get out of bed in the morning, find your pulse and count the beats for 15 seconds. Multiply this number by four. And to strengthen your heart? Exercise! It's a muscle like any other, so it responds to exercise by getting bigger and stronger.

OUT OF SYNC

This is what the Sovereign LORD, the Holy One of Israel, says:
'In repentance and rest is your salvation, in quietness and trust
is your strength, but you would have none of it.'
Isaiah 30:15, NIV

You'd think we'd learn from mistakes. God has *told* us how to find peace in this world. And yet we 'would have none of it,' Isaiah reminds us.

We convince ourselves we've got things *better* figured out than our Father. We go it alone – or we follow a crowd heading in the wrong direction – until our steps begin to falter and the arrhythmia of our hearts has us slowing down and saying, 'Oops. Maybe I should've listened to God.'

If you know something's not right – don't delay. If all is *not* as it should be – then stop. Head back to the place of repentance, rest, quietness and trust, so you can regain your strength and get your heart beating as it should.

WHEN YOUR HEART SKIPS A BEAT

If you have 'butterflies in your chest', you may be experiencing cardiac arrhythmia. This happens when the electrical impulses coordinating your heartbeats cause your heart to beat too fast, too slow, or irregularly. It *may* be dangerous, because your body needs a specific amount of blood pumped, to function optimally. Arrhythmia may also increase your risk of a stroke and heart failure. But don't panic! Pinpoint your triggers. Stop smoking. Drink decaf. Check medication labels for stimulants. And get your heart racing the *healthy* way …. With exercise!

DEVOTION IN THE DUST

But Jesus said, 'Let the children come to Me.
Don't stop them! For the Kingdom of Heaven belongs to
those who are like these children.'
Matthew 19:14, NLT

You may have come across celebrity Christians who deem themselves too important to be crushed by the mob. They separate themselves from weirdly adoring fans by staying in their conference green rooms where it's all power dressing and makeup and hairspray that smells like fame.

Jesus was all about mingling with commoners in the dust of village streets. He loved on the outcasts, the downtrodden, the marginalized, the children. It's hard to think too much of ourselves when we crouch to cup the face of a child. And it's wonderful to know that when we get our hands and feet dirty for the Kingdom, we're in good company.

GOOD DIRT

Several studies show a relationship between resistance to allergies and farm living – or exposure to the 'good' germs that promote overall health. By limiting our children's exposure to germs and dirt, we could be lowering their immunity. Extreme hygiene, especially in childhood, leads to a decline in natural exposure to all sorts of healthy microbes. The concept of let-kids-play-in-the-dirt is a metaphor for building up immunity by moving towards natural living. Only use antibiotics when *absolutely* necessary. Limit the use of antiseptic agents. Spend more time outside. And don't fear the fur! If you have pets at home, don't keep them too far away from your kids.

FOOD FOR THOUGHT

Brain facts 101:

- Brain development begins just 16 days after conception and by six weeks these early neural connections permit the first fetal movements. During the second half of a child's first year, the brain forms synapses at such a rate that it consumes double the energy of an adult brain.

- As much as a fifth of the blood flowing from your heart is pumped to your cauliflower-sized brain, which needs constant blood flow to keep up with the heavy metabolic demands of your body's nerve cells. While your brain accounts for only 2% of your whole body's mass, it uses 20% of all the oxygen you breathe.

- Your brain consists of approximately 100 billion neurons (there are as many stars in the Milky Way). Each neuron has somewhere between 1,000 and 10,000 synapses (junctions between nerve cells), equaling about one quadrillion synapses, responsible for more than 100,000 chemical reactions happening in your brain every second.

- Regardless of your age, your brain can make new neurons and construct new neural pathways. Neuroplasticity is the 'muscle building' part of your brain. When you engage in new experiences or think in novel ways, new pathways are forged. Even as you're reading this, your brain is changing. Challenging our brains significantly slows down memory loss.

- Use it or lose it. The things we do often we become better at, and what we don't use, we lose. That's the reason why repetitive thoughts and actions have such a significant impact. We ultimately become what we think and do.

Above all else, guard your heart, for everything you do flows from it (Proverbs 4:23).

Your great God created a great brain inside of you!

TIME TO REFLECT ...

Are you struggling to find your rhythm, in one or more areas of your life? What *one thing* could you add or cut out, to recalibrate the cadence of your walk with God and others?

Have you set yourself up as being *above* a certain person, or a certain task? Could you jot down your repentance – and find again the peace of humbly serving others, however God calls you to do so?

FOCUSED

Therefore, I have set My face like a stone, determined to do His will. And I know that I will not be put to shame.

Isaiah 50:7, NLT

This Messianic prophecy speaks of Jesus' unflinching follow-through on His sacrificial death on the cross, for us. It showcases His willpower and His resolve to do right by His Father, no matter the cost.

Disappointingly, the strength of mind, grit and self-control Jesus displayed is scarce in our communities. We're too quickly distracted by apps, entertainment, escapism and excuses. Research shows that people who do plenty of media-multitasking have less gray matter associated with willpower and decision-making, and more chance of developing obsessive-compulsive disorder, depression, and anxiety.

How might things change in your world if you practiced focusing uninterruptedly on even just one Bible verse – for five full minutes – once a day? Might it change the trajectory of your day? Your life?

SORRY, JUST SENDING A QUICK TEXT ...

Phone separation anxiety is a thing. When your phone pings, your brain shoots out feel-good dopamine, setting up an addiction response, much like a drug hit. Also, every time you switch your focus from text to email to website, there's a switch-cost. Your brain stumbles – and needs time (15-25 minutes) to get back to where it was, pre-distraction. Checking your phone 15 times a day, with a 15-minute switch-cost, adds up to over three hours of time wasted! Put your phone on silent (better yet on airplane mode!) and enjoy some uninterrupted thought time.

LIVING DUST

... and the dust returns to the ground it came from,
and the spirit returns to God who gave it.

Ecclesiastes 12:7, NIV

Every time a swirl of dust makes you sneeze – or you notice a layer of dust on a bookshelf or countertop – let it remind you that your life is brief and fragile.

This isn't a forlorn or overly philosophical thought. It's just a necessary nudge to appreciate the gift of breath in our lungs and a living spirit within us. One day, these bodies – as healthy as they hopefully are because you're eating, sleeping and exercising like a boss – will return to the ground and somehow, somewhere, end up as part of the food chain, while our spirits soar with God.

What came from dust and returns to dust isn't lasting (Genesis 3:19). Look after it well (while you've got it, for as long as you've got it) even as you surrender to the God who numbers your days (Psalm 90:12).

NOTHING TO SNEEZE AT ...

A sneeze is a nasal reboot, resetting your nose environment and eradicating irritating particles. Allergic sneezes – sometimes accompanied by a scratchy throat and watery eyes – flair up after exposure to an allergen, like mold or dust. Use an antihistamine, or avoid the allergen. A common cold sneeze on the other hand is accompanied by a sore throat and productive cough, while a flu sneeze comes with a dry cough, fever, aches and fatigue. Keep tissues close; keep up your fluid intake; and sleep it out!

BOOST

He must increase, but I must decrease.
John 3:30, ESV

To stay healthy, we need to strengthen our system of disease-fighting white blood cells (leukocytes). Increase immunity, and you decrease the chance of illness.

It's wise to carry this concept into our spiritual lives: always aiming to let Jesus increase while we decrease. More of Him; less of us. That means, more of His compassion and wisdom; less of our prejudice and short-sightedness.

What could you do differently this week to increase the influence of Jesus in your ponderings and proceedings? How could you minimize the attitudes and actions that rise up from selfishness? There's nothing stopping you from trusting God for far greater spiritual health than you've enjoyed up to now.

FIVE STEPS TO IMPROVED IMMUNITY

If a sickness-causing germ gets through your immune barriers, and your immune system isn't as strong as it could be, you'll get sick. To boost your immune system, remember the five S's: Soap, Sleep, Superfoods, Sweat and Six Feet (not under!). Always wash your hands using soap; water alone doesn't cut it. Getting enough shuteye boosts your body's germ fighters. Load up on superfoods containing zinc, vitamin C and selenium (like berries, spinach and brazil nuts). Thirty minutes of moderate exercise stimulates your immune system, and finally, a virus can travel six feet from a cough or a sneeze – so stand clear of snotty kids and co-workers!

RANDOM READING?

Do your best to present yourself to God as one approved,
a worker who does not need to be ashamed
and who correctly handles the word of truth.
2 Timothy 2:15, NIV

You've probably heard crazy stories of people flipping open the Bible any-old-where – randomly pointing to a verse – and taking it as personal truth. Like the guy who opened up to Matthew 27:5 and read that Judas 'went away and hanged himself.' He wasn't encouraged by that. So he tried again. His eyes fell on Luke 10:37: 'Go and do likewise.' Or the guy who searched high and low for a girl called Joy, because God told him, in Isaiah 55:12, 'You shall go out with joy …'

Even a devotional like this runs the risk of taking verses out of context and applying them incorrectly. You get to explore the Word *for yourself!* Arm yourself with the three most important tools for biblical interpretation: context, context, context.

 ## DR. GOOGLE SAYS YOU'RE DYING

You're not feeling great – but you're not keen to visit the doc. You tap your symptoms into a search engine and within four clicks you've diagnosed a brain tumor. Panic ensues – formally known as cyberchondria. Take a deep breath. Google doesn't yet have a healthcare professional's diagnostic skills. Doctors take several factors into account when making a diagnosis, search engines can't, and they also can't safely discriminate between benign issues (headache) and serious disorders (brain tumor). Be careful of basing your life-or-death self-diagnosis on a machine – we all need somebody to lean on, not some bot.

BLOOD BANK

... and through Him to reconcile to Himself all things,
whether things on earth or things in heaven,
by making peace through His blood, shed on the cross.
Colossians 1:20, NIV

G*iving* boosts both physical and mental health. Research
shows that serving others without any expectation of reward
lets you live longer. One study found that those who volunteered
for two or more philanthropic organizations had a 44% reduction
in mortality over five years, even after accounting for prior health
status.

Jesus gave us so much: *all of Himself.* Because of that, we have
plenty to give too. We can always give away the truth that set us
free, sharing how Jesus' blood covers the sins of every human,
of every shape and size. Freely He shed His blood for us – and
freely we get to pay it forward by offering hope to others.

SAVING ME, SAVING YOU

Giving improves physical health and longevity by destressing us. It
activates regions of our brain associated with pleasure, social connection
and trust, and stimulates the release of endorphins and oxytocin. Oxytocin
induces feelings of warmth, euphoria, and human bonding and a good
dose of Oxytocin will cause people to give more generously and feel more
empathy towards one another. The great news is that giving needn't cost
you a cent. You can get all the healthy, feel-good benefits by donating
your time ... or a unit of your blood, which can save up to three lives!

FOOD FOR THOUGHT

The bonus of blood donation: Give and it will be given to you.

✤ Donating blood improves the overall flow of blood that's left behind. If blood has a high viscosity, it will flow like thick syrup and potentially irritate the lining of blood vessels. Repeated blood donations may help your blood flow in a way that results in fewer arterial blockages. Some studies have found that blood donors are a lot less likely to suffer heart attacks.

✤ Regular donations keep the iron levels in your blood on the straight and narrow. Healthy adults have about 5g of iron in their bodies, in red blood cells and bone marrow. For every unit of blood you donate, you lose a quarter of a gram of iron, which gets replenished from the food you eat in the weeks after donation. This regulation of iron levels is a good thing, because too much iron could also be bad news for your blood vessels.

✤ No time for a regular check-up with your doctor? Donating blood gets you a quick once-over! You'll have your blood pressure checked, and your blood will be thoroughly screened back at the lab. If anything is amiss, the national blood service will get in touch.

✤ Don't stress that you need all the blood you can get! Only 470ml of blood is donated – no more than 13% of your total blood volume. In just a few weeks your amazing body will replace all the cells and fluids you've handed over. In time to do it again.

TIME TO REFLECT ...

*Almighty God, show me if I'm finding my sense
of self in a phone – organizing my life around a screen!
Wean me off my addiction, if that's the case,
and help me find my center of gravity in Your grace.
Remind me every day, through sneezes or Scripture,
that from dust You created me – and that's how,
ultimately, this body will end up.
Keep me truth-centered, not tossed about by every random
idea I might stumble upon online or elsewhere.
Boost my spiritual immunity by filling me
with more of Your Spirit, less of my selfishness.
And help me give generously – time, talents, treasures, or even
a pint of my blood. Because You poured out Yours for me.
Amen.*

_____

_____

_____

_____

_____

_____

FROM MILK TO MEAT

For someone who lives on milk is still an infant
and doesn't know how to do what is right. Solid food
is for those who are mature, who through training have the skill
to recognize the difference between right and wrong.

Hebrews 5:13-14, NLT

Spiritual maturity isn't necessarily age-related. Hopefully, we'll all get wiser as we get older: evaluating our life experiences in light of God's truth. But even if you're young – chronologically, or in the faith – there's no reason why you can't outgrow your baby milk and move on to chunkier fare.

Your Father sees what's done in secret, and He rewards (Matthew 6:4). Commit to regular time with Him, in prayer and praise. Taste everything you can in the Bible. Chew and chew and swallow ... and take another bite. Real growth comes from real food. Pray for a holy discontent with spiritual candy floss. Don't be satisfied with anything less than a steak.

MARSHMALLOW MAYHEM

Obesity isn't the result of a simple calories-in-calories-out equation. Calories from refined carbohydrates behave differently from calories from protein or fat. Eating a handful of marshmallows causes an insulin surge that triggers fat cells to soak up calories. But marshmallow calories are 'empty': *sans* the nutrients our bodies need. Recognizing this discrepancy, the brain creates a hunger response that also slows our metabolism, to save the energy we *do* have. The result? We eat more; our metabolism grinds to a halt; we pack on the pounds. Keep your food real!

WHEN YOU CAN'T EVEN

He sat down under a solitary broom tree and prayed that he might die. 'I have had enough, LORD,' he said. 'Take my life …' Then he lay down and slept under the broom tree. But as he was sleeping, an angel touched him and told him, 'Get up and eat!'

1 Kings 19:4-5, NLT

At some point in each of our lives, we get to the end of our-selves. It's the place of believing it'll be better to end it. The world won't even miss us when we're gone.

If you've been there, you possibly – probably? – weren't thinking entirely rationally. Your feelings were *real*, but may not have been founded on fact. Before you do anything drastic, make like Elijah. Have a snack and a snooze. That's not a patronizing, simplistic solution to what is most likely a very real, very complicated prob-lem. But it's a start. And it may put you on steadier footing to face what's in front of you.

IS ADRENAL BURNOUT A THING?

Your adrenal glands are part of the Hypothalamic Pituitary Adrenal axis. The what!? The part of you that controls energy and metabolism. When we're healthy, this system adjusts rhythms of adrenal hormone secretion to meet our immediate needs. When stressed, they release regular doses of the stress hormone cortisol. The adrenal burnout theory holds that eventually the adrenals become frazzled from all the stress and essentially "burnout", causing symptoms like fatigue and low mood. Truth is, this doesn't really happen, and studies have found that the adrenals function just fine, despite being under ongoing stress. To help alleviate any chronic fatigue or mood problems it's essential to identify and manage the underlying causes of exhaustion.

RUN OR ROAR?

The wicked run away when no one is chasing them,
but the godly are as bold as lions.
Proverbs 28:1, NLT

I'm not suggesting you're wicked. Solomon is using antithesis for emphasis and effect. But when we overreact – thinking something is more dangerous than it really is – it's often because we're not trusting God. We've taken our eyes off the Shepherd, who never panics.

There's a time to be safe, rather than sorry. But too often I've rushed my kid to the emergency room … to be told that I should calm down because the cut doesn't need stitches. I've made doctor's appointments – and later sheepishly canceled them. A wiser track to take might be to ask God for discernment, discretion and a sober, measured approach to danger.

Then, instead of awfulizing situations – assuming we're metaphorically being chased by someone or something – we might find ourselves standing firm and fearless.

GREEN MUCUS ALERT!

When your mucus turns yellow or green, it's *not* time for an antibiotic. Antibiotics only treat bacterial infections and have *zero* effect against viruses. Viral respiratory infections are characterized by clear, thin mucus from your nose for the first phase of the illness. Infection fighting cells then move into the area to brawl with the offending bugs. These cells secrete proteins that alter mucus color – causing clear mucus to turn those not-so-lovely shades of yellow and green. This is the normal sequence of events, and dashing off to your doc for an antibiotic won't speed up healing.

HEALED TO HELP

… Jesus went to Simon's home, where He found Simon's mother-in-law very sick with a high fever. 'Please heal her,' everyone begged. Standing at her bedside, He rebuked the fever, and it left her. And she got up at once and prepared a meal for them.

Luke 4:38-39, NLT

Two observations, from this story:

Jesus can heal any fever, no matter how high. So, seek medical help because every good and perfect gift – like smart doctors and excellent meds – comes from God (James 1:17). But don't forget to pray, pray, *pray!*

And incredibly, Simon's mom-in-law, once healed, immediately gets up and serves. You've gotten over a cold, flu or fever, right? We have a choice, on the far side of an illness. To wallow a little longer in the sympathy of others – or to get up and get busy living life again, serving out of gratitude for the way others have served us. It's the best cure for the secondary infection of self-pity.

DON'T GET FEVERISH OVER A FEVER …

When immune system cells meet a virus or bacteria, they head off to your hypothalamus, which responds by increasing body temperature, resulting in a fever. Bugs thrive at normal body temperature, so your hypothalamus tries to fry out the offenders by turning up the heat – so give your amazingly-designed body a chance to sort it out, without meds. Support the war effort with plenty of fluids and rest. If you can't shake your fever after three days, visit your doctor.

HOARSE

I am exhausted from crying for help; my throat is parched.
My eyes are swollen with weeping, waiting for my God to help me.
Psalm 69:3, NLT

Maybe you've prayed and prayed ... *and prayed* ... And your prayers have resulted in nothing but a sore throat. This is faith at the coalface. You don't know what God's doing (is He doing *anything?*) and you don't know if or when He'll come through for you but if He doesn't, it's over. This is the faith of doggedly believing and hoping anyway – because of what God has told you to be true of His character. And this is the faith that is rewarded, by a faithful God (Deuteronomy 7:9).

When you've lost your voice from rasping out unanswered requests – pray one more time. God may seem silent, and slow to answer, but He hears your every heartbeat, and He rescues at the right time. Please don't give up.

SOOTHING WHAT'S SORE

A sore throat can be caused by a viral or bacterial infection, strained vocal chords, or irritants (like cigarette smoke). Time and your immune system will heal a sore throat. In the meantime, you can self-soothe with over-the-counter anti-inflammatories, throat lozenges, numbing sprays, or home remedies like gargling with saltwater and honey, which has promising antibacterial properties to help your throat heal faster. See a doc if your sore throat lasts longer than ten days, or if you have alarming symptoms like difficulty breathing.

FOOD FOR THOUGHT

Lies about longevity: A little bit of *nature*, and a lot of *nurture*.

Evidence-based studies suggest only 20-30% of an individual's longevity relates to genetics; the majority is due to individual lifestyle choices. So, wrinkles on your face? You can only blame your mom for a third of them!

There is no silver bullet that stops or reverses the ageing process. Beware of products making outrageous claims like 'secret formula', 'breakthrough' and 'no side effects'. Many remedies promising incredible results don't undergo rigorous clinical trials, so we've no way of knowing if they're safe. Celebrity product endorsements are often misleading, as are no-risk, money-back or free-trial guarantees. And *see your doctor before* taking a product promising that you'll no longer need to see your doctor!

So ... is there a fountain of youth?

These five lifestyle habits will have a meaningful impact on your longevity – reducing your risk of disease, and improving your quality of life.

- ✤ *Eat better.* The more fresh fruits and veggies you eat, the longer you'll live.
- ✤ *Exercise more.* Every step you take will be adding minutes to your life.
- ✤ *Drink alcohol only in moderation, and don't smoke.* Smoking can reduce your longevity by about ten years.
- ✤ *Prevention is better than cure.* Screen often and take advantage of preventive care by seeing your doctor regularly.
- ✤ *Be safe.* All the healthy habits in the world won't do you much good if you don't bother to wear your seatbelt.

TIME TO REFLECT ...

Every time you intentionally avoid refined carbs – could you use it as a prayer trigger, asking God rather to refine your conversational integrity, or your spending habits, or your work-life balance?

What needs to change in your life, for you *not* to feel (almost permanently) exhausted? Dream big! Then work backwards from that, to a viable solution, and commit to taking steps towards a more sustainable pace.

Do you talk too much? Ask the Holy Spirit to prompt you when it may be better for you to let others lead a conversation. Do you talk too little? Ask the Holy Spirit to prompt you when it's time to speak up or speak out.

_____

_____

_____

_____

_____

_____

_____

_____

_____

DRINKS ON HIM

Is anyone thirsty? Come and drink –
even if you have no money!
Come, take your choice of wine or milk – it's all free!
Isaiah 55:1, NLT

This Scripture speaks of God's immense generosity – and our destitution without it. We *need* His sustenance and quenching. Folks who are wise (and a little cynical) will tell you, 'There's no free lunch.' Mostly, they're absolutely right. There are also, usually, no free drinks. It's quite ordinary and unsurprising for people to expect you to bring or buy your own refreshments to a social event.

Which is why the picture that the prophet Isaiah gives us of our Heavenly Father is so startling. He magnanimously offers His thirst-slaking salvation to *anyone* – resourced or not. Drink deep.

FEVERISH HYDRATION

When you were sick and your mom told you to drink plenty of fluids, she was onto something. Fever is to your body what drought is to the environment, making everything dry, dusty and dehydrated. It's crucial to *replace* fluids quickly and get your body back on track. Even without a fever, germs can dry out your system. Dehydrated mucus in your nose, throat and lungs clogs sinuses and respiratory tubes. When germ-infested mucus hardens it becomes more difficult to cough up – and get rid of. Staying hydrated keeps your mucus running, which is one of our best natural defenses.

MORNING PERSON

The Sovereign LORD has given Me His words of wisdom,
so that I know how to comfort the weary.
Morning by morning He wakens Me
and opens My understanding to His will.

Isaiah 50:4, NLT

First responses upon waking up in the morning – especially when you're in the daily grind of work and kids and general adulting – can range from self-pity to resentment to denial.

Isaiah's words bring a necessary attitude shift. They're part of a Messianic prophecy – which means the 'obedient servant' speaking these lines is Jesus. And He's our example in all things, not so? When He wakes up – 'morning by morning' – His thoughts aren't, 'This is so unfair. Why me? I can't even.' His thoughts are of understanding His Father's will, and comforting the weary.

Would your day develop into something different – something better – if you steered your waking thoughts away from yourself?

🍎 KNACK OF DAWN

Some people are perky in the morning, others smash the snooze button. Research shows that early-risers are healthier and perform better academically. Now you know. The moment you wake up, your brain gets a cortisol burst, priming you for optimal performance. To maximize this positive surge, you need to get enough sleep. Keep your alarm set for the same time every day (yes, weekends too!) because your body's circadian rhythms thrive on routine. And when your alarm beeps, *do something* (push-ups, sit ups, or a jog around the block). This gets your heart pumping fresh oxygen around your body – giving you a healthy kick-start to the day.

DEPRO, BRO

And me? I'm a mess. I'm nothing and have nothing:
make something of me. You can do it;
You've got what it takes – but God, don't put it off.
Psalm 40:17, MSG

According to the World Health Organization, the disease robbing the greatest number of people of productive life isn't AIDS, heart disease or cancer. It's depression. Mental health issues are widely misunderstood and stigmatized. 'Just put on your big girl panties,' people say. Yet, a depressive disorder affects the way you eat, sleep, think and feel. Without treatment, symptoms can last for weeks – or years – significantly impacting life.

Thank God for medicine, and gifted depression counselors. But don't let that numb you into spiritual complacency: you *also* need to take it all to God. He made your brain. He knows – better than you do – the exact state of your soul. He's able to heal. Your situation may feel hopeless, but He promises you wisdom as you navigate depression's deep waters.

WALK OFF THE WORRIES

A study found that people who walked for 35 minutes, six days per week, experienced a 47% reduction in depression levels. Three hours of regular exercise a week reduced symptoms of mild to moderate depression as effectively as Prozac and other anti-depressants. Researchers have even calculated exact exercise guidelines to elicit an anti-depressant effect. Aim to do 3-5 cardio sessions per week, for 45-60 minutes at a moderate intensity. For weight training, do three sets of eight reps at around 80% of your max.

While vigorous activity releases those feel good endorphins we all know and love, it's regular activity that causes growth of nerve cells in the brain – which is what helps improve mood and relieve depression.

DIFFERENT FOLKS, DIFFERENT STROKES

… He gives someone else the ability to discern whether a message is from the Spirit of God or from another spirit. Still another person is given the ability to speak in unknown languages, while another is given the ability to interpret what is being said.

1 Corinthians 12:10, NLT

We all look different. Our bodies work differently. We have differing preferences and aversions.

We also have different gifts, and God uses us and our gifts in different ways, at different times. Don't be jealous of someone else's gift. We're different, sure, but equal before God. The ground at the foot of the cross is flat.

God delights in you (Zephaniah 3:17), so *enjoy* how He's made you – simultaneously admiring and celebrating those around you. His unique design of you? It is what it is, and He calls it very good (Genesis 1:31).

FAST OR SLOW?

Some people look at a donut and put on 3kg. Others eat whatever they like, never gaining a gram. Metabolism is a two-step, 24/7 process: your body breaks down food, then converts that food to energy. Your metabolic rate is made up of, firstly, your basal, or *resting* metabolic rate, which accounts for 70% of your total metabolism, and secondly, the energy you use for everything else (eating, drinking and moving). Three factors regulate your resting metabolic rate: age (metabolism slows down 1-2% per decade after age 25), gender (men's resting metabolic rate is higher than women's), and body size and composition.

DIGEST TEST

Better a small serving of vegetables with love
than a fattened calf with hatred.
Proverbs 15:17, NIV

How we ingest and digest our food has a lot to do with the atmosphere around the table. God has given us food as a necessary (delicious) way to stop. Pause between mouthfuls to talk to those we love. Connect. Recalibrate. And cheerfully recommit to the demands of life, many of which we can't control.

We can't control, for example, our genetics, and whether or not we have a fast metabolism. But we *can* do a *lot* to control the vibe in our homes at mealtimes.

Whether our plates are laden, or we're down to the last tin of tuna in the grocery cupboard, we can choose to serve each other with great love.

EXERCISE TO METABOLIZE

Your body hums along at a pre-set speed determined by gender and genetics, but there are two other factors that have a smaller, yet still significant, impact on your metabolism. The first is thermogenesis, which is the energy you use for digesting, absorbing, transporting and storing the food you consume. This accounts for about 10% of the calories you use daily (and is the reason why *not* eating can slow your metabolism). The second is physical activity (exercise) that accounts for the balance of your daily energy usage. This metabolic component is the most variable of the lot and can boost your metabolism … or not. It's up to you.

FOOD FOR THOUGHT

Legit ways of boosting metabolism

Exercise. You can increase your metabolism, and exercise is the safest, free-est and most efficient way to do it. You don't need a pill or supplement. One study found that the age-related decline in energy expenditure would be approximately 600 Cal/week more in the sedentary compared to the exercising woman.

In practical terms, this age-related difference in energy expenditure, would equate to about a 4kg per year greater increase in your heart rate through cardiovascular exercise is another guaranteed way of boosting your metabolism. Given the amount of energy your heart needs to sustain itself, getting it pumping well above your resting heart rate is going to crank up your energy requirements significantly. The longer and harder your exercise – the better the burn.

Standing up more. Alternating sitting and standing not only keeps you healthy but can also help rev up your metabolism. It's been esti-mated that compared to sitting only, alternating sitting and standing increases energy expenditure by around 10%.

Strength training. Exercise has a significant impact on muscle growth. Muscle mass makes us strong, and as providence would have it, also helps us burn calories – around five times more than its sluggish cousin fat. Strength training boosts your metabolism in two ways:

- Doing the exercise itself burns calories
- It maintains and grows existing muscle mass, especially if weight loss is your goal. Without some form of resistance training, you're likely to lose muscle too

Diet. There are no specific foods that will speed up metabolism, so you can stop putting hot sauce on absolutely everything! Coffee and green tea bump up your metabolic rate slightly – but only temporarily.

What's more important is that when you eat, eat well. Your body actually burns energy while it breaks down food. Without getting in the nutrients you need, your metabolic rate slows in an attempt to preserve the little energy it has.

TIME TO REFLECT ...

*Jesus, thank You that, whether I wake up groggy or galvanized
for a new day, I always wake up to brandnew mercy.
I trust You for enough faith fluids to sustain me today.
Help me to metabolize truth so that it fuels
all my doings in such a way that You are glorified.
Amen.*

_____

_____

_____

_____

_____

_____

_____

_____

_____

_____

_____

_____

BREATHE STRONGLY

I, yes I, am the one who comforts you.
So why are you afraid of mere humans ...?
Isaiah 51:12, NLT

Maybe you're in an incredibly stressful job. Maybe you're in the throes of a deeply damaging family saga. Remember today that God is the One who comforts you.

The Hebrew word for comfort is *naham* and it can be translated *to breathe strongly*.

Try to breathe a little more deeply today, remembering that God goes ahead of you into the future, and He lends you life and breath in the present moment. You can trust Him for enough rest and enough energy to deal with the day's demands. Keep breathing strongly, even as God breathes strongly over you.

BELLY BREATHING IS THE NEW BEACH

Can't get away from it all? Try belly breathing! When you get worked up, your breathing becomes shallow, which limits how much air your lungs absorb. You feel breathless and anxious. Deep belly breathing gets rid of the old air in your lungs, replacing it with fresh air, which lowers your heart rate, stabilizes blood pressure and essentially has the same effect as a day on the beach, without the sunburn risk! Practice makes perfect – because when you're stressed, breathing is the last thing on your mind. Breathe in slowly through your nose, allowing your chest and lower belly to expand fully. Then breathe out slowly ... Watch your belly rise and fall with each breath. Relax.

SOAR

Even youths grow tired and weary,
and young men stumble and fall;
but those who hope in the LORD will renew their strength.
They will soar on wings like eagles; they will run
and not grow weary, they will walk and not be faint.

Isaiah 40:30-31, NIV

We're just past halfway through the year. Maybe you can't imagine how you're going to get to the end of it. You feel you don't have enough strength – and you're probably right. Thank God! He hasn't left you to finish the year on your own. Even now, He's tenderly renewing, refreshing, equipping and establishing you for whatever responsibilities lie ahead.

You can lean as heavily as you like on His limitless strength. Pray that God would lead you to a place of physical and mental rest. He's a well-resourced God. You're free to ask Him anything. But until such time as He sees fit to whisk you away for a holiday or a half-day away from the office, hope in Him for new strength.

DIY DESK HOLIDAY TECHNIQUES

Stuck at the office, and exhausted? Close your eyes and visualize your happy place. Seriously. Creative visualization instantly relieves stress. No actual surf or sand necessary! Next, restructure your workday by working for 50 minutes and resting for ten (step away from your spreadsheet!). Finally, plan your next holiday. Having something to look forward to can boost your mood, and anticipating vacation fun can bring even greater emotional rewards than remembering a trip after you return.

WALK AND TALK

Teach them to your children,
talking about them when you sit at home and when you walk
along the road, when you lie down and when you get up.

Deuteronomy 11:19, NIV

God never intended us to reserve spiritual discussions for church, Bible studies or other ministry events.

You may have a crowd of easygoing, Jesus-loving friends who bring Him into every conversation. Or you may feel there's no one around you with whom you can chat freely about the things of God. If that's the case, let it start with you. Decide to get over the awkwardness and ask God to lend you wisdom and ways of weaving Him seamlessly into exchanges with the people in your world, when you're walking, working, shopping or gyming.

You may be surprised how much they're longing to talk about Him too.

SWEAT-WORKING

Mounting evidence suggests that sitting for long periods is harming our health. In response to this, many companies are embracing sweat-working. Instead of sitting during meetings, employees are encouraged to have walking meetings, or sweat sessions. You can get creative! Have outdoor, standing, corridor or stairwell summits, or try a treadmill desk. Not *every* meeting can be a walking one. But changing just one seated meeting a week into a walking meeting increases work-related physical activity levels. Plan ahead, so no one ends up walking in heels. Stick to smaller groups and have some fun! Enjoying the meeting boosts happy hormones, which in turn boosts both health and productivity.

SLUGGISH

Lazy people want much but get little,
but those who work hard will prosper.
Proverbs 13:4, NLT

Some people seem to have more intrinsic motivation than others. And no matter how intrinsically motivated you are, you probably find that for some tasks you're super motivated – and for others you just can't convince yourself to get cracking.

Could you be brave enough to recognize a procrastination problem, and surrender it to God? Is there an area of your life in which you know you tend to drag your feet? Something you're lazy to do because, as Solomon puts it, you 'want much but get little'? There are some pros to *active* procrastination (read on!) – but *passive* procrastination (denial of reality through indefinite couch time) only leads to plummeting energy levels.

Do you dare to make a move towards getting started on something you've been putting off?

THE PRO IN PROCRASTINATION

When you worry you won't get something done on time, your body goes into fight-or-flight mode, which produces adrenaline, a natural pain killer. Feeling less pain makes doing difficult or undesirable tasks much easier. Adrenaline also improves focus, efficiency and planning. Plus, a big task you're avoiding makes everything else you have to do look more appealing. Active procrastination means you realize you're delaying writing your report, but you're doing something more valuable instead, like studying for an exam. So, *when used effectively*, procrastination can be a powerful motivator and source of inspiration.

DO IT ALREADY

**Don't brag about tomorrow,
since you don't know what the day will bring.**
Proverbs 27:1, NLT

When a friend's husband was critically ill and hospitalized, she told me matter-of-fact in the midst of the trauma and uncertainty, that her baby was due for his vaccinations and so she'd take him to the clinic that day. Of all the things to be concerned about, this could surely have been pushed to the bottom of the list? But she said, 'Well, who knows what tomorrow will bring? Tomorrow may be worse. Today might be as good as it gets. It needs to be done, and I can do it today.'

This isn't fatalistic; just marvelously practical – and somehow empowering. Proverbs 3:27 advises us, 'Don't withhold good from those to whom it is due, when it is in your power to act.' You don't know what tomorrow will look like. Do what needs doing, today.

TO DO OR NOT TO DO?

When a new task or responsibility lands in your lap, take a breath and prioritize. Write down exactly what needs to be completed, and when. Free yourself to focus on what's important and time pressing. You'll subconsciously be thinking about the less urgent tasks on your list and when the time comes to tackle them, you'll work more efficiently. Whatever you do, avoid passive procrastination at all costs. Sofa-dwelling will make your brain foggy, no matter how fascinating the series you're binge-watching.

FOOD FOR THOUGHT

Refresh yourself – not your inbox!

Research suggests that gizmos and gadgets allowing people to read and respond to emails after working hours, could be harming their health.

- *Expectations.* The expectation around responding to emails outside of the office is as much of a job stressor as workload, colleague conflicts or time pressures. Technology designed to *help* employees is doing the very opposite. After-hours emailing negatively impacts your emotional state and that fragile family-work balance, ultimately leading to burnout.

  The problem isn't the time you spend on work emails; it's the *expectation* of *getting* those emails. The expectations drive anticipatory stress: a constant state of anxiety and energy-sapping uncertainty about what may be waiting in your inbox.

- *Exhaustion.* To recover from a long day at the office, we need to switch off completely, mentally and physically. Being constantly contactable via email means that mentally we never leave the office and it also retards our recovery process, so much so that we never fully recover in time before we rinse and repeat.

Don't wait for your boss to tell you what to do!

Draw some after-hour boundaries to curb your email habit. Switch off notifications once you leave the office. If that's impossible or impractical, decide that at least one or two nights a week are email-free evenings. That will *boost* your productivity, and your enthusiasm for your work (and your boss).

TIME TO REFLECT ...

Wherever you find yourself reading this, could you take just three very deep, very slow breaths?

Looking at your schedule this week, where could you go on a thirty-minute holiday, by conjuring up a meaningful moment of rest or celebration or fun – even if you're in the thick of deadlines or other duties? Could you piggyback your toddler around the block? Meet your spouse at the coffee truck during lunch hour? Don't procrastinate when it comes to celebrating life!

Speaking of procrastination – could you jot down something you've been ignoring, because you're hoping it might go away on its own? Name it. Do it.

FEED YOUR SOUL

Dear friend, I hope all is well with you
and that you are as healthy in body as you are strong in spirit.
3 John 1:2, NLT

Scholars describe the soul as the inner life – our thinking, beliefs, attitudes, feelings and memories. We also know a healthy diet goes a long way in keeping us emotionally strong. Your brain is *on*, 24/7. It needs a constant supply of energy, which comes from the food you eat. What's *in* that food makes all the difference. So it's not a stretch to say that what you put into your stomach directly affects your soul.

One commentator writes, 'The body is the means by which the spirit, the soul, and the heart express themselves through visible activity in the material world. And God wants to be made glorious in our bodies. Paul longs in Philippians 1:19-20, "O that I might magnify Christ *in my body*, whether by life or by death."'

How are you sustaining and strengthening your soul?

CHEERFUL CHOW

Serotonin is a neurotransmitter in your brain, regulating sleep, appetite, mood and pain. 95% of your serotonin is produced in your gastrointestinal tract, which is lined with a hundred million nerve cells. So, your digestive system doesn't just process food; it guides your emotions. Studies have compared traditional diets, like the Mediterranean diet (consisting predominantly of whole foods), to typical Western diets (consisting mostly of processed foods). The results showed that the risk of depression is 25-35% lower in those who eat a traditional diet.

LONGTIME FRIENDS

As iron sharpens iron, so a friend sharpens a friend.
Proverbs 27:17, NLT

A recent study followed nearly 1,500 older people for ten years and found that those with a large network of friends outlived those with fewer friends by more than 20%. Friendship isn't just about emotional health; it improves physical health too. Research on the impact of social isolation on physical health has uncovered that the effect of social ties on life span is twice as strong as that of exercising, and equivalent to that of quitting smoking.

Who are your closest friends? Do the names and faces that rise in your mind belong to people who sharpen your conscience and your resolve to live a life that celebrates God's glory and goodness? And if you're struggling to form special friendships, ask God to bring just the right people into your life, and pray you'd recognize them.

🍎 BUDDIES WHO BRING OUT THE BEST

Studies have found that health markers, like blood pressure and waist circumference, were consistently worse amongst people who had fewer social ties. Amongst older age groups, social isolation raised the risk of having high blood pressure by 124%. By comparison, having diabetes raised the risk of high blood pressure by (only) 70%. A good reason to keep your friends close! Healthy friendships encourage healthy behaviors, and improve your mood through the release of oxytocin (the happiness hormone) throughout your body.

CRAY-CRAY

Just kill me now, LORD! I'd rather be dead than alive ...
Jonah 4:3, NLT

Depression is considered to be the leading cause of disability worldwide, affecting an estimated 300 million people. When diagnosed with something like diabetes, folks don't think twice about telling others they're seeking treatment. But when diagnosed with a mental health disorder, they're more likely to keep it to themselves. They don't want to be called crazy, or told to just get over it.

Jonah isn't the only depressive we meet in Scripture. David, Elijah, Job, Naomi, Solomon, Moses, Jeremiah – they struggled with feelings of anxiety or hopelessness. Even Jesus is described by Isaiah as 'a man of sorrows, acquainted with grief' (Isaiah 53:3).

What we learn from Jonah and others like him is that they went to God with their anger, shame or panicked sense of doom. They weren't afraid to admit they needed help, and they didn't allow stigma to keep them stuck.

SMASHING THE STIGMAS

Common myths around mental illness are that it's a sign of weakness, or simply an excuse for bad behavior. People who experience mental illnesses *might* act in seemingly strange or unexpected ways. But it's the illness, not the person, behind these behaviors. That said, people with a history of mental illness are like anyone else: they may occasionally make poor choices (like the rest of us) for reasons unrelated to symptoms of their disorder.

HUMBLED TO BE HELPED

Then they cried out to the LORD in their trouble,
and He brought them out of their distress.
He stilled the storm to a whisper;
the waves of the sea were hushed.
Psalm 107:28-29, NIV

Asking for help is *not* a sign of weakness. It's a sign of boldness, maturity, self-knowledge and humility. We all, somewhere on life's road, get to the end of ourselves and need assistance to move on. Sure, some people seem stronger than others and have an enormous appetite for whatever life dishes up.

Others can manage just one small slice. We're created differently, for different purposes. But no matter how big or small your capacity, don't be too proud to acknowledge that a day will come when you'll need the practical, emotional or spiritual help of another. Seeking support isn't about numbing your pain or masking the ugliness of what's really going on. It's having something or someone to lean on while you face the facts.

ANTI ANTI-DEPRESSANTS?

We call them 'happy pills', but anti-depressants don't make you euphoric – just normal. People with depression and anxiety often have chemical imbalances in their brain. Anti-depressants get the balance right, and reduce symptoms. Also, anti-depressants aren't addictive. Like most medications, they can change the way you feel, so if you stop taking them, you may have a wobble. You're not addicted. Just chat to your doc about slowly tapering your dosage, and don't forget to take the *best* medicine bottled up in your body: exercise!

AMAZINGLY MADE

You guided my conception and formed me in the womb.
You clothed me with skin and flesh, and You knit my bones
and sinews together. You gave me life and showed me
Your unfailing love. My life was preserved by Your care.

Job 10:10-12, NLT

Job's poignant words are actually mid-complaint against God. Job is (understandably) mad, because life isn't working out for him. But his very assertion that God has been intimately involved in every detail of his life – down to the fiber of his body and being – should really shut him up. Job does realize – a few chapters on – that he ought to be enormously grateful.

Today, every time you lift a cup of coffee to your lips – or wave to your kid – or flick a switch – or take a jog – thank God that He knit together the fabric of your muscles and your mind. *You have so much going for you.*

HEAVY MUSCLES?

Despite committing to regular exercise, you might hop onto the scale to find your weight hasn't shifted. Or worse – it's gone *up!* Muscle doesn't weigh more than fat, but one kilogram of fat is bulkier than one kilogram of muscle. Fat takes up more space under your skin. Also, fat and muscle are metabolically different: muscle tissue speeds up resting metabolism, whereas fat mass does the opposite. The more muscle you have, the easier it'll be to burn energy, and fat. You can look and feel better, even if your scale doesn't change.

FOOD FOR THOUGHT

Treadmill or trails?

Even the most hardcore runner has to admit that jogging on a treadmill in a heated gym sometimes beats the chill of an early morning run. Treadmill running is safe, time efficient, winter-friendly and pretty versatile in getting the full range of running benefits. Any running is also better than no running!

That said, when it comes to injury risk, there's an important difference. Most running injuries are overload injuries (muscle, cartilage, bone or tendons wearing down over time). These injuries occur when you repeat a running motion thousands and thousands of times – as you would on a treadmill.

The average runner's foot makes contact with the ground eighty to a hundred times per minute. If you're running on treadmill for an hour, besides the obvious boredom factor, the repetitiveness of the identical motion increases your risk for an overuse injury. Jumping over holes in the pavement on the other hand, or the odd tree stump on a trail run, has you continually changing your stride and using different muscles.

Studies also show that because there's a machine powering the treadmill belt, the way you use your muscles differs from running outdoors. Outside, you rely on your hamstrings to finish the stride cycle and lift your legs up behind you.

On a treadmill, the moving belt does much of that work for you so you don't need to generate the same speed or power. You use your quads to push off – but your hamstrings get less of a workout. So hit the road, Jack.

TIME TO REFLECT ...

*Heavenly Father, You know exactly what's going on
in my head and heart. Please lift my spirits.
And show me if there's anything I'm doing or not doing –
eating or not eating – that's contributing to this funk I'm in.
Thank You for every friend who keeps my boat afloat on
smooth seas. Give me opportunities today
to be the breeze in someone else's sails.
Amen.*

ONE DAY DOWN

This is all the more urgent, for you know how late it is;
time is running out. Wake up, for our salvation is nearer now
than when we first believed. The night is almost gone;
the day of salvation will soon be here. So remove your dark deeds
like dirty clothes, and put on the shining armor of right living.

Romans 13:11-12, NLT

If you didn't sleep well last night, then you probably don't feel like donning 'the shining armor of right living.' The struggle is real. Still, you can trust God for more sleep tonight, and the energy necessary to glorify Him in the hours of today – which is *the first day of the rest of your life.*

You're a day closer to meeting Jesus face to face. You're one day down in terms of time left to change the world. Let that inspire you to do all you can do to shine Christ's light in a dark world.

🍎 LIVING WITH A LUMBERJACK

Snoring is a sleep disorder affecting 40% of men and 25% of women. A snorer wakes his (or her!) partner around twenty times per night. Bed partners of snorers visit their GP more often, and one in three couples report snoring-related relational conflict. Genetics is responsible for 70% of log-sawing; lifestyle factors like smoking, drinking alcohol, breathing in allergens and carrying excess body weight are responsible for the rest. To alleviate snoring, sleep on your side, exercise more, or take up the didgeridoo (true story)!

COST TO COMPANY

But don't begin until you count the cost.
For who would begin construction of a building without first
calculating the cost to see if there is enough money to finish it?
Luke 14:28, NLT

Jesus is talking to a crowd, about counting the cost of discipleship. He's not bullying, manipulating or sweet-talking anyone into following Him. He's saying, *If you want to do this thing, and follow Me? You'd better be sure. It's all-or-nothing.*

He took the task of building His Father's Kingdom unbelievably seriously. He knew that there would be sacrifices involved, for the people choosing to follow Him, and He didn't want those people bailing when things got tough, and thereby discrediting His Name.

We've all heard stories of people who went along with churchy vibes for a while … and then didn't. Because actually, they'd never fully counted the cost, saying, 'Come what may, I'm in.' Have you?

PRICE PER PLATE

Healthy food is expensive. *Or is it?* A study ranking 4000 different foods by price, calorie, weight and portion size revealed that the least to most expensive foods were grains, dairy, vegetables, fruit, protein and processed foods. If you only consider cost per calorie, then sure, bananas are more expensive than donuts. But bananas will keep you going for far longer than donuts, and there's less chance of a post-banana snack attack. To save money, try buying seasonal fruit and veg, buying in bulk, cooking and eating at home and shopping on a full tummy.

BOOSTING THE BODY

Now these are the gifts Christ gave to the church: the apostles, the prophets, the evangelists, and the pastors and teachers.

Ephesians 4:11, NLT

For the church – the body of Christ – to function optimally, we need the wondrous diversity of many skills, talents and perspectives. That's why God gifts different people in such very different ways, and allows us to walk through such very different life experiences.

A healthy church has every spiritual vitamin and mineral necessary – wrapped up inside Jesus-loving people using their unique gifting – for excellent functioning. Whether you're the calcium that puts strength into the bones of the weary, of the vitamin C that keeps away the virus of evil, or the omega-3 that helps others think more clearly – you're necessary to keep your local church healthy. You're part of the wellbeing and the wellspring of the global body of Christ.

 ## SPLIT YOUR VIT

A daily multivitamin is a good way to ensure you're getting all the nutrients you need. Of course, it can't replace a balanced diet, which is always first choice. Food is better absorbed and processed by your body, than a pill. Wholesome meals are also cheaper than multi-medicating. But if you are taking a multivitamin, the recommendation is to *split your vit* – take half in the morning and half at night, because your body can only absorb so many vitamins at any given time.

I SPY, WITH MY LITTLE HEART ...

Guard me as You would guard Your own eyes.
Hide me in the shadow of Your wings.
Psalm 17:8, NLT

Carrots have a reputation as the go-to vegetable for healthy eyesight. Getting shortchanged on vitamin A, a key nutrient in carrots, could certainly contribute to vision decline. But the real star nutrients are lutein and zeaxanthin, pigments found in foods such as dark, leafy greens and certain proteins, like eggs.

A heart-healthy diet is an eye-healthy diet. The connection isn't surprising: your eyes rely on tiny arteries for oxygen and nutrients, just as the heart relies on much larger arteries. So by keeping all of your arteries healthy, you help your eyes and your heart (and everything in between!).

Same-same spiritually. What gets in through our eyes affects our hearts. What we focus on affects our thinking, feeling, believing and deciding. Reciprocally, if our hearts are in a good place with God, we won't want our eyes to settle on anything dishonoring to Him.

SHADY SHADES

Sunglasses aren't just a style accessory; they keep your eyes healthy by protecting them from the sun's ultraviolet (UV) rays! In bright sunlight, your pupils constrict to limit light intake. Wearing sunglasses allows your pupils to dilate from half a millimeter to 5 or 6mm, letting in more light to help you see. Shades without (or with limited) UV protection simply filter the glare, but don't block harmful ultraviolet light. This is *more* harmful to your eyes than *not* wearing sunglasses, and increases your risk of developing cataracts and going blind. Pick a pair that blocks 99% or more of UVA and UVB rays.

TICK TOCK

And God said, 'Let there be light,' and there was light.
God saw that the light was good, and He separated the light from
the darkness. God called the light 'day,' and the darkness He called
'night.' And there was evening, and there was morning – the first day.

Genesis 1:3-5, NIV

Circadian rhythms are 24-hour cycles of physical, mental and behavioral changes, influencing hormone production, hunger, cell regeneration and body temperature. They're even associated with obesity and depression. Understanding how your body clock works impacts your overall health. For example: concentration typically dwindles after 12 PM, so get the number-crunching done early, but leave creativity for later because experts believe fatigue allows the mind to wander more freely to explore alternative solutions. Your body clock is also linked to your biological clock: the antioxidant powers of melatonin protect a woman's eggs from stress.

God created the circadian rhythms that regulate our lives. Pray that He'd make you mindful of how your body works, so you'll be as effective as possible in the daylight hours, and rest as deeply as possible in the dark.

ROUGH MONDAY

Staying up late on Saturday and sleeping in on Sunday leaves you groggy on Monday. It's called social jetlag. Straying from your normal sleep-wake routine confuses your internal clock, leading to difficulty falling asleep on Sunday night, and crankiness on Monday morning. Go to sleep each night and wake up each morning as close to the same time as possible (yup, even on weekends).

FOOD FOR THOUGHT

Don't drink yourself fat!

Shockingly, a 500ml fizzy drink can contain 16½ teaspoons of sugar. When you eat (or drink) sugar, it stimulates the release of dopamine in your brain, a neurochemical that makes you feel pleasure. Your brain likes the feeling, and craves more. As with any addictive substance, over time you need *more* sugar to get the same high, which is a real problem as mounting evidence links sugar to the diseases you fear most: diabetes, heart disease and cancer.

In the 1960s, fats and oils supplied Americans with 45% of their calories. Today, Americans get 33% of their calories from fats and oils, the rest from sugar, and there's been a 300% increase in adult obesity, and a 1000% increase in diabetes. Something's got to give. And maybe it should be those sugary drinks? If you *just can't* drink plain water all day, here are some alternatives:

* Sparkling water (*not* the flavored, sugar-laden kind) adds fizz to your day without the unnecessary extras.

* Milk is a healthy option (without the cookies).

* Fruit juices are more nutritious than soft drinks, but can have just as many calories. Opt for whole fruits, which have fewer calories and plenty of fiber, always better to eat your fruits, rather than drink them.

* If you drink coffee or tea, skip the flavored syrups and the teaspoons of sugar. Choose herbal or fruit teas for extra flavor.

* Watch what your kids are drinking and keep their portions small. Check labels too! 4g of sugar is equivalent to one teaspoon, and kids shouldn't have more than 15g of sugar per day.

TIME TO REFLECT ...

Snoring is often a result of poor lifestyle choices – and it keeps those around you up at night! You might not be a snorer – but are there aspects of your way of life that cause others pain, irritation or anxiety?

What are you watching? Have you counted the cost of that thing, on your physical, emotional, social, intellectual or spiritual health?

Could you jot down a few things you'd like to try, to enhance the circadian rhythms of your life this week?

_____

_____

_____

_____

_____

_____

_____

_____

_____

_____

_____

A BITE OF WORSHIP

Therefore, let us offer through Jesus a continual sacrifice
of praise to God, proclaiming our allegiance to His name.
Hebrews 13:15, NLT

Sometimes praising God is a *sacrifice*. It costs you something and you don't feel like paying. That's why a church-going habit, or meeting up with believing friends, is important – *especially* when you don't feel like it. Because you might not be hungry to worship, but once you're surrounded by the aroma of Jesus-loving others, your appetite for worship wakes up.

The writer of Hebrews also encourages us to motivate and stimulate each other towards love and good deeds (Hebrews 10:24), because when we can't quite get there on our own, we need help. If someone offers you a slice of worship, *take it*. You may realize you're actually famished.

ZERO TO RAVENOUS IN A NIBBLE

You weren't hungry – until you had one of your colleague's chips. Now you're starved! The taste, smell and sight of food triggers craving processes in your gut and brain. Simultaneously, swallowing a few bites lights up your brain's reward centers. So, snacking on chips, salty biscuits and bread before a meal revs up your appetite and blood sugar. Your body releases insulin, driving extra blood sugar into storage, then begs for more! Plenty of chewing knocks down your ghrelin (hunger hormone) levels, so the quicker you swallow something, the more likely you are to eat more of it. Focus on healthy foods that are hard, chewy or crunchy – and you'll naturally eat less.

OLDER AND STRONGER

He gives power to the weak and strength to the powerless.
Even youths will become weak and tired,
and young men will fall in exhaustion.
Isaiah 40:29-30, NLT

Age is generally equated with weaker bodies and brains. But this needn't (necessarily) (always) be the case, because we can depend on the great God who made those bodies and brains, for wisdom to manage our lifestyles better.

Even if you wandered far from God when you were younger, making mistakes and questionable choices which led you to falling in exhaustion, you're older and hopefully wiser than you were even yesterday. That means it's within your power to make a better choice today, which will stand you in good stead for all the remaining tomorrows.

 ## BRAIN POWER

There's no denying it: as we get older, our brains get slower. But if you fancy yourself the next Nobel prize winner, pump up your bike tires and go for a ride! Studies suggest that a tough workout increases levels of a brain-derived protein in your body, believed to improve decision making, higher thinking, memory and learning. People who make time for regular exercise are more productive and have more energy than their more sedentary peers. On top of that, a heart-pumping session can boost creativity levels for up to two hours after you stop sweating.

THE SKY'S THE LIMIT

But those who trust in the Lord will find new strength.
They will soar high on wings like eagles.
They will run and not grow weary.
They will walk and not faint.

Isaiah 40:31, NLT

Not one of us has a perfect body. Some people live with a severe, incapacitating or life-threatening disease or disability. Some people live with a bit of tennis elbow. Still, every single human is let down, at some point, by his or her body. But no matter the level of your physical prowess, you almost certainly have the capability to do *something* – even just *one small thing* – to enhance your physical health.

And when it comes to our spiritual health, the sky's the limit. We have the indwelling Holy Spirit whose joy is our strength (Nehemiah 8:10). When we trust in Him – no matter how faint or weary we've grown – He gives us eagle's wings.

BETTER YOUR BLOOD

You don't have to be an ironman finisher, marathon runner or cross-fit fanatic. Even a little bit of exercise goes a long way towards securing your health. For example, being active improves the way your body regulates glucose and insulin which makes controlling your blood sugar levels a cinch. This is critical in both managing and preventing diabetes. In fact, a recent study found that regular exercise was able to reduce the risk of diabetes by up to 60% – something very few medicines can claim to do!

GOOD TURNED BAD

Every good and perfect gift is from above,
coming down from the Father of the heavenly lights,
who does not change like shifting shadows.
James 1:17, NIV

Inflammation is your body's response to threats like stress, infection, or toxic chemicals. The immune system senses one of these dangers and responds by activating proteins and sending fighter cells that cause redness, swelling and warmth: signs your body is fighting hard. It's a 'good and perfect gift' from God. But sometimes, the immune system overreacts – even attacking the cells it's meant to protect. That's when good inflammation turns bad – resulting in conditions like arthritis.

So many of God's good and perfect gifts can be turned bad – *by us*. Sex – created pure – can be twisted into something sordid – even violent and vengeful. Food – created for nourishment and deliciousness – can morph into gluttony. Even love for our kids can be idolatrously distorted.

Could you ask God to show you if you've misshapen a good and perfect gift from Him?

INFLAMMATION – CAN'T LIVE WITH IT, CAN'T LIVE WITHOUT IT

Poor quality sleep is a major contributor to inflammation, as is lifestyle stress, thanks to high levels of the hormone cortisol that escalates inflammation. Then there's diet. What you eat, or don't eat, has a direct impact on the amount of inflammation you have. Aim to swap out refined and processed foods in your diet for colorful produce and real, whole food. Fresh fare contains hundreds of substances that stop inflammation in its tracks.

GET AWAY

Your strength will come from settling down
in complete dependence on Me ...
Isaiah 30:15, MSG

Taking a vacation makes you smarter! With constant pressure to problem-solve because *I-need-this-yesterday*, your positivity, creativity and strategic thinking dwindles. Your brain simply isn't equipped to maintain relentless stress levels, and operates better when you're not multimedia task-switching (which fatigues the brain's frontal lobe, slowing efficiency and performance). When you're under chronic stress, your body releases cortisol, and too much of that damages the hippocampus (responsible for learning and memory).

Maybe you know all this, so you took a vacation. Except, you've returned more exhausted than when you left. The only way to come home from a holiday changed and recharged is to *settle down in complete dependence on Him*. Just chill, for once, undistracted. It will be difficult at first, to focus only on God. Try just two minutes, once a day. Build that up. Your brain, body and beliefs will be revived.

YOUR BRAIN'S BIGGEST BANG FOR BUCK

Your brain needs *rest and exercise*. So ... build a vacation bucket list. Engage in intellectually stimulating activities (other than working). Keep some routine decisions simple to replenish mental energy (eat the same meal/wear the same outfit every Wednesday). Your brain uses more energy than any other organ (20% of your daily energy intake). Feed the beast! Choose nutrient-dense options (brain food). A sugary treat might make you feel great for a short while, but when sugar levels drop, so does mental energy and mood.

FOOD FOR THOUGHT

Busy day? Boost your breaks

- The Pomodoro technique suggests you work for 25 minutes, take a break for five and repeat. It'll help you fight off distractions, hyper-focus and get things done in short bursts.

- Breaks are vital for productivity. If 25 minutes is too short, take a five-minute break at least *once* every hour. Set reminders on your phone or fitness device.

- During your break, do something that you enjoy – like going for a walk, stretching or getting a cup of coffee. The important thing is to embrace being away from your desk – without slipping into a procrastination trap.

- Some research suggests that you should be on your own to fully detach. An interrupted break has a negative impact on productivity. You get back to your desk and feel like you haven't been away. So try to ensure your break is a decent one, from both your computer and your colleagues!

- Finally, take a break before reaching the absolute bottom of your mental barrel. Key symptoms of bottoming out include drifting thoughts and daydreaming. Take those as your cue to exit right.

TIME TO REFLECT ...

*God, I'm so overwhelmed by information and obligations.
Please order my world. Bring across my screens
and pages the things I need to read. Help me eliminate
distractions in favor of joyful duty, and necessary rest.
Where something good in my life – a gift from You –
has been distorted by sin, convict me.
Thank You for Your kindness that leads me to repentance
(Romans 2:4). Please straighten out what's crooked.
Amen.*

KINGDOM CURES

... Your kingdom come, Your will be done,
on earth as it is in heaven.
Matthew 6:10, NIV

Cancer isn't one disease, but many different diseases, with different causes. So there probably won't be one date in history on which a breakthrough cure for cancer is announced. Instead, every year will bring more and more cures for more and more types of cancer.

Similarly, Kingdom building doesn't happen overnight. Progress is slow. But there *is* progress – on different continents, through different church leaders, kindergarten teachers, advocates, architects and most powerfully, in our own homes. We won't necessarily be able to point to a day in history and say, 'It was *then* we saw God's Kingdom come!' But we could ask ourselves, in our changing of diapers and running of companies, 'What does God's Kingdom look like, here, today?'

CONTEXTUAL HOPE

It may feel like our risk for cancer is growing – but that's because cancer figures are occasionally reported out of context. The number of people who are diagnosed and die from cancer annually has indeed grown – *because the world's population is growing*, and ageing. Less than half the people diagnosed with cancer today, will die of the disease. Some are completely cured, and many more enjoy a good quality of life for years, thanks to effective treatment and management. A few decades ago, less than one in ten children with leukemia survived a decade after diagnosis. Today, thanks to current chemotherapy, the cure rate is almost 80%.

TOUGH LOVE

**For the LORD disciplines those He loves,
and He punishes each one He accepts as His child.**
Hebrews 12:6, NLT

No parent *enjoys* disciplining their kids. It's arduous and emotionally exhausting. But you've done it, and you'll do it again, because if you love your kids, you're willing to do all you can to see them become all God's created them to be. And in the aftermath of discipline, there's so often the joy of seeing even the slight softening of a child's heart.

Sometimes we go through things that aren't nice, but they're necessary. God knows they're good for us. If He were apathetic and indifferent, He'd leave us to our own devices, not bothering to put us through the rigors of discipline. He wouldn't allow suffering to do its work in our souls. Thank God He loves us like He does.

VEGGIE WARS

Bribing your kids to finish everything on their plate in return for dessert, is putting them in danger of not knowing when to stop eating. It takes 20 minutes for your brain to recognize when your stomach's full. Rather encourage your kids to listen to their bodies – to eat when hungry, and stop when full. Don't give up on getting children to eat their greens! The more frequently you offer a food, the more likely your child will be to warm up to it. On average, kids have to taste a new food ten times before they begin to like it.

UP ALL NIGHT

It is useless for you to work so hard
from early morning until late at night,
anxiously working for food to eat;
for God gives rest to His loved ones.

Psalm 127:2, NLT

Pressure to perform can have us working ourselves into a frenzy. We work weekends and into the wee hours of the morning, worrying constantly about finances and the future.

God's Kingdom principles so often seem counterintuitive and counterculture – but they *work* far better than we do, no matter how hard we're working. Following the rhythms of God's wisdom around working and resting will see you achieving far more than you're able to on your own steam. When you fuel your own ambitions you'll eventually be running on empty – possibly even rolling backwards. Accept the rest God longs to give you.

SLEEP YOURSELF THIN

Sleep does a lot more for us than making us less sleepy. It even has a role to play in weight gain amongst adults. Sleep deprivation may alter the hormones that control your hunger. Studies have found that those who were deprived of sleep had higher levels of the appetite-stimulating hormone ghrelin and lower levels of the satiety-inducing hormone leptin, with a subsequent increase in hunger and appetite, especially for foods rich in refined carbs. Let's face it, when you're tired, you reach for whatever is fastest, not whatever is healthiest!

SOMETHING ERE THE END

Moses was 120 years old when he died,
yet his eyesight was clear, and he was as strong as ever.
Deuteronomy 34:7, NLT

Growing old isn't a guarantee for any of us, but we may as well model our lives on those who've done it well: like Moses. He was humbler than anyone (Numbers 12:3) – and God gives grace to the humble (James 4:6). He also prayed that an awareness of life's brevity would lead to wisdom (Psalm 90:12). Moses meekly seized every opportunity to live a meaningful life, making the most of his days.

No matter how old you are, you're getting older every day. Make the courageous call to humbly acknowledge your dependence on God's wisdom – so you can contribute boldly in this transitory life. As Tennyson put it: 'Old age hath yet his honor and his toil; Death closes all: but something ere the end, some work of noble note, may yet be done ...'

NO GRIND, NO MIND

Cognitive decline is 15% slower for those who are mentally active. If you don't engage your brain's faculties, it's likely you'll begin to lose them. Regularly try something new! Brush your teeth with your other hand. Novel challenges present unexpected obstacles, forcing your brain to remodel and find new pathways for processing information. Doing routine, familiar tasks simply reactivates existing circuitry – which can keep your brain going, but won't change or improve it in fundamental ways. This doesn't only apply to elderly folks! You're never too young to start working up a brain-sweat.

NEVER TOO HEAVY

The dagger went so deep that the handle disappeared
beneath the king's fat. So Ehud did not pull out the dagger,
and the king's bowels emptied.

Judges 3:22, NLT

This deeply encouraging Bible verse has almost certainly put faith in your heart today! (Kidding.) But like every other word of the Word, *we can learn from this story*. King Eglon is the fat king being stabbed – and his vast size is clearly his downfall.

Even though God is more concerned about the size of your heart than the size of your jeans (1 Samuel 16:7), this doesn't exempt you from looking after the skin you're in. We each get just one body with which to execute our destiny. If that body is unhealthily overweight, our vigor and verve will be compromised.

Even if weight management has been a lifelong struggle for you, your circumstances aren't beyond God's rescue. Also, He's not looking for supermodels. Just devoted, contented followers happy to serve with maximum vivacity.

BIG BELLY BLIGHT

Being overweight, especially around your belly area, has been closely linked to an increase in breast cancer risk. Being overweight also increases your risk of breast cancer *recurrence*. This higher risk is because fat cells make estrogen, and estrogen can make breast cancers develop and grow. Around 40% of diagnosed breast cancers are detected by women during self-examination, so it's critical to establish a regular self-assessment routine. There are apps – and doctors – that can show you exactly how to do this.

FOOD FOR THOUGHT

The ins and outs of organ donation:

* Since the first successful operation in the 1950s, organ transplants have saved millions of lives, but the need for transplants is increasing faster than organs are becoming available.

* You don't have to be dead to be a donor! A *living* donation involves donating a kidney, part of your liver, or blood stem cells to another person, while you're alive and kicking. Your blood volume returns within 48 hours, the kidney left behind grows a bit bigger to pick up the slack, and your liver will completely regenerate itself.

* Becoming an organ donor makes you a lifesaver. Your heart, liver and pancreas can save three lives. Your kidneys and lungs can help up to four people. Furthermore, you can offer assistance to another fifty people by donating your corneas, skin, bone, tendons and heart valves.

* Even if you have a medical condition, like high blood pressure, you'll most likely still qualify as an organ donor.

* You're never too old to become an organ donor. The decision to use your organs is based on strict medical criteria, not age. It may turn out that certain organs aren't suitable for transplantation, but other organs and tissues may be fine. Don't let anyone look down on you because you are old!

Contact your state or country's organ donor foundation today!

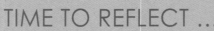

TIME TO REFLECT ...

You may already be an organ donor. (And if you're not, would you prayerfully consider it?) But reflect on how you're donating parts of your *living* self. Are you freely giving away your heart of compassion? Are you contributing to solutions by using the brain God's given you? Write down the ways you could give more of yourself – *all of yourself* – while you're fully alive.

_____

_____

_____

_____

_____

_____

_____

_____

_____

_____

_____

_____

_____

SINGING IN THE STAIRWELLS

God is our refuge and strength,
an ever-present help in trouble.
Psalm 46:1, NIV

Most of life is like taking the stairs. There's no magic elevator to the top and *ta-da!* Life's perfect! The stairs are steep. They can be lonely. And progress is slow. Taking the stairs means settling into the one-stair-at-a-time rhythm of showing up day after day and deciding to be kind and calm. It's saying to your people and mostly to yourself, 'I *know* you've got it in you – just today – to climb one more stair.' Taking the stairs is praying for the small steps and the big leaps. It's asking in humble dependence on God's wisdom because tripping on the stairs is always preceded by arrogantly thinking you can take them two at a time.

And you'll discover in the stairwells surprisingly beautiful acoustics. Despite the slog, you'll still be free to sing to the God who is your ever-present help in trouble, because He'll be there, climbing with you.

STEP UP!

Keen to stay healthy? Then step right up! Climbing stairs is one of the best-kept secrets to increasing fitness and managing weight. It gives you a 50% better workout than walking. Even at a slow pace, you'll burn energy two to three times faster climbing stairs than you would walking. Interestingly, while the rate of energy used is higher when taking stairs two at a time, the burn over an entire flight is more when taking them one at a time. Now you know.

REMEMBER NO MORE

And I will forgive their wickedness,
and I will never again remember their sins.
Hebrews 8:12, NLT

God knows everything about everything. He's aware if the electrons around one atom's nucleus change direction. So if God is all-powerful and all-knowing, how is it that He *forgets* our sin? Surely He stores it somewhere on a divine database?

Because of His love for us, God *chooses* not to hold our sin against us. Jesus paid for it, and tore up the invoice. There's nothing owing against our names. God's way of forgiving is a startling and convicting example of how we can choose to cancel debt – almost as if it was never owed to us. It's within our power to remember people's sin no more.

MAKING MEMORIES

While you *should* aim to forget the offences against you, you don't want to forget to pick up your kid from school! Prolonged stress, chronic lack of sleep and multitasking all affect your brain's ability to make, store, strengthen and replay memories. Very high or prolonged cortisol spikes cut back the connections in your brain's prefrontal cortex and hippocampus, both essential for memory. Your brain needs small breaks after a task in order to lock away new memories. If you're replying to emails while participating in a conference call, your over-tasked mind won't have the capacity to store all the new information it's collecting.

THINK ABOUT YOUR DRINK

Wine produces mockers; alcohol leads to brawls.
Those led astray by drink cannot be wise.
Proverbs 20:1, NLT

Andy Stanley explains why he doesn't drink alcohol at all, by saying that he's never counseled *anyone* who said, 'You know, my life was falling apart, and *then I started drinking* and things dramatically improved!' He goes on to explain that the opposite is generally true. When alcohol arrives on the scene of someone's life story, things usually devolve.

God doesn't ban booze. But He does forbid drunkenness (Ephesians 5:18). Alcohol affects our discernment. It also affects our livers. The word *liver* has its roots in Anglo-Saxon, German and Dutch, arriving in English from the words *lifer* and *leber* and *lever* – because way-back-when folks understood that the liver was linked to life itself. Let's think about our livers – and our lives – and choose our drinks wisely and well.

LOVE YOUR LIVER

Globally, alcohol-attributable liver cirrhosis (severe scarring of your liver) is responsible for nearly 500,000 deaths each year – all of which are obviously preventable. When you drink alcohol, it's your liver's job to process said alcohol and detoxify your blood. Excessive drinking means your liver works overtime. With most organs, like your heart, damaged tissue is replaced with a scar, like on your skin. Marvelously, your liver is able to regenerate and replace damaged tissue with new cells, but alcohol endangers your liver by messing up this regeneration process, causing both inflammation, scarring and ultimately cirrhosis.

REGENERATION

Therefore, if anyone is in Christ, the new creation has come:
The old has gone, the new is here!

2 Corinthians 5:17, NIV

I've read about a church that had a prayer of response printed at the back of their weekly service handout, for anyone wanting to 'accept God'. The prayer read: 'Sorry for my mistakes, God. Thanks for salvation.'

Jesus didn't die for mistakes – like locking your keys in your car. He died for sin – which separates us from His holy, perfect Father. The gospel is about regeneration and transformation and freedom from being the walking dead in this life as we look forward to *eternal* life. And once we encounter God's *changing* grace, we do just that: *change*.

Sometimes change is slow and steady. Sometimes change happens in fits and starts. But change happens. Let's guard against ideologies that carpet-cover sin without expectantly welcoming the new creation.

LIVING LIVER!

Your liver is your largest and most metabolically complex organ, performing over five hundred functions and miraculously able to regenerate itself. But it still needs plenty of TLC. The most prevalent chronic liver malady, and there are many, is non-alcoholic fatty liver disease: the build up of fat in your liver often associated with obesity and diabetes. Another major trigger of liver disease is viral hepatitis, the leading cause of hepatic cancer and most common reason for liver transplantation. To keep your liver living longer? Get the Hepatitis A and B vaccine, focus on personal hygiene, and maintain a healthy body weight.

STILL GOT IT

Now that I am old and gray, do not abandon me, O God.
Let me proclaim Your power to this new generation,
Your mighty miracles to all who come after me.
Psalm 71:18, NLT

Deciding to age well – to age *proactively* – isn't about you. Sure, some people look after themselves for selfish reasons (to remain pain-free for as long as possible, or to pursue hobbies and happiness well into their sunset years). But ageing well is actually about those living in your wake: the generation you're raising, who will ride the waves you've made.

It's up to you to teach the surf skills of wisdom and knowledge and experience and godliness – and the longer you keep your one body strong, the longer you've got to share God's light and love with others, swimming back out into the swell to buoy up those just learning to swim.

NOT DEAD YET!

Arguably, the most prevalent age-related health problem is weight gain. As you get older your metabolism slows and muscle mass dwindles. Obesity is linked to almost every major cause of early death, so this is one you should *actively* (literally!) avoid, by exercising regularly and eating a balanced diet. Your risk for chronic diseases increases as you age, thanks to hormonal changes and exposure to damaging stressors, like smoking. Aside from making obvious lifestyle changes, be proactive about medical screening. The earlier a problem is detected, the earlier it can be treated (and the longer you'll live!)

FOOD FOR THOUGHT

Weight loss: the golden rules

If you're confused about healthy eating – you're not alone. The bewilderment about what a balanced diet means, has meant that most are unsure what to do – so they end up doing nothing at all. Despite the ongoing media debate about diet, there are four golden rules that all experts do agree on:

- Eat more fresh produce. Veggies for the win!
- Eat fewer refined carbohydrates and processed foods (anything that comes in a box or packet). If it comes from a plant, good! If it was made in a plant, not good!
- Be aware of your portion sizes.
- Adopt a change in eating that forms part of your lifestyle, and isn't just a temporary fix. Crash dieting doesn't work! It's natural for anyone trying to lose weight to want to lose it very quickly, but for weight loss to be healthy and more importantly, sustainable, don't deny yourself food. *You do need to eat.* Starving yourself works against your weight loss goals by slowing down your metabolism as your body tries to save the little energy it has left.

Of course no good weight loss plan would be complete without a bit of exercise. Not only will exercise help with maintaining weight loss, it will help you *feel* good while you're doing it. That's something you definitely don't need to feel confused about!

TIME TO REFLECT ...

*Jesus, be in my perceiving, my thinking,
my deciding and my remembering –
even as I trust You to steer my steps.
In this season of waiting, help me to keep climbing
the next stair. Help me to be simultaneously patient
and expectant, because I know You're changing me daily.
Amen.*

MIRACLE MEETINGS

Before [Isaac's servant] had finished praying,
he saw a young woman named Rebekah coming out
with her water jug on her shoulder ... the servant said,
'Please give me a little drink of water from your jug.'
'Yes, my lord,' she answered, 'have a drink.' And she quickly
lowered her jug from her shoulder and gave him a drink.

Genesis 24:15,17-18, NLT

God orchestrated this meeting with Rebekah – which led to marriage, and the birth of a nation. Still, Rebekah *went to the well*. She didn't stay home hoping – or moping.

Whether you're romantic or pragmatic, God is sovereign over your steps (Psalm 37:23). He's able to find your perfect match – the spouse or job or house or university.

Pray that God would supernaturally intersect your circumstances in faith-building ways. Trust Him for miracle meetings, even as you faithfully and cheerfully, like Rebekah, take the next obedient step.

PERFECT MATCH

Surgery can't cure leukemia, because it's a blood and bone marrow cancer. Stem cell transplants can! Stem cells can transform into whatever your body needs – in this instance, healthy bone marrow. The snag is you'll need a matching transplant donor – ideally, your identical twin. Even amongst siblings, the chance of a match is only one in four, so most patients turn to the bone marrow registry for a match, where the odds are 1 in 100,000. All the more reason to become a blood donor (and by default a bone marrow donor too) today!

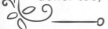

SPLICED

… And you Gentiles, who were branches from a wild olive tree, have been grafted in. So now you also receive the blessing God has promised Abraham and his children, sharing in the rich nourishment from the root of God's special olive tree.

Romans 11:17, NLT

Tree-grafting or bud-splicing is a horticultural technique whereby plant tissues are joined so as to continue their growth together. It's an ancient practice (though you can learn how it's done on Pinterest or YouTube).

In his letter to the Romans, Paul explains the kindness of God in grafting Gentile believers into His family tree – which He planted originally amongst the people of Israel. Paul comforts the Gentile believers with the truth that there's more than enough of God's grace to go around and He's the God who makes a plan to prove His great love for us. Through Jesus, we've become a miracle-part of God's work on the planet: bearing fruit, and offering shade to others who seek refuge in Him.

TRANSPLANT, TRANSFUSE, TRANSCEND

Because of the variety of cells that bone marrow produces (red or white blood cells, and platelets), several diseases affect it – like leukemia, aplastic anemia, lymphoma and other disorders. A bone marrow transplant transfuses healthy marrow cells into a person after their own unhealthy bone marrow has been eliminated through chemotherapy or radiation. Healthy marrow cells are replaced in these patients using a simple blood transfusion – making it possible for them to live whole and happy lives.

SOMETHING SUPERNATURAL

Thank You for making me so wonderfully complex!
Your workmanship is marvelous – how well I know it.
Psalm 139:14, NLT

Pause for a moment to dwell on the reality that inside of you, God created stem cells, which form the foundation of your entire body and act as building blocks for the blood, immune system, tissue and organs.

These cells not only replicate and regenerate themselves, but they also have the ability to differentiate into any kind of specialized cell in the body. The Creator Himself has put something of His creative mark – His image – in you, as these cells are able to become something else entirely, but that something else is still part of entirely unique *you*.

Maybe as you read this, you've got some aches and pains. Some serious, some less so. Still, could you offer up a prayer of thanks for the astoundingly complex body God created to house your soul?

 MAGIC IN THE MARROW

In a bone marrow transplant, stem cells from a healthy person are extracted via their blood and transfused into the person needing the transplant (no painful extraction of actual bone marrow is necessary!) The new stem cells find their way into the host's bone marrow, where they proliferate and differentiate to produce healthy blood cells and platelets. In this way, a stem cell transplant can be a cure for more than seventy diseases.

RADICAL REPLICAS

And you should imitate me, just as I imitate Christ.
1 Corinthians 11:1, NLT

Our bodies are made up of cells that keep on multiplying, imitating each other and replacing each other, so that we keep living, and looking like ourselves. The body of Christ grows like this too. As our churches and communities thrive, we disciple and develop others, inspiring them to copy us as we copy Christ (Philippians 3:17, 1 Thessalonians 1:6). That way we keep on multiplying the strength and resources of the body, replacing ourselves with fresh new cells to carry the cause.

And even as there are different expressions of worship and service across the world, it's electrifying to see the inimitable DNA of Christ's body sparking to life as our compelling love is copied and carried over to others, for God's glory and their good.

COPYING GONE CRAZY

Cancer is the replication and reproduction of cells in our bodies – *gone bad*. Certain changes to a cell's DNA can cause some cells to become cancerous. Essentially, every time a cell prepares to divide into two new cells, it must copy its DNA. Just like us, this process isn't perfect, and the odd typo can occur. This is especially true when cells are growing quickly, like during childhood. But don't worry – be happy! Lying awake wondering if this is happening to you won't solve anything. Just keep choosing a healthy lifestyle every which way you can.

LIBERATED OR LOCKED UP?

You say, 'I am allowed to do anything' –
but not everything is good for you.
And even though 'I am allowed to do anything,'
I must not become a slave to anything.
1 Corinthians 6:12, NLT

We don't have to do *a single good thing* to earn God's favor. It doesn't depend on us, but on what Jesus (already) did. So God's commands aren't about rule-keeping and box-ticking. We've been liberated by love because Jesus fulfilled the law perfectly and did for us what we couldn't do ourselves.

But Paul explains to the Corinthian Christians that a loving Father still sees fit to teach us how to live well. He highlights the truth that many of the things that promise us freedom end up enslaving us. Your credit card promised you the freedom of a shopping spree, didn't it? Now you're enslaved to your bank's high interest rates and relentless debt-collecting.

Have you chased (false) freedom – and become enslaved?

🍎 HEADACHE PILL OR HEALTH HAZARD?

Self-medicating is convenient – but has its shortcomings. OTC medications, for example, can do a great job at masking something serious – and the wrong medications taken in the wrong amounts for the wrong amount of time can cause side effects as serious as organ failure. OTC meds also interfere with the efficacy of prescription medications. As harmless as some medications sound, an addiction to them is anything but. The more often you use them, the higher your risk of dependency.

FOOD FOR THOUGHT

Here are some top tips to turn back time with lifestyle medicine and the natural approach to anti-ageing:

- Engage in active ageing! Staying active is a not-so-secret weapon against all the bad stuff that goes along with ageing, like joint pain and osteoporosis. Exercise augments blood circulation, which keeps your joints healthy and reduces pain. Plus, it strengthens the muscles around your joints, taking pressure off both joints and bone and lessening the risk of falls.

- Always wear sunscreen. UV rays damage all the delicate proteins in your skin resulting in dark spots, wrinkles and fine lines.

- Moisturize, inside and out. Make water your drink of choice and ensure you stay hydrated throughout the day.

- Sleep. Aim for 7-9 hours each night. Sleep lets your body recharge and recover from the day's stressors.

- Meditate. Slow your mind at the end of every day to ensure you stay calm and centered on God's truth.

- Laugh. To LOL not only feels good, it boosts your memory (fewer senior moments) and lowers levels of the age-accelerating stress hormone, cortisol.

The lifestyle choices you make to prevent or lessen the impact of age-related changes to your health can make the difference between hobbling through your golden years or high-fiving your way through them!

TIME TO REFLECT ...

Just like our human bodies, the body of Christ is about replicating cells to bring new life. No one's got it all together. But would you be comfortable with someone replicating your lifestyle, at the moment? Why or why not? Could you write down the good habits you'd love your kids or others to learn from you – and the bad habits you'll commit to kicking, so as not to pass them on?

HATE-TINTED SPECS

But anyone who hates a fellow believer is still living and walking
in darkness. Such a person does not know the way to go,
having been blinded by the darkness.
1 John 2:11, NLT

We can't expect to hear from God – enjoying His fellowship, counsel and guidance – if we're harboring hatred towards one of His other children.

Are you holding a grudge? Are there people who, if or when they fail or get hurt or humiliated, you're secretly (or not so secretly) rather *glad*? You might think you've got things figured out, but if you can't bear to be in the same room as someone else who loves God, you may be 'blinded by the darkness' John writes about.

You'll likely stumble and fall. You don't have to be friends with everyone. You don't even have to *like* everyone. Just get radically, courageously honest about the people you hate, and repent. It may give you a whole new wide-angle on the world.

LIFESTYLE VISION

Globally, some 285 million people are visually impaired: 39 million are blind and 246 million have low vision. Around 90% of the world's visually impaired live in developing countries and the number of blind people increases annually by two million. A number of genetic conditions result in blindness, but 80% of blindness is preventable. The majority of this prevention comes down to lifestyle: what we eat, how much we strain our eyes and whether or not we're screened for any lurking vision-related health problems.

WIDE-EYED WONDER

*I pray that the eyes of your heart may be enlightened
in order that you may know the hope to which He has called you,
the riches of His glorious inheritance in His holy people,
and His incomparably great power for us who believe ...*
Ephesians 1:18-19, NIV

The fact that Paul *prayed* for the Ephesian believers – for the eyes of their hearts to be opened, so they could really see and appreciate what God had invited them into – means that it wasn't a given, that they *got it*.

It's also not a given that we always *get* how blessed we are. We forget that there is always hope, that we have an indescribable inheritance, and that His great power is available to us. Ask God to open wide the eyes of your heart, until you're wonderstruck by His splendor.

PROTECTING YOUR PEEPERS

General ageing, cataracts and disease contribute to low vision risks as you age, while amongst kids, malnutrition and refractive disorders are the most common problems. To maintain your eye health, eat green leafy veggies which are packed with antioxidants to counteract eye damage from sunlight, cigarette smoke and air pollution. If you include spinach and kale in your diet (loaded with the ultimate eye meds, lutein and zeaxanthin), you're up to 50% less likely to develop cataracts. For a sweeter alternative to leafy greens, go with kiwis, grapes and berries. Vitamin-E-rich nuts and seeds, and omega-3-rich salmon, are also prescribed meds for bright eyes.

EYES RIGHT

I will refuse to look at anything vile and vulgar.
I hate all who deal crookedly;
I will have nothing to do with them.
Psalm 101:3, NLT

Perhaps never before in human history has it been so crucial to be intentional about what we look at. Because we don't have to look far to find the dark and the dodgy. The moods in our marriages and the tones of our homes and the atmospheres in our churches and places of work and leisure would almost certainly dramatically change if we all had the psalmist's words flashing as screen savers and plastered above doorways: *I will refuse to look at anything vile and vulgar.*

Has your vision been compromised by filth or deception or deviance? Please don't do any more of today until you've come clean before God, whose kindness leads us to repentance.

SMOKE GETS IN YOUR EYES

Smoking damages your eyes by reducing antioxidants in your body, limiting blood flow to your eyes and lowering pigment levels in your retina. Smokers are four times more likely to develop age-related macular degeneration than non-smokers. For non-smokers living with smokers, the risk is double. Heavy smokers have around three times the risk of developing cataracts and more than twice the risk of developing dry eye syndrome. Smoking also significantly increases your risk of developing diabetes, and subsequently, diabetic retinopathy. Don't let your vision go up in smoke.

CONTRACT LENS

I made a covenant with my eyes
not to look with lust at a young woman.
Job 31:1, NLT

Temptation has three sources: Satan himself (Matthew 4:1); sin running its course in a broken world (Romans 8:21-22); and ourselves – 'our own desires, which entice us and drag us away' (James 1:14).

We can't control the movements of the enemy – but we can refuse to give him even an inch of real estate in our lives (Ephesians 4:27). We can't control how the culture of a wrecked world comes at us unbidden – but we can prepare our hearts to trust God in the tough times by practicing daily trust when all is well (Joshua 1:8). And of course, we *can* control ourselves, because sin is always a choice.

Let's start by making a covenant with our eyes: training our brains to steer our gaze away from anything that might lure us into wrongdoing and regret.

SHIELD YOUR EYES

There are lots of things you can do to keep your vision 20/20, but staying away from a health care practitioner isn't one of them. Regular screening remains the most effective way of preventing lifestyle-related vision loss. Fortunately, there are no needles involved at the optometrist's office! It's guaranteed to be a pain-free experience. Protecting your eyes from physical damage is your first defense. Ensure that you always have your sunnies with you and use protective eyewear when playing sport or DIY projects.

READERS ARE LEADERS

God gave these four young men an unusual aptitude for
understanding every aspect of literature and wisdom.
And God gave Daniel the special ability to interpret
the meanings of visions and dreams.

Daniel 1:17, NLT

God is the source of all wisdom and knowledge, *ever*. He invented education. He created language and literature, music and math. He contrived the cosmos and climatology. It's no wonder we're commanded to seek wisdom because it's better than gold (Proverbs 16:16). The Levite leaders get a special mention in Nehemiah 8:8, for reading and explaining God's Word so others could understand it, and Daniel and his friends, in their captivity, are clearly blessed by God with amazing intellectual abilities.

Gathering information is important. Are you in a season where you've let it slip? Could you read just one article a week – or listen to just one podcast – to broaden the scope of your wisdom and knowledge? If you're already reading voraciously, are you doing something to encourage those around you to do the same?

SCREEN SIGHT

Most of what we read is now on screens. Estimates are that there has been a 35% increase in shortsightedness since the launch of smart phones in 2007. Experts predict that half of all 30-year-olds will be shortsighted by 2033 as a result of screen use. Digital eye strain is an overuse injury. And like other repetitive stress injuries, it will get worse the longer you do the activity. So take regular breaks outside to smell – and look at – the roses.

FOOD FOR THOUGHT

Googly eyes:

Digital eye strain is more likely to occur after the age of 40. That's because your eye's lens loses some of its elasticity with age, which makes quick changes in focusing a tad more challenging.

The first step towards prevention is admitting you have a problem! From there, try making a few changes to your workstation and work routine to protect your eyes in the long run:

- Reduce glare by cleaning your screen and making sure it's the most brightly glowing thing in the room. Same rule applies for not using your smart phone in direct sunlight.

- Sit an arm's length away from your computer screen. Do the high-five test: if you can't properly high-five your computer screen (full arm extension being the key) you're sitting too close. The screen shouldn't be tilted, and should be positioned right at or just below eye level.

- Take blinking breaks. On average you blink about 15 to 20 times a minute. But that rate drops by half when you're viewing text on a screen. Blinking is important because your upper eyelid spreads tears over the front of your eye, or cornea, like a windscreen wiper – akin to moisturizer for your eyes.

- Take a 20-20-20 break (worth mentioning again!) Every 20 minutes, give yourself 20 seconds to check out what's going on 20 meters away from you.

TIME TO REFLECT ...

Loving Father, open my eyes if I'm oblivious to danger or deception in my life. Open my eyes to see things in Your Word I've never noticed before. Open my eyes to those who need my help. And where the world is waving shiny objects in front of me to distract me from Your best plans for me, give me the courage to look away. Amen.

_____

_____

_____

_____

_____

_____

_____

_____

_____

_____

KEEPING COMPANY

Blessed is the one who does not walk in step
with the wicked or stand in the way
that sinners take or sit in the company of mockers …
Psalm 1:1, NIV

Chronic lower back pain is second only to the common cold as a cause of lost working days. It's also one of the most common reasons to visit a doctor or a hospital emergency room.

How we walk, stand and sit, physically, affects our backs. How we walk, stand and sit, relationally, affects our souls. The Psalmist goes on to say, '[blessed is the one] whose delight is in the law of the LORD, and who meditates on His law day and night. That person is like a tree planted by streams of water, which yields its fruit in season and whose leaf does not wither – whatever they do prospers' (Psalm 1:2-3). Are you walking, standing or sitting with people who are crippling you, or increasing your Kingdom influence?

🍎 HOW LOW CAN YOU GO?

The way you sit, stand and move all impact your lower back, which is subject to a lot of mechanical strain. Your lower back supports your entire upper body, keeping you upright through spinal bones and discs, groups of muscles, and countless nerves. Back pain may be caused by injury, or by mechanical or inflammatory spinal conditions. Poor posture, being overweight, heavy lifting and physical inactivity are all common causes, together with spinal degeneration due to age or trauma. Watch your back!

WEIGHTY WORRIES

If you are tired from carrying heavy burdens,
come to Me and I will give you rest.
Matthew 11:28, CEV

You're a strong person. You do what needs doing. You can lift heavy stuff. You can shoulder a load!

For a while. Because no matter how strong you are, you can't do all that, indefinitely. The God who stitched capacity into your mind and muscles knows that very well. We're designed to need other humans, and Him. Could you phone a friend today? Could you call out to your Father in heaven?

Whether you're carrying the heavy burdens of your own making (sin) or the heavy burdens life has thrust onto your back (grief, uncertainty or rejection), Jesus is inviting you to cast your burdens on Him (Psalm 55:22), and rest.

SHEDDING THE LOAD

There's a strong association between obesity and lower back pain – the most obvious being the additional load placed onto your spine. Studies have shown however, a much stronger association between abdominal obesity (belly fat) and back pain, compared to more generalized obesity. It's the same kind of back pain experienced by pregnant women, and for the same reason. Fat in your belly acts like a heavy weight that pulls your lower spine forward, overly arching your lower back, and putting undue strain in all the wrong places. Start shedding the load today by taking the stairs or pounding the pavements!

STANDUP GUY

He said to me, 'Son of man,
stand up on your feet and I will speak to you.'
Ezekiel 2:1, NIV

Scripture is full of encounters of God calling people. And part of the call is to *stand up straight* (Daniel 10:11, Acts 9:6, Acts 26:16). Because although our salvation requires nothing more from us than face-down surrender – a prostrate soul – the way in which we joyfully, thankfully, live out that salvation in the world requires the ability to stand on our own two feet, up straight, shod with a sturdy pair of get-up-and-go's.

Is God nudging you to gather your strength, straighten your spine, stand up, and get moving?

BACK IN BUSINESS

Many of us spend a good chunk of our working life stooped over a computer – which could be the beginning of the end of our back health. After lying horizontal, walking is the activity that puts the least pressure on your spine with standing coming third and sitting the worst of the lot. If your desk is too high, your shoulders are around your ears; too low and your neck hunches over. Make sure your computer screen is at eye level, your feet are flat on the floor, elbows close to your body and wrists straight. This will help you breathe better too (important when gathering your thoughts). Try this right now. Take a deep breath in a slumped position. Now sit up straight and try again. Big difference, right? Slouching reduces lung capacity by 30%!

BRAVE BACKBONE

Train me, God, to walk straight;
then I'll follow Your true path. Put me together,
one heart and mind; then, undivided,
I'll worship in joyful fear.
Psalm 86:11, MSG

The essence of the psalmist's prayer is for an undivided focus. He longs to worship God in Spirit and truth (John 4:24), intentionally and undistracted. So he asks God to *train* him and *put him together*. This smacks of the element of rigorous joy that's part of the Christian life: a determination to discipline ourselves so that we enjoy the freedom from sin that comes with greater godliness.

Perhaps, where you find yourself in your journey with Jesus, God's promises aren't in your hands – *but they're within your reach.* Could you single-mindedly commit to stretching out to grasp the fullness of the life He has for you?

STRONG SPINE

Regular exercise is vital for managing back pain – not only to keep your weight in check, but also to keep all those muscles around your spine strong, stable and in good working order. Pelvic stability and core strengthening exercises work abdominal, back and support muscles that guard your spine. The stronger these muscles are, the more support they provide, and the less pain you will feel. Of course, it's always best to chat to a pro about the best way to do these exercises, or back pain might be the least of your worries!

BLOOMING LOVE

'And why worry about your clothing?
Look at the lilies of the field and how they grow.
They don't work or make their clothing,
yet Solomon in all his glory was not dressed
as beautifully as they are.'
Matthew 6:28-29, NLT

There are at least 400 000 species of flowering plants in the world. Think how many thousands of each kind of plant there are, in forests, cities, office window boxes and country gardens. Think about how many flowers each flowering plant produces in its lifetime. There are quite certainly more flowers on earth than people. And God has crafted and counted each splendid petal.

Allow God's powerful, all-encompassing, *detailed* love to settle your fears today. If flowers make you sneeze, let that serve as a reminder – while you reach for the tissues – that God is your mighty provider, covering you and clothing you. And if flowers *don't* make your sneeze, fill your home or workspace with them, as often as you can.

SNEEZE FEST

Tree pollens tend to trigger the initial seasonal allergic response. This pollen burst is then followed by a lengthier grass pollen surge, lasting from spring into summer and almost all year round in warmer parts. In other words, grass is to blame for causing you the most pain! Flower pollens are only problematic in late summer, when the hills are alive with the sound of mucus!

FOOD FOR THOUGHT

Wake up and smell the roses – or the rancid morning breath?

Even though you brush your teeth at night, you probably don't wake up smelling like roses. Saliva helps to cleanse your mouth, removing any nibbles, chunks and bacteria that could cause bad breath. When you sleep, saliva production slows and your mouth dries out, even more so for snorers. So while you've been in dreamland, those bacteria have been merrily fabricating foul-smelling gas without being washed away. Which is another good reason to drink plenty of water during the day: not only to stay hydrated, but to keep your breath fresh too.

Eat as many crunchy veggies as you can: they help clean your teeth and they promote saliva production. Try keeping some carrot sticks on standby! See your dentist regularly, and assess your toothbrush. You should replace yours every three months or so to ensure those bristles are up to scratch.

Bad breath could also be caused by chronic reflux, some cancers and certain metabolic disorders. If halitosis is something that's been bugging you (or your spouse) for a while, it's a good idea to chat to your doctor about any other symptoms you're experiencing which might give more insight into the cause of your bad breath – whether it's simple or sinister.

TIME TO REFLECT ...

Some social scientists reckon we're the average of the five people with whom we spend the most time. While this is debatable, we certainly do take on the idiosyncrasies – and even the views and biases – of those we hang out with. With whom do you do most of your walking, standing and sitting? Can you trace the influence of these people on your actions, attitudes, words and ways? Write down your thoughts.

FROM LEARNING TO LOVE

And this is my prayer: that your love may abound
more and more in knowledge and depth of insight,
so that you may be able to discern what is best
and may be pure and blameless for the day of Christ.
Philippians 1:9-10, NIV

The world would change, if we all prayed this prayer for people we know and love. Amazingly, this greater and greater love that Paul longs to see flourish in his beloved Philippians is based on knowledge, insight and discernment. It seems the more we understand of God and His ways, the more our love – for Him and others – abounds.

Let's pray for ourselves and let's pray for those we get on well with and those who annoy us that our spiritual acumen would develop more and more – resulting in greater love. Pray too that you'd navigate today excellently, discerning what's pure and blameless.

IS IT THIS, OR THAT?

To treat our health issues, we need to discern what they are. Is your runny nose the result of an allergy (an immune system response to allergens), or a cold (a virus)? The easiest way to tell the difference is by how long symptoms last – which unfortunately doesn't help much when they first strike. A cold usually lasts no longer than ten days; allergies can pester people for months. Depending on your symptoms, your doc might send you for a painless skin prick test, which highlights specific allergens, and with that the best course of treatment action.

RADICAL ERADICATION

'And if your right hand causes you to stumble,
cut it off and throw it away. It is better for you to lose one part
of your body than for your whole body to go into hell.'
Matthew 5:30, NIV

This is a drastic statement from our friend and King, Jesus. He never sugarcoats anything – because He wants us to know the truth, the whole truth and nothing but the truth.

He's encouraging us to *take sin seriously*. Seriously enough to chop off our right hand – our *stronger* hand, usually – if it's the cause of our spiritual faltering. Living minus a right hand would be difficult. It would complicate so many tasks. Jesus is saying, 'That's fine. You'll manage. *Rather that*, than continuing in a life that will condemn you.'

Even as you're reading, what comes to mind? Is God convicting you to cut something out of your life? Be ruthless. Do it today.

DODGING DUST

The most evident way to manage an allergy is to eradicate or avoid the offending allergen. The stickier you are, the more of a pollen magnet you become – so boycott hair gel! Wash your hair, clothes and linen often. Take an OTC antihistamine at night (some of 'em help with a good night's sleep), or use a nasal spray steroid (particularly for persistent allergies). Get some exercise, to improve blood flow to your lungs and nasal passages, and stock up on healthy foods containing antioxidants, probiotics and vitamin C.

WORTH OR WASTE?

Let these false prophets tell their dreams,
but let My true messengers faithfully proclaim My every word.
There is a difference between straw and grain!
Jeremiah 23:28, NLT

Jeremiah goes on to deliver God's words: '"Does not My word burn like fire?" says the LORD. "Is it not like a mighty hammer that smashes a rock to pieces?"' (Jeremiah 23:29). He's confronting the lying prophets who were leading God's people astray, and in so doing he's making a clear distinction between quality (God's sufficient and infallible Word) and quantity (reams of flaky dreams spewed forth by false forecasters).

This is a brilliant and timely reminder for us, in churches, care groups, communities and friendship circles today, to check the quality of the spiritual fare we're consuming. *There is a difference between straw and grain!*

CALORIES THAT COUNT

Central to many weight management programs is a rather thin theory that calories in must be less than calories out. This creates a so-called energy deficit, which triggers your body to start using internal fat stores to meet additional energy requirements. Whether it's bananas or beer, calories are calories, right? Wrong! Your body responds differently to calories from different sources (sugar, carbohydrates, protein and fat). Your weight is further regulated by a complex system of genetic and hormonal factors, as well as neurological input, and not all calories affect this system in the same way. Calorie *quality* is as important (if not more so) as Calorie *quantity*.

LORD FRAUD

'So why do you keep calling Me "Lord, Lord!"
when you don't do what I say?'
Luke 6:46, NLT

People who knew Jesus, loved Jesus, obeyed Jesus and enjoyed His presence, called Him, 'Lord, Lord!' People who didn't actually know Him, love Him, or obey Him, and only sought His presence for their own gain or reputation, also called Him, 'Lord, Lord!' Same words. Different heart attitude. Jesus saw right through them, and He sees right through us.

We're no less flawed and fickle than the people Jesus hung out with when He was on earth. Let's resolve to be upright and scrupulous in our name-calling, not calling Him 'Lord' unless He's on the throne of our lives.

SAME-SAME, BUT DIFFERENT

Theoretically, a calorie is the amount of energy needed to raise the temperature of one gram of water by one degree. Practically, a sugary drink, has 'empty' calories. Compared to an egg, it may have the same *number* of calories, but the body-pathways these calories travel are significantly different. The sweet drink will deliver instant energy, spike blood sugar and then leave you feeling low, and hungry. The same amount of egg calories will keep your blood sugar constant and leave you satisfied. Sugary foods and drinks also spark insulin release, so any excess sugars go straight to fat! It's not surprising then that drinking a can of cola every day has a vastly different impact on your long-term health and energy than whipping up some eggs.

DARE TO DIVERSIFY

Everything that lives and moves about will be food for you.
Just as I gave you the green plants, I now give you everything.
Genesis 9:3, NIV

There are over 20,000 species of edible plants on the planet. Yet, we now get 90% of our food from fewer than 20 species. It's perhaps part of our warped humanity that we dumb down the kaleidoscope of color, taste and texture God intended for us – choosing a handful of the bland and the boring.

God also created a diversity of people and places – yet we tend to gravitate towards the comfort of what's known and familiar, creating echo chambers of mutual agreement. Could you step out in some way this week, moving deliberately in the direction of tasting something new, or talking to someone you wouldn't normally talk to, or taking a different route to work and praying for the people in the houses or offices you pass?

PACKING A CALORIE PUNCH

You can only eat so much in a single day, so spend your calorie budget wisely. The first step is understanding the difference between nutrient-dense calories and empty calories. While all foods contain nutrients, nutrient-dense foods are more beneficial for maintaining optimal health, as they provide more nutrients than calories. Unlike nutrient-dense foods, empty-calorie foods are nutritionally poor food choices, as they contain more calories than nutrients. So, max out your eating budget on nutritious nutrients.

DAY 251

FOOD FOR THOUGHT

Choosing nutrients over calories:

Most empty-calorie foods are highly processed and contain added sugars. You'll find them in vending machines and convenience stores because they have a long shelf-life. So while these foods are usually cheaper and available *everywhere*, eating them regularly isn't doing your waistline, or the rest of your body, any favors.

Check out the average sugar content of some of your favorite things:

Food	Average number of teaspoons of sugar (or equivalent) per serving
Soda, sweetened fruit drinks, iced teas	9 teaspoons per 330ml serving of soda; 12 teaspoons per 330ml serving of fruit drink or iced tea.
Cakes, cookies, pastries, and pies	6 teaspoons in 1/16 of a pie or frosted cake
Sweets and chocolates	3 teaspoons per 30g chocolate bar
Ice-cream and frozen yogurt	3 teaspoons per ½ cup
Condiments	¼ cup of tomato sauce contains around 4 teaspoons of sugar

Top nutrient-dense food picks

Eating nutrient-dense foods is like eating one thing that does the job of three. Top picks would be salmon (bursting with omega-5), eggs (packed with choline to keep your brain sharp), berries (full of antioxidants) and spinach (loaded with vitamins A and C, potassium, calcium, magnesium, fiber and protein).

Don't see food as just a collection of calories. Consider the *effect* of those calories down the line. By cutting out refined carbs and eating more protein and healthy fats, you can work *with* your body's internal weight-control systems, making weight loss more natural.

TIME TO REFLECT ...

*Father God, reinforce my willpower to avoid spiritual
allergens and toxins I know aren't good for me.
Give me the courage to be intentional and discerning about
what I put into my body, mind and soul –
in terms of food, friendships, films and fun.
Teach me to enrich my life with wholesome things.
Amen.*

WOMB WONDER

*You watched me as I was being formed in utter seclusion,
as I was woven together in the dark of the womb.
You saw me before I was born ...*

Psalm 139:15-16, NLT

It's hard to miss the majesty of an almighty Creator when we consider how babies spark to life in the womb – how cells split and accelerate into billions – and later trillions.

But it's also hard to accept that sometimes babies don't develop as they should. Things go wrong. Sin runs its course in a broken world and sometimes there are deformities, disabilities, disappointments and delays. Still, 'we fix our eyes not on what is seen, but on what is unseen, since what is seen is temporary, but what is unseen is eternal,' (2 Corinthians 4:18) and we know that God will never leave or forsake us (Hebrews 13:5). Regardless of what He permits in our lives, He never takes His eyes off us, or our kids, born, unborn or stillborn.

 ## BOOZE OR BABY? YOU CHOOSE.

World Fetal Alcohol Syndrome (FAS) Day is commemorated each year at nine minutes past nine on the ninth day of the ninth month to highlight the importance of healthy pregnancies. During pregnancy, keep your blood sugar regulated with a diversity of whole, healthy foods and plenty of protein. Make sure you're drinking enough water. Get plenty of rest – while you can! And it goes without saying, no smoking, and absolutely no alcohol – not even a drop.

GREED OR GOLDILOCKS?

… give me neither poverty nor riches!
Give me just enough to satisfy my needs. For if I grow rich,
I may deny You and say, 'Who is the LORD?'
And if I am too poor, I may steal and thus insult God's holy name.
Proverbs 30:8-9, NLT

The most common thyroid problems involve abnormal hormone production. Too much thyroid hormone results in *hyper*-thyroidism; too little leads to *hypo*thyroidism. An underactive thyroid causes fatigue, low moods, sensitivity to cold, muscle cramps and weakness. An overactive thyroid causes anxiety, irritability, mood swings, heat sensitivity and difficulty sleeping. Your thyroid epitomizes the Goldilocks philosophy. It works best in balance.

Wisely, Solomon prays a Goldilocks prayer: to be satisfied with what he has, while trusting God to meet his needs. Financially, vocationally or relationally, are you expecting too much, or afraid you'll have too little? Could you pray for not-too-much not-too-little but just-right, as you bring your needs, fears and frustrations to God?

BRINGING THE BALANCE

Your thyroid is small and powerful. Through the hormones it produces, this little gland influences almost all your body's metabolic processes. Thyroid diseases are among the most prevalent of all medical conditions, especially in women, and they are also some of the trickiest to diagnose, because symptoms can be relatively mild and nonspecific. Thyroid disorders range from a harmless goiter (enlarged gland), to life-threatening cancer. It's worth visiting your doctor regularly to check that your thyroid is thriving.

ALIVE AND KICKING

Your love for me is so great that You protected me
from death and the grave.
Psalm 86:13, CEV

If you've ever been around someone right after they've had a near-death experience, you probably found them exhilarated, jubilant to be alive, and motivated like never before to suck the marrow from the bones of their brief, glorious existence. Understandably!

Globally, 6,316 people die every hour. If you're alive to read this, this hour, *then you're not one of them!* You may not have had a recent brush with death, but it's still a great day to be alive! God has staved off the grave for you, for a little longer, because your earth-stint isn't over. He has plans for you yet.

A GRAVE SITUATION?

Graves' disease is the most common of all thyroid conditions. The name isn't an indication of where you'll end up, Graves was the guy who discovered it. It's an auto-immune disorder in which your body gets tricked into attacking its own healthy cells. In this case, your body produces antibodies that cause the cells of your thyroid to go into overdrive and overproduce hormones. Your thyroid could also be thrown out of whack if your intestines become inflamed, which triggers an immune response (up to 70% of your autoimmune system is found in your gut-lymphoid tissue). If you want to avoid being gutted, look after your gut, and it will look after you!

LIFE AND BREATH

Remember Him before your legs – the guards of your house –
start to tremble … Remember Him before your teeth –
your few remaining servants – stop grinding; and before your eyes –
the women looking through the windows – see dimly.

Ecclesiastes 12:3, NLT

The teacher in Ecclesiastes is encouraging us to enjoy God while we have life and strength, youth and vitality, to do so.

Old age and the physical infirmities that inevitably, to some degree or another, accompany it, may rob us of some of the vibrancy of youth.

That said, we don't get to use our physical state as an excuse for disobedience or apathy. No matter how debilitated or decrepit we are, there are constantly people who need our prayers. What's more, we always have a choice to give thanks. May it be said of our generation one day, that even when we had no teeth left in our gums, we sang out our praises of the Most High.

GUARD YOUR GUMS

Globally, 60-90% of school children and nearly 100% of adults have dental cavities, and 30% of people aged 65-74 have no natural teeth. *Oral* health directly affects *overall* health. Without proper oral hygiene (daily brushing), bacteria can reach clinical levels leading to oral infections like tooth decay and gum disease. Bacteria can then leach into your bloodstream and damage blood vessels, causing pregnancy complications, erectile dysfunction, infertility, respiratory conditions, Alzheimer's disease and some cancers. Get busy brushing!

WISE WORDS

Set a guard over my mouth, LORD;
keep watch over the door of my lips.
Psalm 141:3, NIV

In the very next verse, David prays, 'Do not let my heart be drawn to what is evil so that I take part in wicked deeds along with those who are evildoers; do not let me eat their delicacies' (Psalm 141:4). It seems he's aware of a direct link between his mouth and his heart. Because sometimes our mouths drive off before our brains are in gear and we get ourselves into all sorts of trouble.

How could you watch your words, today? *Who* could you watch? Are there some people you admire, because whatever comes out of their mouths always makes the world a better place? Learn from them.

TEETH WILL TELL

Dentists are sometimes the first to spot signs and symptoms of conditions that you might be unaware of. For example, osteoporosis can cause changes in the bones that support your teeth (think receding gums and loose teeth). Off-color gums or tongue may indicate anemia. Tooth enamel erosion may signal reflux or an eating disorder. Diabetics are more susceptible to gum disease, whilst gum disease has the potential to affect blood glucose control and contribute to the progression of diabetes. The good news is that managing one can help bring the other under control.

DAY 258

FOOD FOR THOUGHT

Is ADHD something parents and teachers make up to explain bad behavior?

There's overwhelming scientific evidence that ADHD is a very real condition involving complex neurological, biochemical and genetic factors. Although recent research has identified environmental factors that may increase the likelihood of developing the disorder (like smoking during pregnancy) ADHD is thought to have a stronger genetic explanation.

Whilst on the matter of myth-busting: ADHD isn't caused by too much TV. ADHD affects both boys *and girls*. It's not caused by sugar. And yelling at kids to *pay attention* will not help them overcome the condition, at all, ever.

Are only noisy, disruptive children labeled ADHD?

While many children with ADHD are socially disruptive, the condition can exist in quiet, withdrawn kids. According to the latest guidelines, ADHD is divided into three subtypes (inattentive, hyperactive-impulsive and combined) so the disorder occurs along a broad spectrum.

When can ADHD be diagnosed, and do kids outgrow it?

Diagnosis usually takes place between ages five and seven. While a lot of kids experience a reduction in symptoms during adolescence and adulthood, only a few get over their symptoms altogether. Globally, ADHD affects 4-7% of adults.

Is medication the only way to treat the condition?

Clinical experience shows the most effective treatment is a combination of diet, medication, counseling and academic environmental tweaks. Grab hold of positivity and perseverance as you figure out what works best for your unique child.

TIME TO REFLECT ...

Is God convicting you to clean up your speech? Write down some words or phrases you'll commit to *no longer saying.* Next to those, write down some things you'll say instead. Ask God to set a guard over your lips (Psalm 141:3) and to help you catch quickly any unwholesome or damaging words that slip out.

HUNG OUT TO DRY

My strength has dried up like sun-baked clay.
My tongue sticks to the roof of My mouth.
You have laid Me in the dust and left Me for dead.
Psalm 22:15, NLT

Psalm 22 is a Messianic prophecy. It provides such a vivid illustration of Jesus' death that it's been called 'the Fifth Gospel.' And we *need* these scriptural reminders because we're in danger of becoming blasé about our Savior's sacrifice. We're quick to forget what the crucifixion did to Him: physically, emotionally and spiritually.

The English word, *excruciating*, comes from the word *crucifixion.* It was unbearable. Psalm 22 reminds us that God's love is unbroken – graphically portrayed through the broken body of Jesus, for our broken humanity.

Next time your mouth is a little dry after a jog or a gym session, let it remind you of Jesus – spat on and hung out to dry, for you – and give thanks.

MOUTH-WATERING WINS

Saliva is a seriously underrated bodily fluid. You wouldn't be able to *taste* without saliva! Having a dry mouth causes your gums, tongue and other tissues in your mouth to become swollen and uncomfortable. Germs thrive in this type of setting, which leads to bad breath. Saliva also helps wash away bacteria and food debris from your teeth – so without it you're more likely to develop rapid tooth decay and gum disease. Definitely nothing to spit at! Bear in mind that decongestants, antihistamines, painkillers, diuretics, diabetes and autoimmune disorders may reduce saliva flow.

PRECIOUS PUPIL

For this is what the L ORD Almighty says:
'After the Glorious One has sent me against the nations
that have plundered you – for whoever touches you
touches the apple of His eye ...'
Zechariah 2:8, NIV

The idiom 'to be the apple of someone's eye' refers to something or someone cherished above all others. The 'apple' refers to the pupil of the eye. When we come across this phrase in Scripture, it's translated into English idiom. The Hebrew phrase simply reads 'the dark part of the eye,' which is why Psalm 17:8 is also translated, 'Guard me as you would guard your own eyes.'

It's a staggering thought – *that that's how precious you are to God*. One translation of Zechariah 2:8 says, 'Anyone who harms you harms My most precious possession.'

Next time you bite into an apple, call to mind your priceless worth to the Father.

NATURE'S TOOTHBRUSH

It's not sugar per se that wrecks your teeth – but *how long* your teeth are exposed to it. The longer sugar hangs around on your teeth, the more bacteria build up and converting of said sugar into acid. That's why eating an apple a day won't only keep the doctor away; it'll keep the dentist away too. Eating crisp, firm, fresh foods – 'detergent foods' – is akin to brushing your teeth, so eat them as the final mouthful of a meal if you won't be able to brush your teeth straight after eating.

TOO MUCH OF A GOOD THING

It's not good to eat too much honey,
and it's not good to seek honors for yourself.
Proverbs 25:27, NLT

When you swallow medication, it's absorbed by your stomach, passed into the blood and transported to your liver. Your liver breaks it down and ships it off to your heart, which pumps it out to the rest of your body. While medication is being broken down in your liver, different toxins are produced. This is ok – unless you take *too much* medication, or if you take medication with alcohol. This overloads your liver, damaging cells and increasing your chance of disease.

So it's possible to get too much of a good thing – even good meds. And it's possible to rush ahead of wisdom and grab too much of something – even something good. Are you taking in too much, or taking on too much, of something that's essentially good, but something that could turn bad with excess?

MODERATION MEDICATION

Taking medication regularly means your liver will work hard. The fewer medications, pills and supplements you take the better. When using OTC meds, always read the instructions carefully and avoid using the maximum allowed dose. You can also keep your liver in shape by maintaining a healthy weight, avoiding fad diets and miracle detox cures, eating unprocessed food, drinking alcohol in moderation (if at all), and quitting smoking.

(WITH)HELD

For the LORD God is our sun and our shield.
He gives us grace and glory. The LORD will withhold
no good thing from those who do what is right.
Psalm 84:11, NLT

We sometimes want *more* from God. We feel He's withholding what is clearly (in our view) the very best thing for us. Healing. Financial provision. A spouse. A baby. How can those things *not* be part of His plan for us? Why would He ever withhold them?

Because He's an all-knowing Father – concerned with our growth and His glory. If He's withholding (for now?) something inherently good, perhaps it's not what will make you most like Jesus. God works *all things* together for good, for those who love Him (Romans 8:28), not so we'll be *comfortable*, but so that we'll be *conformed* into the image of His Son (Romans 8:29). God may be withholding something you long for – *but He's still holding you.*

🍎 LESS IS MORE

Countless studies confirm the marvels of modern medicine. Death rates have plummeted. People are living longer than ever. But misconceptions about medicine are as numerous as pills in a pharmacy. One dodgy myth about taking OTC medication is that more is better. When you're in severe pain, you may look at the directions on an analgesic drug label and think, 'An extra dose can't hurt.' Except, *it can*. Recommended dosages are careful calculations. Doubling up can rob you of the medicine's benefits and increase the risk of serious side effects.

NOTHING TO HIDE

So we are lying if we say we have fellowship with God
but go on living in spiritual darkness; we are not practicing
the truth. But if we are living in the light, as God is in the light,
then we have fellowship with each other,
and the blood of Jesus, His Son, cleanses us from all sin.

1 John 1:6-7, NLT

Search engines and social media corporations do infringe on our privacy. But as Christians, it shouldn't *really* bother us. Some aspects of our lives are sacred and we deserve our dignity, but there should be nothing sinister or salacious in our lives – nothing we need to hide for fear of being found out.

If there's something dark in your life that you wouldn't want discovered, it's likely you need to dump it. Would you be brave enough to confess it – bring it into the light – and cast it aside?

Come clean before the people affected by your sin. Move on, free.

FESS UP

Natural supplements and medications aren't necessarily safe. They're not as well regulated as pharmaceutical ones, so the amount of ingredients could vary significantly between products. The label might not warn you, but these meds could also interfere with your prescription medication. Besides causing side effects, some vitamins or supplements can negatively affect the way your body absorbs and eliminates other medicine. So when you talk to your doctor, you need to *over-share* about what over-the-counter supplements you're taking!

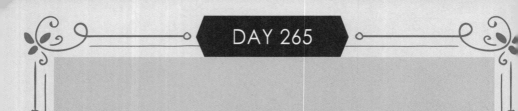

FOOD FOR THOUGHT

Is social media affecting your memory?

Forgetting where you parked your car? Can't remember the name of an old colleague? (Or your spouse?) Age-associated memory loss isn't unusual, but it seems to be creeping up on us a lot earlier than it should.

A likely culprit is technology. True, technology and social media have made our lives easier, but they've also made our memories shorter. Being able to access any information at the tap of a button means you tend to focus less on your own memory, and more on remembering where to find the info.

Choosing filters, finding the perfect camera angle and posting pictures on social media is adding insult to injury and further impacting memory. Social media doesn't come close to the actual experience of being somewhere, and spending time trying to get the perfect shot means *you're* the one that misses the moment!

They may be called cell phones, but don't become a prisoner to yours. Instead, try to soak up new experiences and flush out any brain cobwebs by relying less on Google and more on your gray matter, and be inspired by God's glory all around you.

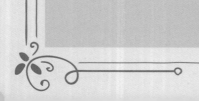

TIME TO REFLECT ...

*Lord, You know the meds, vitamins and supplements I'm
taking, physically. Please provide wise medical counsel,
so that I'll know if I'm taking too much or too little,
or if I shouldn't be taking anything at all.
And where I need spiritual supplements, guide my thinking,
my reading, my listening and my conversations,
so that I take in what I need, to get healthier.
Amen.*

RIGHT BEFORE MY VERY EYES

I have set the LORD always before me;
because He is at my right hand, I shall not be shaken.
Psalm 16:8, ESV

In 1757, Robert Robinson wrote a hymn, penning these now familiar words: *Let that goodness like a fetter / Bind my wandering heart to Thee / Prone to wander, Lord, I feel it / Prone to leave the God I love / Here's my heart, oh, take and seal it / Seal it for Thy courts above.*

Because the truth is, we're prone to wandering. We're quick to forget. We need to be setting God and His Word ever before us, so that reminders of His goodness, grace, love and longsuffering come at us thick and fast and gloriously. Could you make a screensaver for your device today – with a Bible verse you're meditating on – to bind your wandering heart to Him?

PILL PROMPT

For medication to work its medicinal magic – you need to remember to take it! Putting your pills next to your toothbrush seems like a good idea (assuming you're a regular brusher), but certain meds are sensitive to moisture and light, and your bathroom gets a lot of both. The best place to keep medication is in a dry, darkish area, like a cupboard – in their original packaging and away from kids. As for remembering to take them, set a phone reminder. To avoid a nasty aftertaste, swallow your pills with enough water (not wine!) to keep them from dissolving before reaching your stomach.

WHAT REALLY MATTERS

My knees are weak from fasting,
and I am skin and bones.
Psalm 109:24, NLT

Go ahead and read all of Psalm 109. David is in a bad place. He's not thin because he's been dieting. He's thin because he's been mocked, scorned, ridiculed, cursed and persecuted. But amazingly, he's not concerned about *his* status or reputation. He cries out to God to deal well with him, for the sake of *God's* reputation (Psalm 109:21). He has no personal agenda. He surrenders and submits to God's sovereign plans for him, and casts himself again and again on His mercy (Psalm 109:27, 30-31).

David's example might remind us that so much of what we concern ourselves with is not nearly as important as we ramp it up to be, in our own minds. What's more important is how God can use our circumstances – however dire – for His Kingdom and glory.

DIETING DANGERS

There are no regulations curbing radically dubious diets promoted on the internet. This, together with the fact that the human body is a complicated machine, can set you up for disaster. Something that works for a tanned and toned fitness blogger may not work for you. It could even do more harm than good. Hormones, genetics and metabolism vary between people. What gives one person a smaller waist size might put you in hospital. Despite the ever-changing dietary news cycle, what really matters in a healthy diet has *not* changed: Eat more real food; eat less junk food.

SMALL AND SENSATIONAL

And though your beginning was small,
your latter days will be very great.
Job 8:7, ESV

We tend to think of miracles as enormous and obvious and startling. And sure, many miracles are. But actually, there are miracles all around us, all the time. God causes small, incremental growth miracles that aren't necessarily obvious, conspicuous or tangible.

He refreshes us and rejuvenates us in ways that would be impossible by the worldly order of things. He causes spiritual growth – even *physical* growth, restoration and revitalization – despite bodily ageing. In God's Kingdom, you're never a has-been. If you have the indwelling Holy Spirit, you've still got it going on.

GROWING YOUNG

By staying active, you're growing and preserving your brain's cognitive function. A healthy brain is a brain that is full of dense, healthy cellular connections, and exercise has a direct impact on developing this neural network. Regular exercise improves your brain neuron function, increases blood flow to your brain cells and promotes the production of proteins and growth factors that support those cells involved in higher level thinking tasks. Even as you get older, your brain can remodel and re-grow. Exercise promotes this process by boosting old neuron repair and new neuron formation, a process called neurogenesis.

SAD ISN'T BAD

The Lord is close to the brokenhearted;
He rescues those whose spirits are crushed.
Psalm 34:18, NLT

God created the full spectrum of human emotion. Sadness isn't a sin. It's appropriate to feel sad, if say, your puppy drowns, or a friend snubs you, or your kid is admitted to hospital for a battery of tests with possibly life-threatening results.

But perhaps your sadness has been *strangling* of late. The more you tell yourself to get a grip, the more your grip slips. Sit quietly with the thought today that God knows, and God's near. Jesus was 'acquainted with sorrows' (Isaiah 53:3). That means He *gets it.* And He's *got you.*

SOAK UP THE SUN

There's a link between sunshine and your mood. People who put up with long, dark winters in the Northern Hemisphere often suffer from a syndrome known as Seasonal Affective Disorder, with a most appropriate acronym: SAD. This is a type of depression that is directly related to changes in the seasons, specifically shorter days and longer nights. Sunlight contains ultraviolet light, which is absorbed through your skin and produces vitamin D. This in turn boosts your immune system, keeps bones strong and healthy, and promotes happy hormone production – like serotonin, whose levels are directly related to the duration of exposure to bright sunlight. Without sufficient exposure to light, hormones that regulate mood dip, with a direct impact on how you feel.

STILL THE SUN

So the sun stood still and the moon stayed in place until
the nation of Israel had defeated its enemies …
There has never been a day like this one before or since,
when the LORD answered such a prayer.
Surely the LORD fought for Israel that day!

Joshua 10:13-14, NLT

It's amazing that the God who has the power to make the sun stand still lives inside of us. It's highly unlikely that God will cause the sun to stand still for you, at lunchtime today. But He's already done something far greater.

He split history in half by sending His Son to break into the darkness and bring a brilliant light that has never gone out, and will never go out.

As He did for the Israelites in Joshua's time, *surely the LORD fought for you that day!*

SUNSHINE ON A PLATE?

Only a few foods, like fatty fish and mushrooms, contain vitamin D, and generally in very small amounts. Nothing beats the real deal of the sun's rays! Obviously roasting your skin in the midday sun isn't included in the health benefits list. The key is to get *some* sunshine, not all of it! UV light is at its most dangerous between 10 AM and 3 PM, so aim to get outside before or after then. If you do need to venture outdoors over lunch, use your sunscreen, and keep in mind that it only takes around 10 minutes of sunshine exposure to reap its health benefits.

FOOD FOR THOUGHT

Busting the post-lunch energy slump

After lunch your head begins buzzing, your eyes droop and your desk top starts to look cozy ... the morning surge of hormones has petered out, and some degree of brain boredom has set in. What to do?

✤ *Coffee is great; water is even better.* Getting up to refill your glass regularly also gives you a break and gets you off your chair for a bit of exercise.

✤ *Do a lunchtime workout.* This can actually increase productivity enough to counteract the time away from the office. Think a chocolate would do a better job? One study compared people who ate a chocolate bar to those who walked briskly for ten minutes. The chocolate-eaters felt tenser in the hour afterwards, while the walkers were *less* tense and had higher energy levels for two hours post their refreshing saunter.

✤ *Choose a window seat at the office.* Daylight, fresh air and a natural view all boost alertness. Spruce up your desk with some plants. Simply looking at the color green sparks inventiveness!

✤ *Do your most interesting work during the sleepiest time of day (typically 2-3 PM).* Or, divide up your tasks to maximize a balance between variety and productivity. Studies suggest that concentration on anything wanes after an hour (and is pitiful at ninety minutes).

✤ *Take five minutes to make an I-was-thinking-of-you call to someone you love,* it'll reinvigorate you. Kill two birds with one stone and have a giggle while you're at it – laughter is a proven stress buster and will also boost energy levels.

TIME TO REFLECT ...

We need to remember to take our vitamins or meds. We also need to *remember what our Heavenly Father has said to us*. Is there a promise of God you tend to forget – and when you forget it, you tend to freak out? Write it down. Then write it out again in different words. Like, 'God will provide.' Then, 'My Father is rich in wisdom and wealth. He knows all my needs.'

Whether or not you'll get to spend some time in the sun today, could you journal all the ways you've seen the light of God shining through in your circumstances this week?

_____

_____

_____

_____

_____

_____

_____

_____

_____

_____

_____

UNCHANGEABLE

Jesus Christ is the same yesterday and today and forever.
Hebrews 13:8, NIV

One of the great ironies of the faith is that the changeless God, changes us. He's immutable – always the same, utterly consistent, completely reliable, never fickle or flighty. And it's that unrelenting perfection that transforms us into holier – sometimes unrecognizable – versions of ourselves. Hopefully, people who knew us long ago, and know us now, are saying things like, 'You've changed ...'

Because we're not supposed to be the same person we were ten years ago, three months ago, or yesterday. Even as we lean more and more into the unchanging character of Christ, our character should be shifting and miraculously morphing to look more and more like His.

TRANSFORMING TASTE BUDS

News flash: none of us were born loving pizza! Taste preferences tweak over time thanks to repeated exposure. So, when it comes to making healthier choices, the good news is that repeated exposure to healthier options is the obvious solution. Start by gradually reducing processed foods in your diet and replacing them with fresh food. Healthy food is *actually* tastier than takeaways. The more of it you eat, the more of it you'll enjoy. Plus, eating better makes you feel better which makes you want to eat better. All *you* need to do is take the first step!

ESSENTIAL

Yes, everything else is worthless when compared with the infinite value of knowing Christ Jesus my Lord. For His sake I have discarded everything else, counting it all as garbage, so that I could gain Christ and be found in Him, not having a righteousness of my own that comes from the law, but that which is through faith in Christ – the righteousness that comes from God on the basis of faith.

Philippians 3:9, NIV

Omegas are a type of fat your body needs to function optimally. Unlike other fats, omegas aren't simply used for energy, or stored. They're biologically active, playing important roles in virtually all bodily systems, specifically your skin, brain and heart.

Our bodies can't produce omegas-3 and 6 – yet they are *essential* fatty acids. In the same way, Paul points out that we can't produce righteousness on our own – yet it's *essential* for pleasing God in this life, and spending eternity with Him in the next. As much as we might like to think we're self-sufficient, we have to depend entirely on God to fill us and form us and make us essentially righteous.

🍎 FUNDAMENTAL FATS

Omegas, fish oils, fatty acids … What exactly are they? Are they all created equal? And why do we need them? Our bodies *can* produce omega-9, but *can't* produce omegas-3 and 6 – which makes them essential fatty acids, because they need to come from our diets (foods like oily fish, nuts, seeds and avocados) or less ideally, from supplements. In essence, it's essential that you're getting the essentials.

POWERFUL PACKAGE

Here are some of the parts God has appointed for the church:
first are apostles, second are prophets, third are teachers,
then those who do miracles, those who have the gift of healing,
those who can help others, those who have the gift of leadership ...

1 Corinthians 12:28, NLT

If churches were only full of leaders casting vision but never initiating or following through, Kingdom work would never gain traction. If churches were only full of teachers expounding Scripture but never loving their cities or communities, few people would come to know Jesus.

You may feel as if your spiritual gift is insignificant. You may feel unnoticed, unimportant, and un-influential. But God has put together the unique packaging of *you*, for unique purpose. You have a distinctive role to play. *Please offer the world your gifts.*

Even today, ask God for an opportunity to use what He's put inside you, to bless someone else. The gesture may feel inconsequential to you – but you never know how God will use it in someone else's life. Your drop might be another's ocean.

AMAZING OMEGAS

Omega-3s fight inflammation, and also balance out omega-6s, which are *pro*-inflammatory, and primarily an energy source. Omega-9s regulate your immune system and improve heart health, and are considered non-essential because your body can produce them – provided you have the right balance of 3 and 6. Omegas-3, 6 and 9 play unique and significant roles, working together for a healthier you!

STEADYING YOUR STRENGTHS

Then Simon Peter drew a sword and slashed off
the right ear of Malchus, the high priest's slave.

John 18:10, NLT

Peter loved his Master. He was incensed at how Jesus was being treated – enraged at the accusations leveled against Him. And so he reacted! On the Enneagram test, Peter would've been a 6. The loyalist: committed, security-oriented, engaging, responsible, anxious and suspicious. In this situation, he over-played his strengths. His passion and zeal were good, right and beautiful and God used them to build His church (Matthew 16:18). But on that night in the garden, Jesus needed to reign in those strengths, chastising Peter: 'Put your sword away!' (John 18:11).

God put strengths in you to bless others and glorify Him. Ask Him to help you see with honest eyes where and how you may need to bring those strengths back into balance.

OIL EQUILIBRIUM

Processed foods make modern diets extremely omega-6-heavy, which fuels your inflammatory fires. The ratio of omega-6s to 3s should be some-where between 2:1 and 4:1 (not 30:1, as is common!) It's possible to get the omega-6-to-3 balance right, by making dietary changes, starting by excluding highly processed seed and vegetable oils, and replacing them with healthier options like olive or avo oil. It's also a great idea to eat oily fish twice a week, but if you're not a seafood fan, a good fish oil omega-3 supplement will do the trick.

FERTILE HOPE

'Sing, barren woman, you who never bore a child;
burst into song, shout for joy, you who were never in labor;
because more are the children of the desolate woman
than of her who has a husband,' says the LORD.

Isaiah 54:1, NIV

We meet several women in Scripture crushed by the sorrow of infertility: Sarah, Hannah, Elizabeth and others. They cried out to God authentically, transparently, vulnerably. And He showed compassion for each of them, meeting them right where they were at, because His heart is ineffably tender towards women longing to love babies of their own. It's equally tender towards men and the babies they've loved, lost or longed for: like Abraham, David, John.

If you're in this place of pain, please know that whether or not your story ends in miracles, God is near, and He is love.

POLYCYSTIC OVARIAN SYNDROME

Every pregnancy is a miracle. Even couples in prime baby-making condition only have a 20% chance of falling pregnant in any given cycle. A common factor influencing fertility amongst women is polycystic ovarian syndrome (PCOS). Follicles in the ovaries release mature eggs that normally travel to the uterus for fertilization. In women with PCOS, immature follicles bunch together, forming large cysts. The eggs mature within the bunched follicles – which don't break open to release them. So women with PCOS miss their menstrual periods, or have them infrequently. Enlarged ovaries containing cysts can be detected by ultrasound, so don't miss your annual one-on-one with your gynecologist.

FOOD FOR THOUGHT

Winning the PCOS war:

PCOS can mean more than just knowing when to plan a romantic evening. The condition greatly increases your risk of developing diabetes and premature cardiovascular disease including heart attack and stroke. Many women with PCOS are insulin resistant, with 30-40% having pre-diabetes, and 10% having full-blown type 2 diabetes. Polycystic Ovary Syndrome has also been linked to weight gain, which further increases the risk for chronic disease.

The most effective method of treatment of PCOS is lifestyle modification. Paying attention to the foods you eat and your activity levels may help you offset the effects of PCOS.

- Stay in a healthy weight range. Relatively modest weight loss can reduce both insulin and androgen levels, and may restore ovulation.

- Because of the strong relationship between PCOS and diabetes, dietary choices are important both for weight loss and blood sugar control. A crash diet is an absolute no-no as that will just send your hormones spiraling in all the wrong directions, but a low-carb diet might be a good option.

- Exercise is beneficial not only for weight loss, but also for blood sugar control, better sleeping patterns, stress management, heart health and menstrual regularity.

- Birth control pills can regulate your cycle, levelling out your hormone merry-go-rounds. Obviously if you're trying to conceive, being on birth control is counterproductive. Your doc may give you something that targets ovulation specifically. If you're not responding to meds, there are also surgical options to induce ovulation.

TIME TO REFLECT ...

*Father God, thank You for the way
You designed families to create brand new humans
within whole and wholesome, safe and stable home-havens.
I pray for the men and women battling infertility.
You know the deep longings of their hearts.
I daresay You placed them there.
Satisfy them with the blessing of new life,
for the sake of Your Kingdom and glory.
Amen.*

ENOUGH ALREADY

So let us stop going over the basic teachings
about Christ again and again. Let us go on instead
and become mature in our understanding. Surely we don't need
to start again with the fundamental importance of repenting
from evil deeds and placing our faith in God.

Hebrews 6:1, NLT

The writer of Hebrews is issuing a call to maturity. It seems the folks he's writing to are stuck in a hamster wheel of faith fundamentals. They're spinning round and round – covering the same theological terrain – and not moving on.

Maybe you recently met Jesus. Maybe you've known Him for decades. Regardless of where you are in your faith journey, you can always go further. Not one of us ever arrives and you needn't keep on walking the same paths, over and over. Do you dare to allow the Holy Spirit to take you into new territory?

MEANINGLESS MEDS?

Maybe your medicine cabinet is full of the same brand of half-used cough syrups because you tend to stock up on them every time you're sick. What's perhaps more frustrating is that *none of them worked!* There's no evidence showing that cough medicines are more effective than placebos in shortening the length of time you have a cough. Instead, be patient. The average cold and flu-related cough can linger for 18 days. Stay hydrated, get enough sleep and enjoy having a valid reason to spend time on the couch!

COMPULSORY CARE

The LORD is my Shepherd, I lack nothing.
He makes me lie down in green pastures,
He leads me beside quiet waters, He refreshes my soul.
He guides me along the right paths for His name's sake.

Psalm 23:1-3, NIV

Note that the reason David (the psalmist) lacks nothing is because the shepherd *makes* him lie down. He *leads* him beside quiet waters and He *refreshes* and *guides* David. The scene is tranquil and comforting, but these are all strong, active verbs – because God knows that we need help to rest and regroup.

Do you resist the promptings of God to slow down, or pause to think, or rest? What are you afraid will happen, if you suspend the crazy pace of your life to breathe deeply for a minute, and listen to the Shepherd?

STANDING SLOWLY

Sometimes when you get up from your desk or hop out of bed, you're met with dizziness and blotchy vision. It's called orthostatic hypotension, and is caused by a sudden drop in your blood pressure. When you're sitting or lying, it's easy for your heart to circulate blood throughout your body. As soon as you stand up, gravity sends your blood to your ankles. Your heart and blood vessels need to react quickly to ensure your brain gets all the blood it needs. It takes only a few seconds for these corrective measures to kick in, and while your body waits, you feel dizzy. Better to stand up slowly … Jumping out of bed is overrated anyway!

HEY, SOUL

Why, my soul, are you downcast?
Why so disturbed within me? Put your hope in God,
for I will yet praise Him, my Savior and my God.

Psalm 43:5, NIV

We probably don't speak to our own souls enough. We complain a lot. And we're quick to tell other people how to live their lives – but we're slower to take our own advice to heart.

Maybe this idea freaks you out, but what if you set some phone reminders, to *address your soul*, once or twice a day? The songwriter of Psalm 43 demonstrates how we might give ourselves a talking to. He actively engages his own mind and emotions in introspective dialogue. He's taking his thoughts captive, as Paul instructs us to do (2 Corinthians 10:5).

He's rallying himself to take his focus off whatever depresses him, and instead hook his hopes onto God, where they belong.

 ## MOOD BOOSTING FOR FITNESS MINIMALISTS

Research has found that simply getting up and moving can improve your mood and reduce feelings of depression. In fact, light physical activity showed the *biggest* emotional benefit, compared to moderate and high intensity exercise. This is good news, because if you're suffering from depression, one of the hardest things to do is whip on your active wear and head to the gym. Just *doing something* is way better than doing nothing – especially since going for a leisurely walk, gardening or doing Thai Chi in a lift – can lift your mood!

THOUGHT FEAST

And now, dear brothers and sisters, one final thing.
Fix your thoughts on what is true, and honorable,
and right, and pure, and lovely, and admirable.
Think about things that are excellent and worthy of praise.
Philippians 4:8, NLT

To be devoted, joy-filled Jesus-followers, we need to engage our brains, not just our emotions. Just as we need to remind our souls to *put* our hope in God (Psalm 43:5), we need to remind our brains to *fix* our thoughts on all things worthy and worthwhile.

What food are you offering to your thoughts? We have a choice: to feast on rich, wholesome truth, or the meager pickings of social media feeds. Fatten your focus and your feelings at the truth banquet God has prepared for you.

FEARSOME FATS AND WHERE TO FIND THEM

They say we should avoid all fat, as it contributes to weight gain and high cholesterol. Who is "they?" And what do they know!? Dietary fat is essential for optimal functioning. Fats are an energy source and important building blocks of our cells. They help with absorption of the fat-soluble vitamins A, D, E and K and play a role in blood clotting and wound healing. Our brain alone is made up of 60% fat. So it's safe to say we can't live *without* fat! Avoid trans fats at all costs (the kind in packaged, processed foods), but go gung ho for *good* fats like avocados, extra virgin olive oil, coconut oil, eggs, cheese, fatty fish, nuts and seeds.

SEEING GREEN

Now Israel loved Joseph more than any other of his sons,
because he was the son of his old age.
And he made him a robe of many colors.
But when his brothers saw that their father loved him
more than all his brothers, they hated him
and could not speak peacefully to him.
Genesis 37:3-4, ESV

J oseph's colorful robe became a suffocating cloak of jealousy for his brothers. It was the tangible proof that their father loved Joseph more than he loved them. The cloak was many colors; they only saw green.

But the robe was *actually beautiful*.

Has someone beautiful in your life become loathsome and ugly to you, because of jealousy? Could you step back – and simply appreciate their beauty for what it is? Jealousy is really a disgruntlement with God. You're mad because of the colors He's splashed across another's life. Trust Him to pick the paint palette of *your* destiny.

 ## SHADES OF GRAY?

Some think if you're color blind, you only see black, white and gray. Color blindness is more appropriately called color vision deficiency. It's caused by a malfunction of one, or all, of the three types of cone cells in the eye. Most folks with the condition struggle to distinguish between shades (rather than not seeing color at all). To check whether you have color vision deficiency, see your optometrist. You might try using color-filtering lenses, which correct the balance of signals sent from objects to your three sets of cones.

FOOD FOR THOUGHT

Arthritis isn't a single disease, but rather an umbrella term for over a hundred different conditions characterized by inflammation. Inflammation is your body's response to outside threats like stress, infection, or toxic chemicals. When your immune system senses one of these dangers, it responds by activating proteins and sending fighter cells to the danger area, which causes inflammation. When it comes to your joints, all these extra blood and immune cells start to cause irritation, and over time, permanent damage. The end result? Pain and stiffness. While arthritis can't be cured, there are certain things that you can do to ease, and often prevent, discomfort.

Firstly, exercise. It might seem strange to suggest movement when you're feeling sore, but during gentle exercise, your body releases substances that lower inflammation. Exercise also strengthens the structures around your joints. Some say if you run, the constant jarring on your joints increases your risk of developing arthritis by wearing away healthy cartilage. Not true! You don't have to hang up your running shoes! Provided your knees are in good shape, you have no higher risk of arthritis than someone who doesn't run. In fact, evidence suggests runners may have a *lower* risk.

Secondly, watch what you eat. Your body sees high carbohydrate and processed foods as alien life forms and responds by releasing substances that increase inflammation. By swapping out processed foods for fresh food, your whole body benefits, not just your joints.

TIME TO REFLECT …

Glance back at what you've read this week. Is God nudging you to move on from needlessly going through the (same) motions in a particular area of your life? Is He commanding you to rest? Do you feel convicted to speak strength to your soul and fortify your thoughts with robust truth? Has your vision become jaded by jealousy? Come, unedited, to your Father. He's waiting.

_____

_____

_____

_____

_____

_____

_____

_____

_____

_____

_____

_____

_____

NIGHTMARE

You will not fear the terror of night,
nor the arrow that flies by day ...
Psalm 91:5, NIV

An estimated 10-50% of kids have nightmares terrifying enough to disturb their parents. Children's nightmares may stem from listening to a scary story, watching a movie, or feeling anxious during the day because of school, or a death in the family. But 85% of adults have nightmares too.

Whether you're having bad dreams, or whether you're lying awake haunted by a memory, or petrified by what may or may not happen in your imminent future: your Heavenly Father promises to 'cover you with His feathers. He will shelter you with His wings. His faithful promises are your armor and protection' (Psalm 91:4). Give Him your fears – enormous or seemingly insignificant.

MONSTERS UNDER THE BED

While we know for certain monsters don't exist, dreaming is an uncertain area of neuroscience and psychology that's hard to study, since each person's dream world is inherently subjective and hard to document. It seems, however, that physical aggression and fear are what make up most of our dreams. Once we enter REM sleep, when dreaming takes place, our brain works differently to how it does during the day. Parts of our brain slow down; others speed up. We think in pictures, symbols and emotions that often incorporate aspects of our waking lives. Nightmares occur during REM sleep. Certain medications, daily stresses, a scary series, a traumatic event or anything interfering with good quality sleep could all be considered nightmare triggers.

SWEET DREAMS

I lay down and slept, yet I woke up in safety,
for the LORD was watching over me.

Psalm 3:5, NLT

It's hard to fight fear in the dark hours before the dawn when thoughts race fast and furious beyond any apparent hope to control them. If you're battling insomnia and anxiety, or if the responsibilities you bear render nighttime silence unbearable, then maybe instead of staring at the ceiling you might try preaching a bit of gospel truth to yourself.

The Lord is watching over you. He promises to guide you with His wisdom and sustain you with His strength. Paul reminds Timothy that, 'God has not given us a spirit of fear and timidity, but of power, love, and self-discipline' (2 Timothy 1:7). Breathe deep and slow, and trust God for sleep.

DEEP SLEEP DIY

For sound sleep, garner good sleep hygiene. Keep a consistent bedtime routine and ensure your room is cool, dark and quiet. Put your day to bed before you put yourself to bed: don't take unresolved fights, bills or spreadsheets under the bedsheets with you. Turn off all gizmos and gadgets at least an hour before you hit the hay. Exhale your stress with some belly breathing, prayer and meditation on Scripture. And avoid nightmare fodder: keep clear of scary series, horror movies and the late news!

FIT FOR LIFE

But grow in the grace and knowledge of our Lord and Savior
Jesus Christ. To Him be glory both now and forever! Amen.

2 Peter 3:18, NIV

You'll have noticed a golden theme-thread throughout this devotional: a healthy lifestyle can be summed up by the three words, *eat*, *move*, and *sleep*.

It sounds simple, because it is. A healthy lifestyle doesn't have to be complicated at all. With the endless tweets, blogs, articles and news reports about *this* diet and *that* exercise routine, it's easy to get caught up in the fine print. Focusing on the details makes you lose sight of the bigger picture, which essentially is:

- ❦ Eat real food
- ❦ Move throughout the day
- ❦ Prioritize sleep

The Christian life is really that simple too. *To know God, and to make Him known.* We do that through feasting on His Word, exercising our spiritual muscles through the disciplines of prayer and serving others, and resting in Him through total surrender.

THE FIRST DAY OF FOREVER

Switching to a healthier lifestyle doesn't happen overnight, nor does it need to happen in a day. You begin by making small changes and smart choices that you can stick with in the long term. And never forget, just because you don't *feel* sick, doesn't make you healthy. That's why making changes *before* you develop a chronic condition is critical. It may be an old maxim, but it's still as true today as it ever was: prevention is better than cure. As a practical example – medication may reduce your risk for a heart attack or stroke, but only healthy choices can eliminate the risk almost entirely.

DEM BONES, DEM DRY BONES

… I was carried away by the Spirit of the LORD to a valley filled with bones. He led me all around among the bones that covered the valley floor. They were scattered everywhere across the ground and were completely dried out. Then He asked me, 'Son of man, can these bones become living people again?' 'O Sovereign LORD,' I replied, 'You alone know the answer to that.'

Ezekiel 37:1-3, NLT

The rest of Ezekiel's living vision unfolds in the subsequent verses of Ezekiel 37.

God vividly illustrates the miracle of salvation: how He takes the dry bones of our disillusionment and the death and destructiveness we've brought upon ourselves and others through our sin – and He renews, revives and totally regenerates us.

No matter how bone weary you are of the life you find yourself inhabiting – *there is always hope.*

CUPPA CALCIUM?

Calcium is the building block of healthy bones. If you're not getting enough calcium from your diet, your body starts to extract it from your bones to supply other organ systems that also require it, like your nervous and cardiovascular system. The average adult needs 1000mg/day of calcium. A cup of milk has around 300mg of calcium, so you'd need 3-4 servings a day. If you're a dairy, spinach or other high-calcium food fan, don't change a thing. As a rule, aim to get your calcium fix from your diet, but if you feel you may be lacking, speak to you doctor about whether a supplement might be an option for you.

MIRACLE IN THE MARROW

Don't be impressed with your own wisdom.
Instead, fear the LORD and turn away from evil.
Then you will have healing for your body
and strength for your bones.

Proverbs 3:7-8, NLT

The beginning of dry bones beginning to walk around in our churches and cities is always humility. It's us coming to God with no delusions of grandeur.

It's us coming to God knowing that our human perspective and insight and understanding is at best very limited, and at worst utterly misguided and bound to let us down.

If we want to see revival in our communities – a strengthening of our bodies and bones – we need to turn away from the intoxication of all things sick and sensational, and acknowledge our total dependence on God's wisdom and ways.

SOAK UP THE STRENGTH

As important as it is to make sure you get enough calcium, it's equally important to make sure you don't lose calcium – and that it is absorbed properly. Calcium can only be absorbed when vitamin D is around, but other things prevent calcium absorption: like salt! Postmenopausal women with a high-salt diet lose more bone minerals than other women of the same age. Many fizzy drinks contain phosphoric acid, which increases calcium excretion in your urine. That spells trouble for anyone at risk for osteoporosis. Caffeine, too, can leach calcium from your bones, but provided your daily intake of calcium is sufficient, you don't have to give up your healthy coffee addiction altogether.

FOOD FOR THOUGHT

Here are some answers to your osteoporosis FAQs!

How does healthy bone differ from osteoporosis?

Healthy bone is strong – about four times as strong as concrete! It has a hard outer shell and a spongy interior. Unlike concrete, bone is living tissue, constantly being broken down and built up in a process known as remodeling. Most of your adult skeleton is replaced about every ten years.

Our body creates new bone faster than it breaks it down until about age 30, when we typically reach peak bone mass. Osteoporosis ensues when new bone creation doesn't keep up with old bone removal. The outer shell of bone becomes thinner, and the inner spongy bone becomes less dense.

What are the symptoms of osteoporosis?

Usually, you're blissfully unaware of any changes to your bones – until you fall. Once your bones have weakened, fractures can happen from falls or bumps that ordinarily wouldn't be considered bone-breaking.

Which lifestyle habits impact bone health?

Smoking! Nicotine and cigarette chemicals upset the hormonal balance that bones need to stay strong, killing off bone-making cells and stimulating bone-breaking cells. Because smoking damages blood vessels, it also damages nerves in toes and feet, which can lead to more falls and delayed recovery. A sedentary lifestyle is also a problem. Mechanical muscle-pull on bone is the only physiological way to stimulate bone formation, so without exercise, bone loss happens faster. Lastly, alcohol directly interferes with the body's ability to absorb calcium – a building block for healthy bones.

TIME TO REFLECT ...

*Lord, give me wisdom to keep my physical bones strong
so I can serve You with robust energy for a long time yet.
Strengthen my spiritual bones too so I can carry the cause,
and carry others, without faltering. I want to be strong
enough to stand where You have me,
for as long as it takes, and strong enough to step into
whatever You're calling me to, when the time is right.
Amen.*

_____

_____

_____

_____

_____

_____

_____

_____

_____

_____

SLOWED BY SIN

Get rid of all bitterness, rage, anger, harsh words,
and slander, as well as all types of evil behavior.
Instead, be kind to each other, tenderhearted,
forgiving one another, just as God
through Christ has forgiven you.

Ephesians 4:31-32, NLT

In a school fun run, my son kept stopping to wait for his (slower) (larger) friend to catch up. As a result, he didn't run his fastest time. It was nice of him to wait for his friend, but it made me think how we slow others down, spiritually, when we carry the excess weight of 'bitterness, rage, anger, harsh words, and slander ...'

Lugging around unforgiveness will make us heavy, slow and lethargic, spiritually and emotionally. We're the ones who suffer most. Sin keeps us from running our best times. But because our sin affects those around us, it may keep others from running their best times too.

JELLY BELLY?

Fat that lies around your belly is more harmful to your health than fat anywhere else on your body. It produces its own set of hormones that change how your body responds to insulin, which can increase your risk of developing diabetes. Over time, hormones released from your belly fat increase your risk of high blood pressure, heart attack and stroke. Grab a tape measure! For women, a waist circumference of more than 80cm is on the risky side. For men, it's anything more than 94cm. Blast off belly fat by being active, today!

PUT OFF, PUT ON

You were taught, with regard to your former way of life,
to put off your old self, which is being corrupted
by its deceitful desires; to be made new in the attitude
of your minds; and to put on the new self,
created to be like God in true righteousness and holiness.

Ephesians 4:22-24, NIV

The Christian life isn't a logical formula, because Jesus *plus nothing* leads to abundant life in this world and eternal life in the next.

But if you need a practical process for *how* you might live that abundant life, then Paul's instruction to the Ephesians is helpful: replace your old behavior with new behavior.

Putting on the 'new self' leads to revival, revitalization and refreshing. And we're holistic beings, so a change of heart on the insides of you leads to a radiant change of face on the outsides of you (Psalm 34:5).

REPLACE TO REJUVENATE?

It's one thing to replace bad habits with good ones. But should we also be replacing our hormones? And will it make us live longer? Some hormone levels change as we age, but no research shows that hormone therapies directly add years to life. Your doc may well advise hormone replacement therapy, but this would be for known hormone deficiencies, rather than anti-ageing.

DAY 297

GROWING GOD'S WAY

It's not important who does the planting,
or who does the watering.
What's important is that God makes the seed grow.
1 Corinthians 3:7, NLT

It's possible we think a bit too much of ourselves and the work we do for God's Kingdom. We take pride in our gifts – gifts that actually have nothing to do with us because they're to be used for others, not for us, and because, 'What do you have that God hasn't given you?' (1 Corinthians 4:7).

We also need reminding (often) that *God* is responsible for any fruit harvested from the use of our gifts, *not us*. He's the author of all life. He grows people and plants and He births volcanic islands in the ocean and He causes people who love Him to grow more and more into the likeness of His Son. Let's never take credit for growth-work we aren't capable of accomplishing.

GROW FIGURE

Growth hormone is made by your pituitary gland at the base of your brain, and plays a fundamental role in growth, development and organ tissue maintenance. There's evidence-based support for growth hormone supplementation for children who don't produce enough growth hormone of their own. But there's no conclusive evidence to suggest that taking growth hormone can slow down ageing in any way. Some studies show promising results supporting the use of growth hormone to increase muscle mass, but there are lots of unanswered questions about potential side effects too. The research continues!

LIVE EXPECTANTLY

So He will do to me whatever He has planned.
He controls my destiny.
Job 23:14, NLT

Someone inflexibly stuck to a selfish agenda might find this kind of truth irritating and stifling. But really, it's incredibly liberating. We can relax in the love of a Father so very strong, and so very capable, to achieve His best plans for us. We aren't passive in the process of God working out His will and way through our lives; but it takes some of the stress out of feverishly trying to control outcomes we're incapable of controlling.

Today might be your last day. Just sayin'. But you needn't get all Chicken Licken about it – worrying the sky's going to fall on your head. Just make the wisest choices at your disposal, with the available knowledge, and eagerly wait on God for the rest.

LIFE EXPECTANCY

Vitamins A, C and E are currently at the helm of anti-ageing research. Studies show that centenarians have a unique profile in which high levels of vitamin A and E are linked to their extreme longevity. Of course, diet and exercise are also critical to long life, as are prioritizing sleep, seeing your doctor regularly, maintaining good friendships (this alone can increase longevity by 32%), and getting up off that couch! One study found that each hour people spent sitting watching TV after age 25 was linked to a deduction of 22 minutes from their overall life expectancy.

TENACITY IN THE TEDIUM

Whatever your hand finds to do,
do it with all your might …
Ecclesiastes 9:10, NIV

In our culture of instant gratification, we're quick to give up on something if the results aren't immediate. Is your marriage tough, and not what you expected it would be? Get a new one! Has your kid *not* turned into a perfect human after one lecture? Put her in therapy!

Our spiritual attention span has become so short that we're unwilling to put in the days and decades of spiritual discipline necessary to yield a crop of righteousness. Perhaps we need to start reminding ourselves and each other that it's ok to focus on just one thing – even one mundane, possibly boring thing – and simply keep at it with all our might, for as long as it takes.

THE BEST OF BOREDOM

Boredom is the frustrating experience of wanting, but being unable, to engage in satisfying activity. In other words, a bored person can't engage the internal (thoughts or feelings) or external (environmental) factors necessary to produce a gratifying pastime. Digital technologies have enabled constant engagement, yet it now seems we feel lost and bored in any moment that's without distraction or entertainment. Some people thrive on this constant stream of info but others simply don't. The key is finding a balance between chronic boredom and constant engagement. It's that balance that can be beneficial for our minds and even our productivity.

FOOD FOR THOUGHT

It doesn't have to be hell to be healthy!

Jumping on and off the diet bus is neither good for your health nor your waistline. Hitting the healthy path doesn't have to happen in one day either. Make small, permanent changes that you can live with until they can become habit, and then pick another small change to tackle. Do the best you can with what you have, but don't forget to live a bit too. Don't feel guilty about a massive meal or a high-carb weekend. Pick right back up where you left off as soon as you can and keep heading in the right direction.

What then shall we eat?

Nutrition is a rapidly changing science, with new evidence emerging all the time. The following dietary strategies for maintaining health and preventing disease are strongly supported by the peer-reviewed scientific literature, i.e. this is what the experts agree on:

Recommended

- A diet rich in non-starchy vegetables, especially green leafy vegetables
- Moderate intake of whole grain sources of carbohydrates
- A diet high in fiber
- Dietary fats which are rich in omega-3 fatty acids and mono-unsaturated fatty acids
- Adequate protein intake from a variety of sources, including fish, meat, poultry, eggs and nuts
- Regular dairy consumption (milk, yoghurt, cheese)

Not Recommended

- Sugar-sweetened beverages
- Foods with added sugar
- Highly processed foods and refined carbohydrates
- A diet with a high-glycemic load
- Trans-fats or partially-hydrogenated vegetable fats.

TIME TO REFLECT ...

Do you tend to look for a quick fix or a silver bullet to solve your fears or to fast track past your frustrations? If things aren't panning out the way you hoped in one or more areas of your life, what truth do you need to tell yourself about God?

_____

_____

_____

_____

_____

_____

_____

_____

_____

_____

_____

_____

_____

JUST BE

We are merely moving shadows, and all our busy rushing ends
in nothing. We heap up wealth, not knowing who will spend it.
Psalm 39:6, NLT

Waiting on God is hard. It feels monkish, impracticable, boring and counterproductive. It makes us feel awkward and fidgety and irritable.

But sometimes, for good ideas to flow, we have to stop thinking for a moment. At least, stop thinking of the next thing we have to *do* – and try to just *be* for a bit. Elijah took a break in the shade to regain strength to carry on (1 Kings 19:5). This wasn't a waste of time; it was essential. God healed and restored him. David took breaks from shepherding to write songs. Jesus took breaks for downtime with His disciples, and for prayer (Luke 5:16).

If all your 'busy rushing' is getting you nowhere, create space in your schedule this week – *to just be*.

BOREDOM, OR SPRINGBOARD?

Passive activities, like attending work meetings, can lead to *greater* creativity, because being bored promotes daydreaming, which in turn allows us to make fresh, innovative connections. It's an unlikely concept in our workaholic world, but occasional, passing (not chronic) boredom could result in creative breakthroughs. On the other hand, if you're feeling bored more often than not, it could be a sign that your job isn't a good fit, or that you aren't being challenged. This could spark an important conversation with your boss. Boredom may be the catalyst for moving on to bigger and better things!

TODAY DON'T DELAY

Remember what it says: 'Today when you hear His voice,
don't harden your hearts as Israel did when they rebelled.'
Hebrews 3:15, NLT

All over God's Word, He asks us to wait (like in Isaiah 40:31, Psalm 27:13-14, Proverbs 3:5-6, Lamentations 3:25, Psalm 33:20-22 and Psalm 130:5-6). He asks us to wait on Him. To be patient. To be prayerful and cautious and to act with discernment, discretion and wisdom. *Except when it comes to repentance and obedience*. Then, it's in our best interests to *act fast*.

If God is calling to you today – and He is, ever and always – don't delay. You have no idea what blessings hang in the balance. Act fast. Run to Him with your stories and your secrets. He longs to set you free.

ACT F.A.S.T.

A stroke, or brain attack, occurs when part of your brain loses blood supply and stops working. It's a life-or-death medical emergency – so act FAST if you suspect it! F is for FACE: Ask the person to smile. Check for drooping on their face. A is for ARMS: Can the person raise both arms? Can they lift both simultaneously or does one arm drift downward? S is for SPEECH: Ask the person to repeat something. Is their speech slurred or strange? And T is for TIME: Get help immediately. Make a note of when symptoms began. For each minute a stroke goes untreated, a person loses almost two million neurons. The FASTer you act, the better!

HOODWINKED

The serpent was the shrewdest of all the wild animals the LORD God had made. One day he asked the woman, 'Did God really say you must not eat the fruit from any of the trees in the garden?' … 'You won't die!' the serpent replied to the woman.

Genesis 3:1, 4, NLT

Making bad things look good is Satan's ancient trick. You'd think by now we'd have learned, but alas, we still fall for it.

Yet we're never powerless to face the enemy. Pray God would retrain your brain to love the good and the beautiful – as opposed to the dark and the hideous.

Ask Him to replace your heart of stone with a heart of flesh, so you'll love what He loves (Ezekiel 36:26). And pray you'd see as God sees, so you'll recognize the bait-covered hooks of the enemy for what they are, and steer clear.

TRICKED OUT OF TREATS

The foods we crave most are often (nutritionally) the worst. But we *can* train our brains to light up at the sight of healthy nosh! Taste preferences can transform through repeated exposure. So, when it comes to making healthier choices, repetitive exposure to better options is the obvious solution. Also, *think about your habits.* Do you munch something sugary at 3 PM daily to see you through the rest of the afternoon? Besides giving your brain an addictive sugar rush, you're programming a bad habit. Rather shake up your daily routine and avoid the afternoon slump altogether.

THOUGHT REVAMP

Don't copy the behavior and customs of this world,
but let God transform you into a new person by changing
the way you think. Then you will learn to know God's will for you,
which is good and pleasing and perfect.

Romans 12:2, NLT

Paul's words to the Romans are wonderfully hope-crammed. No matter how desperate your situation, there's always a way out because God can 'transform you into a new person by changing the way you think.' No relationship or political situation or financial crisis or educational debacle is beyond redemption. You name it, God can cause it for your good and His glory.

Even if there's absolutely nothing you can do to change your situation, *you* are still in the situation, and God can change *you*. And not just change you.

Transform you into a new person. Never underestimate the power of God in and through you, as you surrender your thinking to Him.

🍎 FOOD MATH

If your diet is more processed than fresh, it'll be super challenging to stop eating processed foods altogether. Move towards health by adding in more fresh produce at every meal. In other words, *add don't subtract*. Because processed food dulls your taste buds, the less of it you eat, the less of it you'll want and the more you'll start appreciating flavors and textures of healthier options. Also, choose healthy foods that *you* like. If you can't palate kale, don't eat it! There are other delicious, equally healthy options.

FAST FOCUS

'But when you fast, comb your hair and wash your face.
Then no one will notice that you are fasting,
except your Father, who knows what you do in private.
And your Father, who sees everything, will reward you.'

Matthew 6:17-18, NLT

Jesus doesn't say, 'If you fast …' He says, 'When you fast …' He assumes this spiritual discipline is part of our lives. We don't *have* to fast, to score points with God. If we were all about earning our salvation, Jesus needn't have died. But God knows how easily distracted we are. He knows that denying ourselves something (whether it's a particular meal or food item, or a series you're watching) is a great way to focus our spiritual attention, and remind us to pray.

Jesus also knows how vain we can be, so He makes it clear that fasting isn't about impressing people. He encourages His disciples to *hide* their hunger. Only God needs to know.

ON AGAIN, OFF AGAIN

Done correctly, intermittent fasting (*consciously* skipping a meal) can lead to weight loss, better glucose control, lowered diabetes risk, improved concentration, and increased energy levels. When *feasting*, your body gets its readily-available energy from what you eat – rather than from stored fat. Once your cells have had their fill, insulin stockpiles leftover glucose as fat. When *fasting*, your body pulls energy from fat stores. Intermittent fasting essentially makes cells more sensitive to insulin, teaching your body to use food more efficiently, and to burn fat for fuel.

FOOD FOR THOUGHT

To fast, or not to fast?

Before you consider fasting, consider this:

- *Hunger.* If you normally eat every three hours, your body will get hungry every three hours. Once you retrain your body *not* to expect food all day every day (or first thing in the morning), these side-effects become less of an issue.

- *Constipation.* Less going in means less coming out! Your body should readjust fairly quickly.

- *Headaches and dizziness.* These are common but disappear as your body adapts.

The real key is to make smart food choices when you *do* eat. Nutrient dense options, including nuts, eggs, cheese, green veggies and protein are your best choices, because these don't cause any radical blood sugar changes that also cause your appetite to spike.

Also, fasting isn't for everyone. Don't fast if you are:

- Underweight

- Pregnant or breastfeeding

- Under 18 (you're still growing!)

- Suffering from an existing condition (e.g. diabetes) or taking chronic medication.

Chat to a doc before plunging into intermittent fasting. Also, changing up your diet in this way requires a fair bit of willpower. Don't fool yourself that by skipping breakfast you'll be able to catch up by eating a loaf of bread for lunch! Ensure your meals continue to be balanced, regardless of when you eat them.

TIME TO REFLECT ...

*God, give me good ideas of how I might fast,
to focus unswervingly on You. Then, steer my thoughts
towards what I should be praying about.
I want to commit myself entirely to Your will,
Your way, in Your strength, and for Your glory.
As I seek You, impress Your will upon my heart and mind.
Amen.*

FEARLESS AND FREE

In my distress I prayed to the LORD,
and the LORD answered me and set me free.
The LORD is for me, so I will have no fear.
What can mere people do to me?
Psalm 118:5-6, NLT

Whether you're facing exams or a crushing work deadline, stress can make you sick. We know stress can be *good* – promoting focus and hard work. But unmanaged, it can lead to anxiety, tears, panic attacks, sleepless nights, colds and flu. There are some practical things you can do to boost your immune system in pressured times – read on! – but start by boosting your spiritual immunity.

From the midst of the overwhelming demands you face, *pray*. Take it from the psalmist who had been there and done that: God will answer you, and set you free, because He's *for* you. You needn't fear the pressure, or the people imposing it.

ALL SYSTEMS GO

Your immune system is exactly that: a *system*, not a single entity. For *your* system to function well, your first line of defense is a healthy lifestyle. That means, no smoking (which is *not* a stress-reliever – it actually fosters heightened anxiety levels). Rather, sleep better and exercise more, and focus on getting enough vitamin C as well as fat soluble vitamins A, D and K and the minerals selenium and zinc. Lastly, washing your hands (with soap!) holds the record for being the most effective germ-spreader preventer.

SMART

Their purpose is to teach people wisdom and discipline,
to help them understand the insights of the wise.
Their purpose is to teach people to live disciplined
and successful lives, to help them do what is right, just, and fair.
Proverbs 1:2-3, NLT

Education is an enormous priority for most families and societies, and so it should be. Yet we've all known extremely intelligent, highly educated people *who don't live well*. They've accumulated knowledge – but very little wisdom.

Even as you're studying for exams or up-skilling yourself at the office or online, pray God would increase your *heart* knowledge: your understanding of His will and His ways and His plans and priorities for the human race and the planet He designed for us to live on. Pray God would maximize the brainpower He's given you, for His glory and the good of others.

MUNCHING FOR MEMORY

Your brain weighs around 1.4kg – a fraction of your overall body weight, yet it gobbles up a third of your daily energy intake. This myriad of neural connections needs lots of fuel! For your brain to function at its cognitive best, it needs healthy blood flow to deliver oxygen and nutrients, and healthy neural pathways to ensure messages are passed freely between each connection. The foods you eat can either help or hinder these processes. Steak and eggs are excellent brain foods, but if you want a brilliant brain, add fish, nuts, avo, olive oil, green veggies and berries to that mix.

SHAKEN AND STIRRED

The churning inside me never stops;
days of suffering confront me.
Job 30:27, NIV

Job's description of how he's experiencing stress is so vivid, so apt. Maybe your responsibilities right now – or the decisions you're wrestling with – have you ceaselessly churning on the inside. The soul-noise of all that churning can drown out reasonable, rational thought, and can definitely affect your memory and efficiency.

Find one minute today (go into a bathroom stall at the office if there's no other place to be alone) and stand still, with your eyes closed. This needn't be weird. Just allow the rushing of your thoughts to settle, and still. Don't try to solve anything. Just be. If you *must* think – think this simple prayer lifted from Frances Ridley Havergal's ancient hymn: *Take my life and let it be, ever only all for Thee.*

🍎 SIT, SIP, CHEW ...

Some simple interventions can have a significant impact on your brain function and memory. Like, sit and be still. Mindful meditation improves concentration and reduces stress, which benefits memory. Likewise, coffee significantly improves memory retention over 24 hours and enhances glucose control and blood flow, both vital for memory. So by all means, relish that cappuccino! But note: we're talking *coffee, not caffeine.* Caffeine tablets and energy drinks carry uninvited health risks. An alternative to coffee is chewing gum. It improves focus, by increasing oxygen intake and activity in your hippocampus, which boosts memory and creates stronger connections in your brain.

PEACE OUT

'I am leaving you with a gift – peace of mind and heart.
And the peace I give is a gift the world cannot give.
So don't be troubled or afraid.'

John 14:27, NLT

Peace of mind and heart was Jesus' parting gift to His followers. Clearly, it was important to Him that His friends didn't suffer from stress and anxiety. He wasn't promising them an easy, pain-free life – but He was offering them a *peaceful* one.

Because peace is one of those paradoxical states of being that we can experience internally no matter what kind of chaos reigns around us. Jesus explains that we won't find peace in anything on offer in the world. Peace comes from Him alone, and it comes from knowing, as the psalmist says, that God is 'the source of all my joy' (Psalm 43:4). Could you bring your tears and your tired thoughts to your King today, and trust Him for peace?

BURNT-OUT BRAIN?

Like your body, your brain gets tired. Mental exhaustion is a thing. If you realize your brain is in an energy slump, get up and move. That'll send a rush of oxygen and nutrients to weary brain cells. Next, nosh some nutrient-dense brain food for all-day fueling. Finally, take a mental health break. Whether it's a mini-break or a week away, time off is essential to fighting mental fatigue. Even on your busiest day, make sure you take a lunch break – or just ten mindful minutes to breathe and gather your thoughts.

LORD OF THE FEAST

'The wedding feast is ready, and the guests I invited
aren't worthy of the honor. Now go out to the street corners
and invite everyone you see.' So the servants brought
in everyone they could find, good and bad alike,
and the banquet hall was filled with guests.

Matthew 22:8-10, NLT

This story is about a king who threw a massive party for his son's wedding. But everyone he invited had better things to do, so he told his servants to round up anyone – the poor, the destitute, the good, the bad and the ugly – and bring them to the feast. Jesus' point is that God is generous to invite us into His Kingdom, and we'd be fools to put off His invitation because we selfishly, stupidly, think we've got better things to do.

If you know you've put off accepting God's call in favor of your own agenda, it's not too late to say yes. Even if you show up late to the feast, He'll save you a place, and a plate.

LATE NIGHT FRIDGE RAID

Rumor has it, eating dinner after 9 PM causes weight gain. It doesn't. But mindlessly eating sugary snacks just might. There's no magic pumpkin hour when your metabolism suddenly slows down, but after-dinner snacks usually consist of empty calorie foods munched while mindlessly watching TV. This type of eating increases insulin release, responsible for storing leftover energy as fat. Eating too close to bedtime also causes indigestion, which interferes with your hunger-regulating hormones and that hungry-all-the-time feeling.

FOOD FOR THOUGHT

Say NO to year-end burnout!

The final stretch of the year can feel like the hardest. There's the looming stress of the holiday season, and pressure to finish (or start!) all the things you haven't gotten around to. A few changes can put the brakes on burnout, ensuring a more enjoyable culmination to the year.

✤ *Me-time*. Christmas functions and get-togethers are great, but fuses may be short and there's seldom time for *you*. Allocate 10 minutes every day, just for you. Read a book, listen to your favorite music, or simply be. Prioritizing yourself, even for a few minutes, can vastly improve your mood and boost stamina.

✤ *Exercise*. It's the best stress outlet, *especially* when life is busy. Even just a walk or short bike ride will reduce your cortisol levels and increase your happy hormones. Regular workouts can make it easier for you to fall asleep at night, replenishing your energy for the next day's craziness.

✤ *Slow down on technology*. It's easy to feel productive when you're constantly engaging with devices, but often they only distract you, and prevent your brain from relaxing and recharging. Unplug for a couple of hours each day.

✤ *Pray and meditate, to put life back into perspective*. This helps you manage stress from the inside out. More importantly, it gives you a chance to connect to your body and focus on the present. Slowing down while taking a moment to acknowledge your inner-feelings clears your mind for the day ahead.

TIME TO REFLECT ...

Maybe today you don't need to journal your deepest thoughts and the longings of your heart. Maybe today you just need to make a list. Get your ducks in a row. (Or make sure the ducks are at least in the vicinity of your pond.) Jot down the nagging to-dos that are keeping you up at night or distracting you at work or in conversations with your kids. Try turning some of those worries into time-sensitive goals, to inspire you to get busy ticking them off.

OUTTA HERE

They brag about themselves with empty, foolish boasting.
With an appeal to twisted sexual desires, they lure back
into sin those who have barely escaped from a lifestyle of deception.
They promise freedom, but they themselves are slaves of sin
and corruption. For you are a slave to whatever controls you.
2 Peter 2:18-19, NLT

O ne of the coolest things about being a grownup is that *you get to leave*. You can get up and go, at any time. Without explanation, excuse or somehow needing to validate your choice. I'm not talking about walking out on marriage or child-rearing or responsibility. *I'm talking about walking out on false teaching*.

And really, we need to teach this to our kids too. They can't just get up and walk out of Math class, but if they're uncomfortable with spiritual teaching from the mouth of an adult, they can respectfully leave. Ask the Holy Spirit to show you clearly – *immediately* – when something you're hearing isn't from God. Then run.

FADDISH AND FALSE

Fad diet detector 101 – Generally, a fad diet claims one or more of the following: It guarantees weight loss; it promises quick, easy results with no dieting or exercise; it claims you can eat all you want; it comes in a bottle or as a pill; it involves eating only one food or food group; or it claims you can still eat chocolate or ice-cream … *Run* from these false promises! Literally. The running will actually do you good.

WORSE OFF

And when people escape from the wickedness of the world
by knowing our Lord and Savior Jesus Christ
and then get tangled up and enslaved by sin again,
they are worse off than before.

2 Peter 2:20, NLT

Read all of 2 Peter 2. It's a warning, and it paints a startling picture of what happens when we lean into God – and then get lured back into old sin patterns and ways of life. We're left worse off than before. Jesus set us free, and we're free indeed (John 8:36).

There's no reason good enough for us to go back to what enslaved us before. Would you commit to praying for insight into your lifestyle habits and the trends of your friendship circles, and ask God to show you where you're sacrificing your freedom?

🍎 FATTER FOREVER?

Fad diets often leave you fatter than before. You begin your diet by cutting back on daily calories. Rapid weight loss occurs, as much as 3-4kgs in two weeks. But then, weight loss slows. Metabolic rate slows. Weight loss stagnates, motivation plummets and previous eating patterns resume. Weight increases because your body is guarding against future 'famine'. After a few weeks, not only has the lost weight been put back on, but *more* weight has been gained overall, resulting in the dieter ending up heavier than before the diet began. All this is counterproductive for sustained weight loss, and dangerous for your heart. Better to choose a balanced, sustainable eating plan.

SLOWLY DOES IT

The Lord isn't really being slow about His promise,
as some people think. No, He is being patient for your sake.
He does not want anyone to be destroyed,
but wants everyone to repent … And remember,
our Lord's patience gives people time to be saved …

2 Peter 3:9, 15, NLT

Because we live chockablock lives in a hurried culture of instant everything, it often seems to us as if God moves slowly in our lives … far more than He ever moves quickly. Peter explains, 'The Lord isn't really being slow.' Rather, He's being kind. Remind yourself and your people that we can trust our Father's timing and timeline.

What seems slow to us is steady sovereignty and perfect, unblinking control, always for our good and His glory.

STEADY AND SUSTAINED

It's natural for anyone trying to lose weight to want to lose it quickly but the golden rule is that to lose weight *safely*, you need to lose it *slowly* (approximately 0.5kg per week). This way, you avoid stripping out valuable calorie-burning muscle, your losses will be maintained, and you won't suffer the misery that serial dieters endure, from continually denying themselves the necessary quantities of food to sustain good health. Becoming overweight happens 1 kilogram at a time, and so does prevention.

GRATITUDE ATTITUDE

Give thanks to the LORD, for He is good!
His faithful love endures forever.
Psalm 136:1, NLT

It's easy to lose sight of all we have to be grateful for. We're a fickle bunch, us humans. We're quick to get disgruntled and entitled. I've caught myself complaining that there's not enough space in the fridge or freezer for the groceries I've just bought … I mean, *what an amazing problem to have?*

How differently would your day be framed if you chose to give thanks for something – just one thing – in every situation or conversation you find yourself in today, or for every task or responsibility? If you really feel there's nothing to give thanks for, you can always give thanks, as the psalmist did, for God's goodness and His faithful, everlasting love. Regardless of the ebb and flow of your circumstances, His love never changes.

DAILY DOSE OF THANKS

A little gratitude goes a long way, not just for your soul, but for your health too. Gratitude has physiological benefits, like lowered blood pressure, less anxiety and improved mood. Expressing gratefulness also improves interpersonal connections, which has its own set of health benefits. Gratitude essentially does three things: it highlights the good we have in our lives, it offsets negativity we're exposed to, and it connects us with others, strengthening our relationships. In other words … diametrically opposite to stress! In fact, one study associated gratitude with a 23% decrease in cortisol levels. The more grateful you are, the less stressed you'll be.

ALWAYS SOMETHING

Be thankful in all circumstances,
for this is God's will for you who belong to Christ Jesus.
1 Thessalonians 5:18, NLT

We don't have to be all Pollyanna about our thanksgiving. It's unlikely that you'll feel grateful for losing your job, or your car keys, or a loved one. We don't have to be fake – insincerely cheerful – to glorify God. But no matter what our circumstances, *inside of those circumstances* we can find something for which to be grateful.

Paul says it's God's will for 'you who belong to Christ Jesus' to give thanks. That's reason enough to give thanks: you belong to Jesus! You could also give thanks for the reality that your state of affairs – for which you're battling to give thanks – won't last forever, and heaven awaits.

COUNTING BLESSINGS

One fascinating study found that two specific activities, counting blessings and writing thank you notes, improved health profiles and reduced the risk of depression by around 40%. There is also a strong connection between gratitude and impulse control. Grateful people are generally able to make better decisions, especially when it comes to their health. What's more, feeling grateful soothes your nervous system and helps you sleep better and longer. Start adding gratitude to your daily to-do list. It won't cost you a thing, doesn't take much time and the rewards could be life-changing.

FOOD FOR THOUGHT

Parental guilt: It's a thing.

Our hectic lifestyles often mean we end up feeling guilty for not helping our kids with homework, or being at every sports match or drama rehearsal, or cooking them organic, free-range, low-sugar meals every night, or solving their learning difficulties and complicated social interactions. We set impossible standards for ourselves as parents, and we seldom reach them!

If you've actually sinned against your kids ... ask their forgiveness, and God's. *Then move on in freedom.* Guilt paralyzes, but conviction mobilizes. Conviction activates the area of the brain involved with taking another person's perspective and being empathic, which helps us identify ways in which we might do things differently.

Consider these tips for managing parental guilt:

- Make sure you get enough time to reset and recharge, so you've got energy to be the best parent you can be.

- Take off the superhero cape. Be realistic about the expectations you have of yourself and your children.

- Channel your feelings of guilt into action. Try to see things from another perspective, and consider ways to rectify situations.

- Find a reliable source of advice, and stick with it. Google is awesome for helping with all those science projects, but can be confusing when it comes to figuring out how to parent. Do some research and find a site with information and advice you can relate to. Better yet, walk the parenting path in the footsteps of an older, wiser friend or mentor.

TIME TO REFLECT ...

Lord Jesus, how can I ever thank You for loving me more than You loved Your majesty? Thank You for giving up the pleasure and perfection of heaven to put on skin and sacrifice Yourself so we could be saved. Help me to live thankfully – focused outwards on the thousands of blessings surrounding me. I want my life to be characterized by gratitude and joy. Give me eyes to see beauty in a broken world. Amen.

_____

_____

_____

_____

_____

_____

_____

_____

_____

_____

IMAGINE

Sing a new song to the LORD!
Let the whole earth sing to the LORD!

Psalm 96:1, NLT

Many of us see creativity as an untouchable attribute that some people just have, and others just don't. But the truth is, *everyone* can be creative.

Maybe you're not a sculptor, singer or songwriter. *You can still be creative*. The definition of creativity is 'the ability to transcend traditional ideas, rules, patterns and relationships, and create meaningful new ideas.' Simply using your imagination counts as creativity.

We're all made in the image of God the Creator. There's something of His creative ingenuity inside each one of us. Enjoy expressing the unique, pre-packaged creativity that God carefully folded up inside of you.

MOOD AND HEALTH VIBES

Creativity – even doodling in book margins – boosts your mood and health. Distraction from consciously thinking about a problem frees your brain to problem-solve more creatively. A study found that singing not only improves your posture and the way you breathe, but can also boost your immune system. This same study found that after an hour of singing, stress hormones were lower and immune fighter cells, higher. You needn't belt out your favorite tune for an hour a day, but in the same breath don't be afraid to sing in the shower – the louder the better!

GET ON THE FLOOR

Praise His name with dancing,
accompanied by tambourine and harp.
Psalm 149:3, NLT

Perhaps you're not into interpretative dancing and flag waving during worship services. (Though you might be – and that's cool. Good for you.) But you can still use your whole body to revel in God's goodness.

Whether you're dancing at a wedding or with your kids in the kitchen, you can call it worship if the attitude of your heart is one of gratitude for God's goodness in giving us life and breath and music and movement. How wonderful that you can get on the dance floor (or the kitchen floor) and enjoy the body God's put you in.

SHAKE YOUR BOOTY

Dancing is excellent exercise, providing you with infinite freedom to channel your creativity. Dancing also improves muscle tone, heart health, balance and co-ordination, and lowers your risk of dementia (because busting out new moves engages neurons in your brain). It's also hard to dance and stay mad. Other forms of creativity, like writing, painting and drawing, have also been found to help fight off stress and anxiety. What's more, studies show that regardless of whether you're creating it or just appreciating it, art has a positive impact on your brain. The options to be creative are endless. Open a blank document and start writing. Grab your phone and take a picture. Start a conversation. Build something. As long as you're contributing, not consuming, anything you do can be creative!

FIGHTING FAMINE

Feed the hungry, and help those in trouble.
Then your light will shine out from the darkness,
and the darkness around you will be as bright as noon.
Isaiah 58:10, NLT

Globally, poor nutrition causes 45% of deaths in children under five years old. When you consider how far civilization has progressed, this seems unthinkable – and unacceptable. Jesus always had time for kids. He even advised us to be more like them (Matthew 25:40).

As His followers, our indignation should burn more than most against malnutrition, child neglect, human trafficking, domestic violence and other atrocities.

Could you get behind an organization involved in feeding, educating and equipping children so they can soar into the cloudless sky of a brighter future?

ENTITLED, OR GRATEFUL?

The best place to start changing the world is in your own home. You can give your kids the gift of perspective by encouraging them to appreciate the good food you put in front of them. But don't force your kids to finish every last morsel on their plates, as that can disrupt their innate self-regulatory instinct (they actually know when they've had enough). Also, don't use dessert as a reward for finishing a meal or eating veggies. This strategy, unfortunately, makes kids less likely to appreciate healthy foods, and makes desserts more desirable. Besides that, with all the negotiating that goes on, family meal times can become a lot less appetizing for everyone!

PILLOW PRAYERS

My child, don't lose sight of common sense and discernment.
Hang on to them, for they will refresh your soul ...
You can go to bed without fear;
you will lie down and sleep soundly.

Proverbs 3:21-22, 24, NLT

If you're battling to sleep at night, there may be a physiological or psychological reason (read on). But don't discount the power of prayer. Ask the Holy Spirit to pinpoint what's causing your tossing and turning.

Ask Him to convict you if there's something you're clutching – instead of surrendering. Ask Him for sleep! And if sleep still eludes you, for whatever reason, redeem the time by praying even more. Pray for anyone and anything that crosses the teeming highways of your thoughts. You may even find that praying unceasingly – unsleepingly – is the very thing that has you drifting into dreams.

SLEEPLESS?

If you're struggling with wakeful nights, the first step is to figure out *why*. The causes of insomnia can be broken down into three Ps. Firstly, predisposing conditions, as in, your genetics. Secondly, precipitating circumstances, such as stress, a death in the family, or divorce. And thirdly, perpetuating conditions like poor sleep hygiene (an unhealthy sleeping environment or routine). If you can't find the reason for your restlessness, check in with your doc sooner rather than later.

TEETH FOR TRUTH

*... when I was with you I couldn't talk to you
as I would to spiritual people.
I had to talk as though you belonged to this world
or as though you were infants in Christ.
I had to feed you with milk, not with solid food,
because you weren't ready for anything stronger ...*
1 Corinthians 3:1-3, NLT

If we were only meant to drink all our food, God wouldn't have given us teeth for chewing. We've got molars and incisors and we can sink them into steaks or spinach or cucumber sandwiches. They're not really for soup.

Spiritually, we can lazily content ourselves with a liquid diet – only ever sipping on milk – even though God has a buffet of solid truth to satisfy us. Milk is part of God's nurturing, nourishing plan for infants and animals. It's miraculous stuff at the start of life. But there's more: a truth-table, where you can feast.

🍎 MILK AND MUCUS?

Provided you don't have a dairy allergy, there's little evidence to support *any* relationship between dairy consumption and mucus production. If you do feel as if dairy consumption creates more mucus, it probably has to do with the texture and temperature of the milk. Studies showed that when people complained of a cough after drinking cold milk, their cough disappeared after drinking warm milk. Use yourself as a science experiment. If reducing dairy works for you, go with it. If not, rest easy, you won't need to cancel your music production because of mucus production.

FOOD FOR THOUGHT

De-worming musical earworms

An earworm is a sticky song – a song that gets stuck in your head. The song, or often just one line of it, plays on … and on … and you can't get rid of it! Most adults report hearing them on a weekly (if not daily) basis.

Earworm songs tend to have some predictable characteristics. The songs you've heard recently are also the most likely to get lodged in your cranium. But sometimes an experience triggers an earworm response of a song you haven't heard in years. Under the right circumstances, most songs can be earworms, but researchers have identified a hallmark of earworm-causing tunes. Along with their predictable melodies, they also tend to contain an unexpected shift in pitch or tempo that your brain finds memorable.

Most researchers believe people get earworms either to match or to change their current state of arousal – to boost energy, or to calm down. But if you're slowly going insane, because of *Hey Macarena* … then there are some ways to de-worm.

Putting your mind to a mentally demanding task usually shifts attention away from internal music. Chewing gum can also help. But it seems the most successful way to remove earworms is to confront the enemy. By intentionally listening to the offending song or singing it out loud, your brain may just find some closure and relief and get rid of any worms … at least temporarily!

TIME TO REFLECT ...

Journal your thoughts and prayers around the creativity your Creator has imprinted in your mind and muscles. How do you love to be creative? What kind of beauty are you drawn to? What breaks your heart – and what ideas come to mind when you think of leaning into that space, to make a difference?

FREE TO FEAST

So now that you know God (or should I say,
now that God knows you), why do you want to go back again
and become slaves once more to the weak
and useless spiritual principles of this world?

Galatians 4:9, NLT

Because we live in a cause and effect world, we tend to think we have to *do* something to *deserve* something. We're excited, relieved and amazed to know Jesus died the death *we* should have died – but after a while we find ourselves wanting to die that death too.

We self-flagellate – making life difficult and complicated – because somehow that makes us *feel* more spiritual. God doesn't demand we starve ourselves of His grace, mercy and forgiveness. Rather, we can feast on it, as children and heirs of the King (Ephesians 1), because we're free indeed (John 8:36). We have permission to enjoy that marvelous position.

STARVE OR FEED A FEVER?

Your immune system is only as strong as its energy source – *what you feed it*. Without energy, it's useless against even the smallest bug. To 'starve a cold' is simply to starve your body's defense against it. The same applies to fevers. Weirdly enough, we actually *need* fevers. They're our biggest bug-busting tool. Germs enjoy a temperature of 37.5 degrees. It's at this average body temperature that they thrive and wreak havoc. By cranking up the furnace, your body creates a very uncomfortable germ environment. But, your body needs extra energy to do so. Keep it fed!

BAD MATH

Do not add to or subtract from these commands I am giving you.
Just obey the commands of the LORD your God that I am giving you.

Deuteronomy 4:2, NLT

God made sugar, and He called it good. Our brains metabolize glucose (a kind of sugar) to function. But high-fructose corn syrup is an *added* chemical that's crept insidiously into our food supply and now represents over 40% of caloric-added sweeteners, as it delays the expiration date of most foods for a lower price, while maintaining a relatively good taste.

Just as we can err on the side of starving our bodies of nutrients, or adding too much sugar to everything, we're not above leaving out bits of God's Word that don't suit us, or adding things into God's Word that He never intended to be there. The first makes us liberals; the second, conservatives. Let's strike the balance of taking God at His Word – nothing added, nothing taken away.

ADDED SUGARS SUBTRACT FROM HEALTH

The biggest dietary driver of type 2 diabetes is high-fructose corn syrup. Fructose makes a beeline for your liver and triggers lipogenesis (the production of fats like triglycerides). Triglycerides floating around your blood stream are associated with everything from fatty liver disorder to heart disease. Unlike glucose, fructose doesn't stimulate the release of insulin from your pancreas, nor the production of leptin (your hunger-regulating hormone). High-fructose corn syrup can be found in most processed food or drink. Check your labels and do the math!

SUIT UP

Put on all of God's armor so that you
will be able to stand firm against all strategies of the devil.

Ephesians 6:11, NLT

Paul issues an emphatic command to the Ephesian believers. Put on *all* of the armor, so you can stand against *all* the enemy's schemes. He's not playing games.

There's an all-or-nothing urgency about this instruction to put on truth, righteousness, peace, faith, salvation, and the Word of God.

But when we're living in peaceful (mostly) western societies, we can be lulled or numbed into very un-war-like thinking. It may be hard to sense the enemy's threat on an average Tuesday at the office. It may even seem a little crazy to think there's any threat at all.

But 'we are not fighting against flesh-and-blood enemies, but against evil rulers and authorities of the unseen world, against mighty powers in this dark world, and against evil spirits in the heavenly places' (Ephesians 6:12). We need to be ready.

PROBIOTIC PROTECTION

When antibiotics annihilate both bad and good bacteria, we experience side effects like diarrhea, gastrointestinal problems and yeast infections. Enter probiotics, essential for our survival! In addition to assisting digestion, these bacteria produce folic acid, niacin, and B vitamins in our intestinal tract. They crowd out bad bacteria, producing acids that inhibit their growth, and stimulating our immune systems to fight them off. We need helpful bacteria to multiply, thrive, and act as our protectors.

FATTENED

You have spent your years on earth in luxury,
satisfying your every desire. You have fattened yourselves
for the day of slaughter.

James 5:5, NLT

James takes exception to those who've lived for selfish, wanton pleasure, at the expense of, and in denial of, people in desperate need – even people facing death (James 5:6).

Today's societies are fairly orderly and sanitized. It seems unlikely you're taking pleasure in another's destitution. But it might be worth analyzing how our consumerism and our habit of expecting immediate gratification might affect our planet, or the people producing the things we crave. You and I might not be physically fat, but we still tend to live lives that aim to *satisfy our every desire*, as James puts it.

Maybe you could fast from something today – a food item, a habit, an expectation – to consider how you've fattened your life with selfishness, and how you might thin it out with generosity.

BACTERIA TO BEAT OBESITY

Gut bacteria may have an impact on insulin sensitivity – impacting how your body responds to carbs and stores fat. Studies done on mice showed that when gut bacteria of obese mice were put into healthy (skinnier) mice, the fit slender rodents put on weight, even though their diet hadn't changed. Other studies done on men (not mice) found that poor gut diversity leads to increased fat storage and poor insulin sensitivity, which in turn was linked to inflammation, diabetes, obesity and depression. Healthy gut, healthy you!

GOOD TO GO

Standing at her bedside, He rebuked the fever, and it left her.
And she got up at once and prepared a meal for them.
Luke 4:39, NLT

Jesus visits Simon, whose mom-in-law is really ill. Jesus heals her – and she wastes no time. It's as if she thinks, 'I am good to go! Let me be useful!' If God has seen fit to heal you, how are you channeling your gratitude and your energy? It's not easy to be in a fantastic mood when we're laid low by sickness.

But if we're in a place of health and strength, there's possibly not much stopping us from smiling a little more, or speaking a little more gently and considerately. Let's decide to make the mood in every room we enter. Let's use our get-up-and-go to make a positive, life-giving difference to those around us.

HAPPY GUT BUGS

Recent evidence suggests that certain bacteria influence mood by producing compounds that travel from your intestine to your brain. There's even a name for this feel-good superhighway: the gut-brain axis. Feeding your gut the right things results in a brain that feels less anxious and distressed. One study found that after four weeks of taking a probiotic supplement, people's reactivity to sadness was reduced. Simply meaning that when participants did feel a bit down, they were better able to get over it, and were less vulnerable to dysfunctional thoughts that could lead to a lingering depressive episode.

FOOD FOR THOUGHT

A yoghurt a day keeps gut troubles away …?

To improve your gut diversity, it's important to keep your gut working. First and foremost, make sure you eat a good serving of fiber each day. The best source of fiber? Green, leafy veggies, which give you tons of nutrition while feeding your bacteria. By filling up on healthy fiber, you're also more likely to keep your weight in check, which is an added bonus, since obesity adversely affects gut diversity.

Secondly, get sufficient sleep! A healthy sleep cycle helps your body produce the hormones melatonin and prolactin, which improve bacterial balance and aid digestion.

Thirdly, eat the right foods. Yoghurt is a brilliant source of good bacteria, but not the only one. Cheeses, especially cottage cheese, Gouda and parmesan, are all very gut-bacteria-friendly. They're collectively known as fermented foods: good micro-organisms break down the food, making nutrients easier for your body to absorb.

If you're dairy intolerant, no worries! Scientists have successfully bottled these good bacteria in the form of a supplement. However, before popping any old probiotic, read the fine print. Check the product label for *live and active cultures*, particularly lactobacillus. It's the most effective bacteria for breaking down food, absorbing nutrients, and fending off unfriendly organisms. Bifidobacterium probiotics are also up there with the best.

An important tip on probiotic supplements: keep 'em cool. The number of living bacteria in probiotic yogurt decreases at room temperature, so make sure you stash your probiotic supplements in the fridge for maximum efficacy.

TIME TO REFLECT ...

*Heavenly Father, today I pray for the health
of my physical and my spiritual gut. Help me pay attention
to what I put into my body for my overall health
and wellbeing. And help me pay attention to the Holy Spirit,
who so often gives me gut feelings in situations
requiring of me a wise and courageous reaction.
Keep me from ignoring the inner tug of conviction. Help me to
be obedient by bravely going with my gut, for Your glory.
Amen.*

KEEP WATCH

Then He returned to the disciples and found them asleep.
He said to Peter, 'Couldn't you watch with Me even one hour?'
Matthew 26:40, NLT

Jesus asks His disciples to stay up with Him while He prays in the Garden of Gethsemane. He's 'crushed with grief to the point of death' (Matthew 26:38), because His death is imminent. He desperately needs their companionship. They fall asleep. He chides them. They fall asleep again. He addresses Peter personally, and it's as if He's saying, 'Dude, seriously? An *hour*?'

Not only did Peter fall asleep when he should've been wide awake, he also denied – *three times* – even knowing Jesus. And yet this is the same Peter upon whom Jesus built His church – the global body of Christ we're part of today. How enormous is the grace, mercy and compassion of our patient, longsuffering God, who uses us despite our fallibilities, and our inabilities to sleep or stay awake.

SWITCH OFF

It's 2 AM. You're staring at the ceiling – desperate to fall asleep, again! Since it takes just four seconds of light exposure to switch on your wake-up hormones, checking your phone is not a good option. Better to get up. Yup, the longer you lie worrying about not sleeping, the more your brain starts associating bed with being awake. Rather, distract your brain by tidying the kitchen or reading in the lounge. When your eyelids start drooping, head back to bed. Take some deep breaths to slow your heart rate, and you should drift off shortly (and sweetly).

SHOES OFF

When the LORD saw Moses coming to take a closer look,
God called to him from the middle of the bush, 'Moses! Moses!'
'Here I am!' Moses replied. 'Do not come any closer,'
the LORD warned. 'Take off your sandals,
for you are standing on holy ground.'

Exodus 3:4-5, NLT

Exodus 3:6 goes on to say, 'When Moses heard this, he covered his face because he was afraid to look at God.' It's a massive moment. God is tangibly revealing Himself to Moses and Moses is awestruck by His holiness. God even instructs him to take off his shoes in this sacred space.

It's a staggering thought that we get to come into God's presence anytime, anywhere, because Jesus has put us in right standing with Him and so really, *all ground is holy ground*. Let's never be flippant about that privilege. Let's let our words be few (Ecclesiastes 5:2) before our magnificent God.

BAREFOOT BENEFITS

Your body depends on a complex process to keep you upright. Your brain monitors balance via sensors in your feet, activating different muscles (multiple times per second) to regulate your stability. Shoe-confined feet have limited joint motion and sensory input. They're in contact with the same surface all day, which dampens the signal your brain receives about your foot activity. The result is that your brain over- or under-reacts when an adjustment to steadiness is needed. For strong, stable feet, and poise … dare to go bare!

SOLES FOR SOULS

For shoes, put on the peace that comes
from the Good News so that you will be fully prepared.
Ephesians 6:15, NLT

Our feet carry us into all sorts of situations, every day. How might it revolutionize your world if, every day, you prayed that God would give you *soles for souls*?

What if, every time you walked through someone's front door, or into a classroom or a boardroom, a mall or a canteen, you walked in with feet of peace, 'fully prepared', as Paul says, to offer the hope and harmony of the gospel of Jesus Christ?

 ## BETTER TO BE BARE

Studies show that standers perform 10-15% better on cognitive tests when barefoot than when wearing hard-soled shoes. Knowing that should encourage you to take a step in the right direction! The world is a germ-infested place, sure, but as long as you don't have any open wounds, your skin does a pretty good job of protecting your feet. It's damp, dirty socks inside of shoes that really harbor bacteria. You needn't forgo shoes completely, of course. But don't scoff at the opportunity to kick them off when you can. Besides keeping your feet healthy, and improving your balance, bare feet keep your brain on its toes!

STRESS OR CELEBRATION?

So prepare your minds for action and exercise self-control.
Put all your hope in the gracious salvation that will come to you
when Jesus Christ is revealed to the world.
1 Peter 1:13, NLT

Holiday stress often comes from unrealistic expectations. Our tidings of comfort and joy are drowned out by the pressure we feel to do, be and buy it all.

Studies suggest holiday stress and overindulgence explain the soaring rate of fatal heart attacks reported over December and January. We have high hopes for a holiday where everyone is together, and getting along. But that's countered by battling gift-shopping crowds, preparing or indulging in rich meals, and dealing with difficult family members.

To survive and *thrive* over this festive season: relax, and manage your expectations. Let's be proactive. Let's prepare our minds for action, exercise self-control, and put our hope in Jesus, not in our friends, family or family-in-law, or the gifts we give or get.

DECK THE HALLS WITH TINSEL – OR TENSION?

To release the ever-tightening grip of holiday stress, count your blessings, not your burdens. Keep up your exercise routine, and guard against stress-eating. Manage what's on your year-end plate (social gatherings, gifts or Christmas pudding) by focusing on quality, not quantity. And remember, this is the season of giving. Give your time – the best gift of all. Doing something for someone else triggers a rush of endorphins, those feel-good hormones that keep depression and stress at bay.

LOVE ATTACK

If someone slaps you on one cheek, offer the other cheek also.
If someone demands your coat, offer your shirt also. Give to anyone
who asks; and when things are taken away from you, don't try to get
them back. Do to others as you would like them to do to you.

Luke 6:29-31, NLT

Nobody enjoys the pounding headache, tightened chest or queasy stomach that can accompany stress, but it's easy to overlook these warning signs in the end-year madness.

Stress can put you in constant fight-or-flight mode, which negatively affects your organs and is linked to diabetes, impaired immunity and gastrointestinal problems. None of this makes for feeling festive!

Artists and athletes visualize their ideal performance ahead of time, which helps them hit the target. Do the same! Mentally rehearse some Christ-like actions and attitudes so you're ready to go on the love offensive, this Christmas.

If you know your mom-in-law will tell you how to roast the potatoes (or raise your children), prepare yourself by bowling her over with your calm, selfless response.

DECREASE THE DRAMA

First up: sleep, exercise, eat well, and keep your sense of humor. Laughter enhances your intake of oxygen, stimulates your heart, lungs and muscles, and increases endorphin release. As hard as holiday eating can be, aim to fill up with healthy fats and proteins at each meal to keep your hanger at bay and your stress levels muted. Keep (Christmas) calm, and carry on.

FOOD FOR THOUGHT

Raising healthy adults

Childhood obesity is a risk factor for chronic diseases such as hypertension, stroke, type 2 diabetes, respiratory disease, cancer, arthritis and heart disease during adulthood, not to mention obesity's impact on self-esteem and social development. Overweight children and adolescents are more likely to become obese adults. One study found that approximately 80% of children who were overweight or obese at 10 to 15 years old were obese at 25.

Get a load of this: obese children under age 3 *without* obese parents are at low risk for obesity in adulthood. But parental obesity more than doubles the risk of adult obesity among both obese and non-obese children under the age of 10. Parents, your child's health begins with *your* health! Our kids imbibe our attitudes and behaviors. Kids whose parents encourage them to exercise and eat well, and model those healthy behaviors themselves, are more likely to be active, and healthy eaters, as they grow up.

Start by pulling the plug on passive pastimes (anything with a screen!) and find a sport or hobby everyone in your family enjoys. Global recommendations are that kids should enjoy 60 minutes of vigorous physical activity each day. Make it fun!

Just as you might secretly smuggle extra veggies into dinner (adding grated carrot to lasagna works a treat), there are heaps of sneaky ways to add extra activities to your kids' day. Involve them in gardening, cleaning the house or washing the car. It'll take the load off you too.

TIME TO REFLECT …

Take a few minutes to surrender your December to God. It's a busy month, and it's probably come at the end of a busy year. What are your goals? When you get to the other side of Christmas, what decisions will you be glad you made? With which friends or family members are you most likely to experience a bit of conflict over the holiday season? Write down their names, and commit to praying for them.

MERCY AND MORTALITY

Then this message came to Isaiah from the LORD:
'Go back to Hezekiah and tell him, "This is what the LORD,
the God of your ancestor David, says: I have heard your prayer
and seen your tears. I will add fifteen years to your life ..."'

Isaiah 38:4-5, NLT

Take time to read all of Isaiah 38. It gets real. And it's such a moving account of our mortality – a sobering message to 'set your affairs in order, for you are going to die' (Isaiah 38:1) – and God's mercy in sometimes offering us an extension, in this life, until we meet Him in the next.

It's a powerful prompt to settle your relationships and responsibilities in such a way that, if this day were your last, the life you left behind would only be a blessing. It's also a great reminder to look after our health, doing all we can, by God's grace and sovereignty alone, to add years to our lives.

BLIND TO YOUR MOLES?

Malignant melanoma develops when normal pigment-producing skin cells (melanocytes) become abnormal, grow extremely quickly, and invade surrounding tissues. Here's a quick DIY skin cancer check. It's as easy as ABC (and D and E). **A**-symmetry – is half your mole unlike the other half? **B**order irregularities – rough or poorly defined edges? Common moles are smooth and have even borders. **C**olor changes? Nonthreatening moles are usually a single shade of brown or black. **D**iameter – larger than 6mm? **E**volve – has it grown bigger and become more prominent? A yes to any of those MCQ's requires an urgent visit to your doctor.

DETERMINED TO BE DOWN

To what can I compare this generation?
It is like children playing a game in the public square.
They complain to their friends, 'We played wedding songs,
and you didn't dance, so we played funeral songs,
and you didn't mourn.'
Matthew 11:16-17, NLT

Jesus rebukes His overly critical listeners for always finding fault. He says, 'For John didn't spend his time eating and drinking, and you say, "He's possessed by a demon." The Son of Man, on the other hand, feasts and drinks, and you say, "He's a glutton and a drunkard, and a friend of tax collectors and other sinners!" But wisdom is shown to be right by its results' (Matthew 11:18-19).

Humans haven't changed since Jesus' time. We're still quick to make excuses and find grounds to stay unhappy. Maybe you could make this Christmas season a reason to rejoice no matter how things roll. You have a choice. Pain is inevitable. Misery is optional.

EXCUSES, EXCUSES

Let's avoid holiday weight gain by deciding *not* to make excuses! Despite the delectable food around at this time of year, research shows the average weight gain over a six-week festive season is only around 0.5kg. However, weight gain is greater amongst those who are already overweight. Also, this weight gain is usually half the total amount of weight you'll gain over the course of a year. Ouch! Let the Christmas spirit enthuse you to exercise, instead of lead you into lethargy!

EAT, DRINK AND BE MERRY

This day shall be for you a memorial day,
and you shall keep it as a feast to the LORD;
throughout your generations, as a statute forever,
you shall keep it as a feast.
Exodus 12:14, ESV

There are dozens of references to feasting in Scripture. People feasted to mark special family occasions (Genesis 21:8). And people feasted because God commanded it (Leviticus 23:1-2). Sumptuous food is evidence of the goodness of God, and it's meant to be relished.

God has designed life with opportunities to rest and reflect around tables. Of course, like all His good gifts, we can twist appropriate feasting into gluttony and greed.

Before we head any further into the holidays, perhaps we could make some heart-attitude, health-aware decisions around how we'll feast fittingly – so we still fit into our jeans come January.

EASY AS PIE

If you're keen to maintain-not-gain this holiday, try the PIE principle: Proximity, Indulge and Exercise. The biggest risk factor for overeating is being around food (*proximity*), so stash the Christmas chocolates out of sight. Dish up your food in the kitchen, not from the table – where you'll stare at it … and likely give in to that second helping. *Indulge*. Most of us will eat too much of *something*, but let's avoid eating too much of *everything*! If you're going to indulge, pick the one thing you most enjoy. After a meal why not go for a walk as a family, and while you're at it, make *Exercise* part of the holiday vibes.

HAPPY STRESS-MAS

For the word of God is alive and active. Sharper than any double-edged sword, it penetrates even to dividing soul and spirit, joints and marrow; it judges the thoughts and attitudes of the heart.

Hebrews 4:12, NIV

There's a 5% increase in heart-related deaths during the holiday season. Research shows the number of cardiac deaths is higher on December 25th than on any other day of the year, and second highest on January 1st.

These events have been labeled the Merry Christmas Coronary and Happy New Year Heart Attack. Emotional stress is a big contributor: interacting with relatives, absorbing gift-buying financial pressure, entertaining or traveling. Changes in diet and alcohol consumption play a role too.

Your Christmas tension may also stem from stressed-out 'thoughts and attitudes of the heart.' Don't let your devotional time with God slip, just because it's the holiday season and you're *so over* this year. Allow the Word to penetrate even between your 'soul and spirit, joints and marrow.' Being honest before God, and possibly one or two trusted loved ones, might give you the chance to avoid disaster.

HOLIDAY HIJACK

If a heart attack threatens to hijack holiday festivities, don't delay getting treatment for fear of disrupting the celebrations! A cardiac event would've been brewing for some time before becoming alarmingly apparent. Hypertension is a silent killer, with the first symptom being a heart attack in almost 50% of cases (a third of which are fatal!) Give yourself an early Christmas gift of a medical checkup.

MORE BLESSED

And I have been a constant example of how you can help those in need by working hard. You should remember the words of the Lord Jesus: 'It is more blessed to give than to receive.'

Acts 20:35, NLT

Psychologists and neuroscientists have identified a typical state of endorphin-induced euphoria – a 'helper's high' – reported by those engaged in charitable activity. These studies showed that the same area of the brain activated by food or sex (namely, pleasure) lit up when participants thought about donating to charity. A Harvard study found those who contributed time or money were 42% more likely to be happy than those who didn't.

'Tis the season to be merry. It's about peace on earth and goodwill to all (Luke 2:14). And it's about giving: God giving us the priceless, reality-altering gift of His Son who would live and die and be raised to life again, for us. It's fantastic to *receive* gifts at Christmas. But it really is even better to *give* them.

TAKING THE MERRY OUT OF CHRISTMAS

Incidences of depression and suicide are particularly high at this time of year. Most affected are those who've experienced a recent loss, or those without a social support network. Teens and students are more inclined towards suicide at this time of year because of exam stress. When we engage in good deeds, or random acts of kindness – we naturally reduce the physiological changes that occur when we're stressed. Altruistic emotions can physiologically trump our stress response and simultaneously boost our health.

FOOD FOR THOUGHT

Don't become a Christmas coronary statistic! Are you experiencing any of these symptoms?

- If it's not food poisoning from Christmas dinner, then crushing chest pain associated with nausea, vomiting and sweating could mean something more serious. Call for help immediately, even if your symptoms don't *feel* life-threatening. They could get worse fast.

- If you feel like Santa didn't make it up the chimney and landed on your chest, then something may be up. People often describe heart attack induced chest pain as 'deep pressure' or 'being crushed'.

- Tingling in your arms is another significant heart attack symptom. It can also show up in your neck, right arm, teeth and stomach. Feeling pain in other areas of the body besides your heart is known as referred pain and occurs when the nerves surrounding your heart become agitated, sending pain through the nerves in your spine to other locations in your body, specifically your left jaw, shoulder and arm.

- What feels like indigestion might be masking a coronary episode. It's even more confusing when you burp and feel relief. Take an antacid and see what happens. If the discomfort doesn't disappear within half an hour, call your doctor or take a trip directly to the E.R. and don't pass GO!

TIME TO REFLECT ...

*Jesus, I want this festive season – which is supposed to be
all about You – to really be all about You! Help me glorify You
in the way I eat, shop, wrap, bake, celebrate and relax.
Give me wisdom to look after myself and my loved ones well.
Remind me, Holy Spirit, to exercise and sleep,
despite the lethargy and the late nights of the holidays.
Bring to mind the lonely and those who've lost hope,
so I can love them, with company or cooking.
Amen.*

_____
_____
_____
_____
_____
_____
_____
_____
_____
_____

CHEW ON TRUTH

How well God must like you – you don't hang out
at Sin Saloon, you don't slink along Dead-End Road,
you don't go to Smart-Mouth College.
Instead you thrill to God's Word,
you chew on Scripture day and night.

Psalm 1:1-2, MSG

Psalm 1 juxtaposes a life joyfully dedicated to God, and a life bent on selfishness and ending in destruction. There's *joy* promised to those who 'chew on Scripture day and night', and who don't rush to take part in activities where other people are mocked, or where ungodly advice is spewed.

Solomon also reminds us in Proverbs 19:2 that 'enthusiasm without knowledge is no good; haste makes mistakes.' Slow down long enough to check you're not getting caught up in a moment, wolfing down inevitable disaster. It's always a good idea to chew slowly and intentionally on goodness and truth. Don't waste a morsel. Savor and swallow.

PLATE RACE

Rushing through a meal is one race you don't want to win. Besides leaving you bloated, and often still hungry, inhaling your meal poses health risks, including weight gain and insulin resistance (not forgetting choking!) Once food arrives in your belly, hormones are released, telling your brain you're full. Eating too quickly means you're likely to overeat before this message (which takes around 20 minutes) goes ping in your brain's inbox. Savor the flavor instead, enjoy your entire meal experience, and give your belly time to get in touch with your brain before heading for seconds.

RECKLESS RAGE

Control your temper, for anger labels you a fool.
Ecclesiastes 7:9, NLT

No one wants to be labeled a fool – disregarded, disrespected, disliked and definitely taken un-seriously. Someone may be labeled a fool for espousing stupid ideas, or for jumping into something with both feet before checking the depth. Here Solomon, the teacher of Ecclesiastes, bluntly informs us that unleashing our anger, unchecked, will also have people calling us fools.

Would you be honest today about the specific people or places that have you losing control of your temper? In which situations are sparks of fear or frustration quickly and easily ignited? Are you being wise (not foolish!) – looking after yourself physically and emotionally by sleeping enough and eating enough?

HANGER PANGS

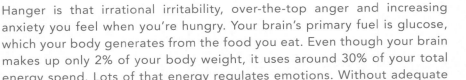

Hanger is that irrational irritability, over-the-top anger and increasing anxiety you feel when you're hungry. Your brain's primary fuel is glucose, which your body generates from the food you eat. Even though your brain makes up only 2% of your body weight, it uses around 30% of your total energy spend. Lots of that energy regulates emotions. Without adequate fuel, the part of your brain responsible for curtailing angry impulses simply doesn't have enough resources to exert self-control. Have a *snack* attack instead of a snap attack! Tone down your rage by ensuring you don't let your energy levels dip so low your brain thinks it's starving! Fill up on healthy fats which curb those hangry emotions. It'll leave you, and those around you, happier *and* healthier.

SLEEPING HOPE-SEEDS

Jesus also said, 'The Kingdom of God
is like a farmer who scatters seed on the ground.
Night and day, while he's asleep or awake,
the seed sprouts and grows,
but he does not understand how it happens.'

Mark 4:26-27 , NLT

Jesus goes on to say, 'The earth produces the crops on its own. First a leaf blade pushes through, then the heads of wheat are formed, and finally the grain ripens. And as soon as the grain is ready, the farmer comes and harvests it with a sickle, for the harvest time has come.' (Mark 4:28-29) Just as the trillions of cells in your body work 24/7, whether you're awake or asleep, God is at work, 24/7, building His Kingdom.

You scatter seeds. You water and watch. That's about all you can do. God causes those seeds to sprout and push through soil and thrive. Don't lose heart if you don't see results now, or ever. Get some sleep. Even then, God will be growing things in the dark.

MORE SLEEPING, LESS SNACKING

Your hungriness is regulated by ghrelin (which increases appetite) and leptin (which reduces appetite). A balance of the two is important for a healthy appetite and a healthy weight, and sleeping plays a significant role here. Poor sleep results in higher ghrelin levels and lower leptin levels, resulting in an increased appetite, especially for sugar-rich, high-carb foods. Don't 'weight' – move sleep back to the top of your to-do list!

ABSOLUTE AFFECTION

Oh, dear Corinthian friends! We have spoken honestly with you,
and our hearts are open to you. There is no lack of love on our part,
but you have withheld your love from us. I am asking you
to respond as if you were my own children. Open your hearts to us!

2 Corinthians 6:11-13, NLT

Paul is being incredibly vulnerable in these verses. He's appealing to his Corinthian readers – fellow believers for whom he's poured out his life in ministry – to be as honest and openhearted with God and others, as he's been with them.

The Greek word translated in these verses as *love* or *affection* is literally *bowels.* This sounds weird to us but it wasn't weird to Paul's readers. Paul has loved them from the depths of himself, offering all of himself, for all he knows they can become.

Who is God asking you to love like this? Could you reach deep within yourself, to reach out to that person today?

IRRITABLE INTESTINES?

If you persistently experience belly pain, cramping, bloating, diarrhea or constipation, you may have Irritable Bowel Syndrome (IBS). It's caused by signaling problems between your brain and digestive tract, problems digesting certain foods, and stress or anxiety. IBS sufferers may have unusually sensitive intestines or problems with intestine muscle movement. To manage the condition, you, your doctor and pharmacist should work together to determine what's triggering your symptoms. Treatment includes tweaking your diet, taking supplements (like probiotics), getting regular exercise, enough sleep and managing stress.

SWEEP THE TEMPLE

Don't you realize that your body is the temple of the Holy Spirit,
who lives in you and was given to you by God?
You do not belong to yourself, for God bought you with
a high price. So you must honor God with your body.

1 Corinthians 6:19-20, NLT

The context of these verses is sexual immorality. Paul's message isn't subtle: flee from it! (1 Corinthians 6:18). But the principle applies to all of life: what we do with our bodies and what we put into our bodies should glorify God because our bodies belong to Him.

Brendon Burchard said, 'Most people would feel guilty for destroying someone else's property. Yet they wreck the very temple their Creator gifted them.' What choices can you make today to ensure that, as far as it depends on you, your body will be as useful as possible, for as long as possible?

NAUGHTY OR NICE?

Cholesterol gets a bad rap, but what you might not know is that it's something you couldn't function without. Cholesterol is produced by your liver and plays a critical role in digestion, the production of hormones, and contributes to the structure of every cell in your body. Fortunately, your liver is a competent cholesterol factory, so you'll never run dry. Eggs are one of the richest sources of cholesterol in your diet, which is why you've traditionally been told to go easy on the "over-easys". But no more. Large-scale studies have found weak relationships between dietary cholesterol (eggs) intake and blood cholesterol levels. So eggs have been egg-sonerated!

FOOD FOR THOUGHT

The menace of the muffin top

Subcutaneous fat lies directly under your skin – your love handles in other words. It isn't as hazardous to your health as visceral fat though, which lies deep undercover in your abdominal cavity, padding the spaces between your organs.

If you can't find a tape measure but need to know if you're at risk of too much visceral fat, grab a piece of string or dental floss. Measure your waist midway between your lowest rib and the top of your hip bone. Breathe out slightly. Don't be sneaky and squeeze the string (and your waist) into submission. Then wind the string length-wise around your credit card. Gentlemen, you can wind that string around your card no more than 11 times; ladies, no more than 9.5 times. Any more than that and you have too much belly fat.

Body mass index is a widely used method for gauging obesity. It takes into account your height and weight, spitting out (via a complicated formula) a single number which places you on a body weight continuum. Although BMI can tell you you're carrying extra padding, it can't tell you *where* the padding is – which is the most important factor affecting your health. Research suggests we should consider the tape measure (or credit card) measurement as well, to give us a more complete picture.

The good news is that it *is* possible to lose your belly fat! When you lose weight, your body prioritizes the loss around your tummy (it knows!). If you lose just 5-10% of your overall body weight, you can reduce your hazardous handles of belly fat by as much as 30%.

TIME TO REFLECT ...

Try making a health to-do list for the week ahead. Could you tweak your shopping list with healthier food choices? Could you schedule in (set reminders!) a couple of early nights, or some slow, uninterrupted mealtimes? Could you keep a healthy snack in your handbag or glove compartment for moments of low blood sugar (and low tolerance)? Could you be proactive about minimizing your stress this week, or managing explosive situations so your anger doesn't get the better of you?

_____

_____

_____

_____

_____

_____

_____

_____

_____

_____

ANCESTRY AND INFLUENCE

But if you refuse to serve the LORD,
then choose today whom you will serve.
Would you prefer the gods your ancestors served
beyond the Euphrates? Or will it be the gods
of the Amorites in whose land you now live?
But as for me and my family, we will serve the LORD.

Joshua 24:15, NLT

It's hard to outrun the influence of your ancestry. Whether we realize it or not – and certainly whether we want it to be that way or not – our parents, and our parents' parents and even further back than that, shape our worldviews, biases and beliefs.

That's why when Joshua addresses the Israelites, reminding them of their history and challenging them to nail their colors to the mast, for God, it's encouraging and inspiring to realize we have a *choice*. If our ancestors worshiped God, how beautiful that we can do likewise, walking the paths they've worn smooth for us.

If our ancestors rejected God, how incredible that we get to blaze a new trail, for our children, and our children's children.

BEATING YOUR GENES

Bad genes, really? Studies have found that simply walking for an hour each day can reduce the genetic influence towards obesity, by 50%. On the other hand, a sedentary lifestyle marked by watching television for four hours a day increased the genetic influence by 50%. So, it's entirely possible to outrun your genes. Your DNA is not your destiny!

DESERT FLOODS

For I am about to do something new. See, I have already begun!
Do you not see it? I will make a pathway through the wilderness.
I will create rivers in the dry wasteland.

Isaiah 43:19, NLT

Isaiah's prophecy encapsulates Christmas. Our Father and Creator broke the drought of human history by sending His Son, and floods of abundant life (John 10:10).

Perhaps you've had to fake it, this festive season, because your heart feels more arid wasteland than fertile field. But no matter what's transpired in the past year to dry up your hope, Jesus can create 'rivers in the dry wasteland' of you.

He's doing something new. Every time you fill up your water bottle at the cooler or the sink today, give thanks for the streams of living water available to you and yours, this Christmas and always.

🍎 MORE THAN MOST

Some people need to drink more water than others. Certain diseases (like diabetes) and medications (for heart disease, stomach ulcers or depression) influence how parched we feel. Also, elderly people may have a poorly-regulated thirst mechanism. In these cases, your body may not send you reliable thirst signals, so "drinking to thirst" would not be an appropriate approach. There are also situations in which you'll want to drink more: hot, humid weather causes you to lose more water through perspiration, and if you're sick with a fever or vomiting you'll be losing extra liquids too. Pregnant or breastfeeding women also require extra water, as do avid exercisers. Drink up, don't dry up!

JOY TO THE WORLD

For a child is born to us, a son is given to us.
The government will rest on His shoulders.
And He will be called: Wonderful Counselor, Mighty God,
Everlasting Father, Prince of Peace.

Isaiah 9:6, NLT

You're not alone, this Christmas. And thankfully, you're not in control, this Christmas. The Christ child born in Bethlehem governs your life, our world and universe, as Father, Counselor, and Prince of Peace. Breathe in and out, and give thanks, this Christmas season, that you are in excellent hands.

You may have already unwrapped some Christmas gifts today. Thank God for the good things we get to enjoy in this life. And thank Him for your health, and the health of those you love. Consider, even today, how you might treasure the gift of your own wellbeing, stewarding it excellently, so you can be God's gift to others, in the year ahead.

DEAR ME. MERRY CHRISTMAS. LOVE ME.

When you wake up on Christmas morning one year from now, what health gift will you be glad you gave yourself? Fitness? Firmness? Whole-Food-ness? Or simply overall Fabulousness?

AFTERMATH

Why, my soul, are you downcast?
Why so disturbed within me? Put your hope in God,
for I will yet praise Him, my Savior and my God.
Psalm 42:11, NIV

There are lots of reasons we might feel let down in the aftermath of Christmas. We'd been looking forward to Christmas for weeks – maybe months – and the celebrations were awesome! But now it's all over. Or we'd built up in our minds the joy and profundity of family reconnections – and things didn't quite roll how we hoped. Or we ate (or drank) too much and today we feel lousy. Or even – because none of us is above being this shallow – we didn't get the gifts we wanted.

Speak some truth to your disappointed, dejected soul. Today is the first day of the rest of your life and there's always something to look forward to because Christmas is coming again, and so is eternity.

BAD HAIR DAY

Believe it or not, waking up with bad hair has a greater impact on your day than you might think. A survey found that waking with a dodgy hairdo leads the average woman to spend an hour and a quarter feeling moody and miserable. What's more, the average woman spends around 156 days a year with limp, greasy, uncontrollable or lifeless locks. That's a lot of grumpy days. Here's wishing you a more manageable mane in the year ahead!

FAITH FOR THE FUTURE

With this news, strengthen those who have tired hands,
and encourage those who have weak knees.
Isaiah 35:3, NLT

The good news Isaiah is offering to those with 'tired hands' and 'weak knees' is that the future is always better than the past.

Isaiah 35:1-2 reads, 'Even the wilderness and desert will be glad in those days. The wasteland will rejoice and blossom with spring crocuses. Yes, there will be an abundance of flowers and singing and joy! The deserts will become as green as the mountains of Lebanon, as lovely as Mount Carmel or the plain of Sharon. There the LORD will display His glory, the splendor of our God.'

If you're struggling to glimpse the goodness of God – if your hands are tired and your knees are weak – please don't give up. Our loving, wise, powerful Creator-King is in the restoration business, and He's not done with you yet.

THE TIME IS NOW

Evidence suggests that afternoon workouts might have an edge over morning workouts. Generally, physical performance is best, and risk of injury is reduced, between 3 PM and 6 PM, because joints and muscles are as much as 20% more flexible later in the day. If you enjoy tennis or squash, then afternoons are ideal too: eye-hand coordination is better and muscle strength peaks between 2 PM and 6 PM. The lungs also function more efficiently at around 5 PM. However, any exercise, at any time, is always a good thing and your body won't judge! Just do it.

NEW YEAR, NEW YOU!

While 75% of people stick to their New Year's resolutions for at least a week, only 45% are still on target six months later. Perhaps the most important determining factor for goal-setting success is your belief that you have the power to change your situation.

Studies show that those who believe self-control is unlimited have a far better chance of succeeding at New Year's endeavors. In other words, if you blame your genes for your obesity, rather than your fast-food addiction, you might not make much progress. If, however, you feel in control of your own health and chalk your health shortcomings up to a lack of effort, your potential to succeed is dramatically increased.

Get your systems in place before January 1st and take these last four days of the year to journal your thoughts around physical and spiritual health goals. Tell friends and family about the changes you're making, so you're accountable to someone other than yourself.

The temptations in your life are no different from what others experience. And God is faithful. He will not allow the temptation to be more than you can stand. When you are tempted, He will show you a way out so that you can endure.
1 Corinthians 10:13, NLT

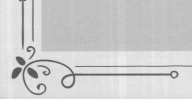

NEW YEAR, NEW YOU!

What spiritual goals are you setting for the New Year? Are they realistic, actionable and measureable?

If you want to pray or read your Bible more, be specific. For example, *I want to pray for ten uninterrupted minutes, five days a week, at 5h45, because the kids wake up at 6h00.* If you're leading a full, pressured life, it may be unrealistic, and probably impossible, to read through the whole Bible before the end of February. But you could download a Bible reading plan, and *commit*.

If you want to plug into community more than you have done this past year, how much time can you carve out in a week, for a life group or volunteer slot or dinner with friends? Set time-sensitive reminders, and *commit*.

Keep in mind that sticking to your resolutions, or achieving your goals, will mean managing the tension between what you *want now* (the immediate) and what you *value most* (the ultimate). Will you do what you want to do, or will you do what you'll wish you'd done, looking back? So consider what you *really* value more: eating dessert tonight, or feeling great about your body in your favorite jeans a month from now? Binge-watching a series, or spending time building relationships that leave the world better than you found it?

Those who say they live in God should live their lives as Jesus did.
1 John 2:6, NLT

NEW YEAR, NEW YOU!

How might it change the trajectory of your life in the year ahead if you set just one goal in each of the following areas of your life: Eat, sleep and move? Remember, your goals will be different from anyone else's. Be simultaneously as ambitious and as realistic as you possibly can be. Can the goal fit into a tweet? That's a way to keep it manageable in your mind – simple, concise and clear – instead of an overwhelmingly complex or daunting goal.

For example,

I aim to have cut the sugar in my coffee by half, by June.

I aim to be drinking no sugar in my coffee, by December.

By the end of the year, I'll run 5km without needing to stop and walk.

I'll plan for at least seven hours of sleep per night, for at least five days a week.

Speaking of sleep – as you put this year to bed, allow Paul's words to sink in and settle your soul …

So now there is no condemnation
for those who belong to Christ Jesus.
Romans 8:1, NLT

NEW YEAR, NEW YOU!

Father God,
Thank You for being with me every day of this past year.
Thank You that You'll be with me every day of the next.
Thank You that Your love for me is unshakeable,
and Your plans for me are perfect. Come what may
– whether I'm abandoned or acclaimed –
help me live only to please You. I surrender all to You –
my insides and my outsides. Take me and make me,
for Your glory.
Amen.

For we died and were buried with Christ by baptism.
And just as Christ was raised from the dead by the glorious power
of the Father, now we also may live new lives.
Romans 6:4, NLT

ABOUT THE AUTHORS

Dr Michael Mol is a medical doctor, international speaker, best-selling author, tele-health entrepreneur and founder of HelloDoctor. He is executive producer and CEO of TruthTV. He's a husband to one, father to three, friend to few, a stranger to many, but not to God. www.drmichaelmol.com

Dalene Reyburn is a well-loved speaker and best-selling author. She contributes to various online magazines and devotionals and shares truth, courage and hope at www.dalenereyburn.com. She has a master's degree in Applied Language Studies. She and her family make their home under African skies.